The
HOLLYWOOD
BOOK of LISTS

The HOLLYWOOD BOOK _of_ LISTS

FROM GREAT PERFORMANCES AND ROMANTIC EPICS TO BAD REMAKES AND MISCASTING DEBACLES

STEPHEN J. SPIGNESI

CITADEL PRESS
Kensington Publishing Corp. www.kensingtonbooks.com

CITADEL PRESS books are published by

Kensington Publishing Corp.
850 Third Avenue
New York, NY 10022

All Kensington titles, imprints, and distributed lines are available at special quantity discounts for bulk purchases for sales promotions, premiums, fund raising, educational, or institutional use. Special book excerpts or customized printings can also be created to fit specific needs. For details, write or phone the office of the Kensington special sales manager: Kensington Publishing Corp., 850 Third Avenue, New York, NY 10022, attn: Special Sales Department, phone 1-800-221-2647.

First printing July 2001

10 9 8 7 6 5 4 3 2 1

Printed in the United States of America

Library of Congress Control Number: 2001092633

ISBN 0-8065-2212-7

This is, rightly so, for
Jim Cole

Screenwriter,
Director,
Actor (I'm being generous on this one)
and, above all, friend

"Hope is a good thing,
and no good thing ever dies."

Contents

Acknowledgments

Special thanks to . . .

Lee Mandato
Jim Cole
Mike Lewis
John White
Mick Garris
Charlie Fried
Dave Hinchberger
George Beahm

Ann LaFarge
Donald Davidson
Carol Cady
Bruce Bender
Kensington Books
Pam Spignesi
The Internet Movie Database

"So, where's your hose, Mr. Lombardo?" and Other Reasons to Love Hollywood

The title of this introduction refers to a line Denise Richards says to Matt Dillon in the 1998 camp classic, *Wild Things*. Richards and her girlfriend Nicole (Neve Campbell) have come by to wash Dillon's jeep as part of a school fund-raising project . . . but Richards has her eyes on "Mr. Lombardo" for more than just guidance counseling, as we soon learn. When Dillon opens his front door, she says the "hose" line with such innocence that its double entendre stands out blatantly. This is one of those fun cinematic moments when we forget we're watching a movie and are completely caught up in what's happening on the screen.

Other memorable moments (for this writer anyway) include the look on Al Pacino's face as his brother Freddo (John Cazale) is executed in *The Godfather;* the restaurant scene in *This Is Spinal Tap* when cold sores suddenly appear on the lips of Michael McKean and Christopher Guest; Joe Pesci's "I amuse you?" scene in *GoodFellas;* the moment in the *Ben-Hur* chariot race when the guy in the green is caught beneath the horses' legs and dragged beneath a chariot for what seems like forever; Shirley MacLaine's "Give my daughter the shot!" scene in *Terms of*

Endearment; the laser vasectomy scene in *Goldfinger;* Leonardo DiCaprio's final scene in *Titanic;* Matthew McConaughey's "Now, imagine she's white" scene in *A Time to Kill* (even though it was originally supposed to be Samuel L. Jackson's speech); Robert De Niro's "You talkin' to me?" scene in *Taxi Driver;* the "Say hello to my little friend" scene in Pacino's *Scarface;* the "Academy of the Overrated" scene in Woody Allen's *Manhattan;* Alec Baldwin's, ahem, "pep talk" in *Glengarry Glen Ross;* Tom Hanks's hospital scene in *Philadelphia;* the heroin overdose scene in *Pulp Fiction;* the "I Should Have Known Better" sequence in *A Hard Day's Night;* the "In your eyes" scene from *Say Anything;* the "fava beans" scene in *The Silence of the Lambs;* the "You had me at hello" scene in *Jerry Maguire;* the airport scene in *Casablanca;* the eerie opening montage of *Citizen Kane;* the Orgasmatron scene in *Sleepers;* the "Berserker" scene in *Clerks;* the opening "Best of My Love" tracking shot in *Boogie Nights;* the tango scene in *Scent of a Woman;* the "Summer Wind" scene in *The Pope of Greenwich Village;* Karl's "I aim to kill ya" scene in *Sling Blade;* the trunk scene in *Jackie Brown;* the "I'm walkin' here!" scene in *Midnight Cowboy;* the resurrection scene in *E.T. The Extra-Terrestrial;* the *"Bonanza"* scene in *Tin Men;* Paul Newman's closing in *The Verdict;* the "So, I called it in" scene in *Fargo;* the "Sophie's choice" scene in *Sophie's Choice;* and, of course, any scene from *Showgirls* (Sorry. Couldn't resist).

Hollywood is one of America's greatest creations and it is one of our biggest exporters: American entertainment—in all its wonderful forms—is *what the world wants.*

The Hollywood Book of Lists looks at the movies, the stars, the scandals, the oddities, TV, and other facets of that unique American "invention" known as Hollywood. (Hooray for it.)

NOTE: Throughout *The Hollywood Book of Lists,* we provide lists of movies for your viewing pleasure. Some are theme lists; some are star-based movies (Robin Williams, Abbott and Costello, etc.). These are not meant to be complete filmographies; but rather lists of some of the most memorable and noteworthy films in the categories or by the stars. All are definitely worth your time.

The HOLLYWOOD BOOK of LISTS

16 Celebrity Nicknames

You think you were the only one who was tortured by often cruel (but usually on-target) nicknames when you were young? Check out these celeb nicks and get even more depressed by realizing that these folks ultimately went on to fame and fortune, while most of *us* (if we were lucky, that is) had to be grateful just to be rid of our nicknames!

Robert De Niro "Bobby Milk" De Niro was called this because his skin was really white when he was young.

Cameron Diaz "Skeletor" This gorgeous *There's Something About Mary* star was super-skinny as a teen. She's filled out some since then.

Jenna Elfman "Bucky Beaver" What else? Elfman had a really pronounced overbite and there ain't nothing kids like more than a visible physical abnormality.

Hugh Grant "Whippy" Grant's *Mickey Blue Eyes* costar James Caan gave him this nickname, which is short for "Whippet." Why? Because whippet dogs are incredibly nervous and Grant apparently has the same kind of personality as these hyper canines.

Geri Halliwell "Pancake" This Spice Girl was *really* flat-chested when she was young. Like Cameron Diaz, she has, ahem, filled out some since then.

Whitney Houston "Nippy" This diva was nicknamed after a comic strip character who was always getting into mischief. Hmmm.

Samuel L. Jackson "Machine Gun" This nickname referred to Jackson's really bad childhood stutter. Imagine what *Pulp Fiction* would have been like if he had never gotten rid of it?

Val Kilmer "Psycho" Apparently Kilmer has thrown a few on-set tantrums (according to the Hollywood grapevine) and was christened with this nick because of them. He reportedly is not very fond of this sobriquet. (Who would be?)

Lucy Lawless "Unco" Short for "uncoordinated."

Tommy Lee "T-Bone Steak" As all of you who have seen the Pamela and Tommy Lee sex video can attest to, he is incredibly well-endowed. This nickname refers to the size of his johnson. (Reportedly, he likes this nickname.)

Sophia Loren "Stechetto" This is the Italian word for "stick" and it was given to Loren because she was like a toothpick when she was younger. She, too, eventually filled out.

John Malkovich "Mad Dog" This brilliant actor apparently has something of a temper. Yeah, I'd say "Mad Dog" might suggest such a personality trait, wouldn't you?

Ricky Martin "Kiki" This is a family nickname.

Rebecca Romijn-Stamos "Jolly Blonde Giant" Duh.

Will Smith "Captain Correction" Smith got this nickname for chastising and correcting his classmates when they cursed.

Kate Winslet "Blubber" The British actress was fat when she was younger. She looked pretty good in *Titanic,* although her weight fluctuated drastically throughout the film.

7 Decades of "Best Pictures" at a Glance

Did you know that since the 1930s there has *never* been a decade in which *all* the directors of the Oscar-winning Best Picture also won the Best Director award? (The worst showing for directors was the thirties, when only five of the Best Picture winners also won the Best Director prize.)

The closest the Academy came to a sweep was the sixties, when nine of the Best Picture winners also won Best Director. But even though *In the Heat of the Night* won Best Picture in 1967, Norman Jewison lost out to Mike Nichols, who won Best Director for his work on *The Graduate.*

This happened again most recently in 1998, when *Shakespeare in Love* won Best Picture, but its director, John Madden, lost to Steven Spielberg for the latter's *Saving Private Ryan.*

How can this happen?

After all, a picture doesn't direct itself, right? And if a movie is considered the Best Picture of the year, then why isn't the person who helms it considered the Best Director of the year?

The answer lies in the way the voting system of the Academy of Motion Picture Arts and Sciences is structured. And it's simple: Each member of the Academy votes within his or her own category: actors vote for actors, cinematographers vote for cinematographers . . . and directors vote for directors.

But *everyone* votes in the Best Picture category, and so it is possible (and quite probable, as the record proves) that an often painful-to-watch picture like *Saving Private Ryan* would lose to the more mainstream *Shakespeare in Love,* and yet the Academy's roster of directors would recognize Spielberg's achievement with *Ryan* and award him Best Director.

In the following list, when the director of a Best Picture also won Best Director, it is indicated with a double asterisk (**).

The 1930s

1930   *All Quiet on the Western Front* (Lewis Milestone**)
1931   *Cimarron* (Wesley Ruggles)
1932   *Grand Hotel* (Edmund Goulding)
1933   *Cavalcade* (Frank Lloyd**)
1934   *It Happened One Night* (Frank Capra**)
1935   *Mutiny on the Bounty* (Frank Lloyd)
1936   *The Great Ziegfeld* (Robert Z. Leonard)
1937   *The Life of Emile Zola* (William Dieterle)
1938   *You Can't Take It With You* (Frank Capra**)
1939   *Gone With the Wind* (Victor Fleming**)

The 1940s

1940   *Rebecca* (Alfred Hitchcock)
1941   *How Green Was My Valley* (John Ford**)
1942   *Mrs. Miniver* (William Wyler**)
1943   *Casablanca* (Michael Curtiz**)
1944   *Going My Way* (Leo McCarey**)
1945   *The Lost Weekend* (Billy Wilder**)
1946   *The Best Years of Our Lives* (William Wyler**)
1947   *Gentleman's Agreement* (Elia Kazan**)
1948   *Hamlet* (Laurence Olivier)
1949   *All the King's Men* (Robert Rossen)

The 1950s

1950   *All About Eve* (Joseph L. Mankiewicz**)
1951   *An American in Paris* (Vincente Minnelli)
1952   *The Greatest Show on Earth* (Cecil B. DeMille)
1953   *From Here to Eternity* (Fred Zinnemann**)
1954   *On the Waterfront* (Elia Kazan**)
1955   *Marty* (Delbert Mann**)
1956   *Around the World in 80 Days* (Michael Anderson)
1957   *The Bridge on the River Kwai* (David Lean**)
1958   *Gigi* (Vincente Minnelli**)
1959   *Ben-Hur* (William Wyler**)

The 1960s

1960   *The Apartment* (Billy Wilder**)
1961   *West Side Story* (Robert Wise**)
1962   *Lawrence of Arabia* (David Lean**)
1963   *Tom Jones* (Tony Richardson**)
1964   *My Fair Lady* (George Cukor**)
1965   *The Sound of Music* (Robert Wise**)
1966   *A Man for All Seasons* (Fred Zinnemann**)
1967   *In the Heat of the Night* (Norman Jewison)
1968   *Oliver!* (Carol Reed**)
1969   *Midnight Cowboy* (John Schlesinger**)

The 1970s

1970   *Patton* (Franklin J. Schaffner**)
1971   *The French Connection* (William Friedkin**)
1972   *The Godfather* (Francis Ford Coppola)
1973   *The Sting* (George Roy Hill**)
1974   *The Godfather Part II* (Francis Ford Coppola**)
1975   *One Flew Over the Cuckoo's Nest* (Milos Forman**)
1976   *Rocky* (John G. Avildsen**)
1977   *Annie Hall* (Woody Allen**)
1978   *The Deer Hunter* (Michael Cimino)
1979   *Kramer vs. Kramer* (Robert Benton**)

The 1980s

1980   *Ordinary People* (Robert Redford**)
1981   *Chariots of Fire* (Hugh Hudson)
1982   *Gandhi* (Richard Attenborough**)
1983   *Terms of Endearment* (James L. Brooks**)
1984   *Amadeus* (Milos Forman**)
1985   *Out of Africa* (Sydney Pollack**)
1986   *Platoon* (Oliver Stone**)
1987   *The Last Emperor* (Bernardo Bertolucci**)
1988   *Rain Man* (Barry Levinson**)
1989   *Driving Miss Daisy* (Bruce Beresford)

The 1990s

1990   *Dances With Wolves* (Kevin Costner**)
1991   *The Silence of the Lambs* (Jonathan Demme**)
1992   *Unforgiven* (Clint Eastwood**)
1993   *Schindler's List* (Steven Spielberg**)
1994   *Forrest Gump* (Robert Zemeckis**)
1995   *Braveheart* (Mel Gibson**)
1996   *The English Patient* (Anthony Minghella**)
1997   *Titanic* (James Cameron**)
1998   *Shakespeare in Love* (John Madden)
1999   *American Beauty* (Sam Mendes**)
2000   *Gladiator* (Ridley Scott)

The "Movies About Game Shows" List

Now all we need is for Alex Trebek to star in a thriller about a *Jeopardy* contestant whose signaling button doesn't work because it's been sabotaged . . . by VANNA WHITE! (We can call it *The Deadly Wheel of Jeopardy.*) (Sorry.)

1. *Champagne for Caesar* (1950)
2. *Queen for a Day* (1951)
3. *Shock Treatment* (1981)
4. *Prize of Peril* (1984)
5. *The Running Man* (1987)
6. *Deathrow Gameshow* (1988)
7. *Little Man Tate* (1991)
8. *White Men Can't Jump* (1992)
9. *Quiz Show* (1994)
10. *Mallrats* (1995)

For Your Consideration . . . An Introduction to the "A to Z" Lists

2 *"Signature Movies" of 380 Favorite* *"Household Name" Actors and Actresses*

Throughout *The Hollywood Book of Lists* are 380 favorite actors and actresses and the names of two (*only* two) of their movies.

Now don't get in a tizzy: I'm not saying that the two movies listed for each are their *best* films, or even their *most popular* ones. What I'm saying is that these might be considered their *signature* films—those that showcase juicy roles in which the actor gets a chance to shine; impeccably written and creatively directed vehicles that elicit a memorable performance. Bottom line? These are the two movies you should rent if you want a quick-and-dirty education on the talent of the actor or actress in question.

A caveat: You may not agree with my two choices (especially when we're dealing with a Donald Sutherland or a Sharon Stone, each of whom seems to have done about a million movies), but one of my criteria was award-winning (or award-nominated) performances. Thus, for Miss Stone, *Casino* made the cut, *Basic Instinct* did not. (One "natty dugout" scene does not a signature performance make.)

Whether or not you agree with my two picks, you *will* agree that the two movies selected give us a look at the performer at his or her best.

(Also scattered throughout the book are many fascinating "Tales of Oscar"—interesting bits of Oscar information gleaned from years of AMPAS's history.)

NOTE: The Academy of Motion Picture Arts and Sciences now comprises thirteen branches: Actors, Art Directors, Cinematographers, Directors, Executives, Film Editors, Music, Producers, Public Relations, Short Films and Feature Animation, Sound, Visual Effects, and Writers.

- -

Naked ambition

The gold-plated, 13-1/2 inch tall, 8-1/2 pound (originally 6-3/4 pound) Academy Award is a statuette of a naked man plunging a sword into a reel of film. It was designed by MGM's Cedric Gibbons, who explained that the five holes of the reel represented the five branches of the Academy of Motion Picture Arts and Sciences. He did not indicate what the guy represented.

- -

For Your Consideration . . .

The "A" List

F. Murray Abraham *Scarface* (1983); *Amadeus* (1984)

Ben Affleck *Good Will Hunting* (1997); *Chasing Amy* (1997)

Danny Aiello *Moonstruck* (1987); *Do the Right Thing* (1989)

Alan Alda *Crimes and Misdemeanors* (1989); *And the Band Played On* (1993)

Karen Allen *Raiders of the Lost Ark* (1981); *Starman* (1984)

Nancy Allen *Dressed to Kill* (1980); *Blow Out* (1981)

Woody Allen *Manhattan* (1978); *Mighty Aphrodite* (1995)

Kirstie Alley *Look Who's Talking* (1989); *Deconstructing Harry* (1997)

Ursula Andress *Dr. No* (1962); *Casino Royale* (1967)

Julie Andrews *The Sound of Music* (1965); *10* (1979)

Ann-Margret *Carnal Knowledge* (1971); *Magic* (1978)

Anne Archer *Fatal Attraction* (1987); *Short Cuts* (1993)

Alan Arkin *The In-Laws* (1979); *Glengarry Glen Ross* (1992)

Bess Armstrong *The Four Seasons* (1981); *Nothing in Common* (1986)

Patricia Arquette *True Romance* (1993); *Flirting With Disaster* (1995)

Rosanna Arquette *The Executioner's Song* (1982); *Pulp Fiction* (1994)

Ed Asner *Roots* (1977); *JFK* (1991)

Dan Aykroyd *Trading Places* (1993); *Sneakers* (1992)

62 Movie Stars and the Jobs They Held Before They Became Movie Stars

It's always a bit of a culture shock to learn what incredibly famous people did to earn a living before they became big stars.

I'm not sure we really want to picture the dignified Warren Beatty working in the Lincoln Tunnel as a construction worker. It's too jarring an image for those of us who are Beatty fans.

Likewise picturing Harrison Ford as a cook; Lorenzo Lamas as a McDonald's french fry cook; Barbra Streisand as a switchboard operator; diminutive Paul Williams as an oil-field worker (Paul Williams!?); or perhaps most bizarre, hulking Gerard Depardieu as a door-to-door soap salesman.

This list looks at 62 of the best-known celebrities and what they did before they became big stars . . . at a time when they were, well, more like the rest of us!

Danny Aiello *Bus terminal announcer*
Eddie Arnold *Hearse driver*
Lauren Bacall *Theater usher*
Roseanne *Window dresser*
Warren Beatty *Lincoln Tunnel construction worker*
Sandra Bernhard *Pedicurist*
Ray Bolger *Accountant*
Richard Boone *Roustabout*
Carol Burnett *Hatcheck girl*
Glen Campbell *Cotton picker*
Richard Chamberlain *Supermarket clerk*
Sean Connery *Coffin polisher*
Bill Cosby *Shoe salesman*
Kevin Costner *Stagehand*
Joan Crawford *Department store clerk*
Ruby Dee *Translator*
Gerard Depardieu *Door-to-door soap salesman*
Kevin Dobson *Railroad ticket taker*
Patrick Duffy *Mower of lawns*
Keir Dullea *Carpenter's apprentice*
Charles Durning *Boxer*
Peter Falk *State of Connecticut Budget Bureau administrator*

Harrison Ford *Cook*

John Forsythe *Waiter*

James Garner *Poolroom manager*

Whoopi Goldberg *Morgue beautician*

Robert Goulet *Stationery salesman*

Charles Grodin *Pinkerton night watchman*

Jerry Hall *Manure shoveler*

Dustin Hoffman *Psychiatric attendant*

Bob Hoskins *Fire eater*

Alan King *Bandleader*

Burt Lancaster *Acrobat*

Lorenzo Lamas *McDonald's french fry cook*

Cyndi Lauper *Dog kennel cleaner*

Jon Lovitz *Hospital orderly*

Fred MacMurray *Saxophone player*

Dean Martin *Bootleg runner*

Lee Marvin *Plumber's apprentice*

Walter Matthau *Floor scrubber*

Robert Mitchum *Coal miner*

George Murphy *Coal loader*

Jim Nabors *Typist*

Bob Newhart *Accountant*

George Peppard *Disk jockey*

Ronald Reagan *Radio sports announcer*

Robert Redford *Oil-field worker*

Cliff Robertson *Reporter*

Yakov Smirnoff *Bartender*

Mary Steenburgen *Waitress*

Barbra Streisand *Switchboard operator*

Preston Sturges *Cosmetics inventor*

Rip Torn *Short order cook*

Lee Van Cleef *Accountant*

Jean-Claude Van Damme *Masseur*
Dick Van Dyke *Advertising executive*
Raquel Welch *Weather girl*
William Wellman *Stunt pilot*
Cornel Wilde *Macy's toy salesman*
Paul Williams *Oil-field worker*
Nicol Williamson *Metalworker*
Jonathan Winters *Apricot picker*

23 Beloved Cult Movie Stars

Cult stars live on and develop fan followings that span generations. These 23 have been consistently popular since their earliest work. Many defined a genre (Abbott and Costello, Charles Bronson, Jackie Chan, Cheech and Chong, Traci Lords, the Marx Brothers, Monty Python, Seka, the Three Stooges) while others had such enormous appeal that they became cultural icons (James Dean, Jayne Mansfield, Marilyn Monroe, Roy Rogers).

Proof of the pudding: For many of these stars, their careers have never been healthier . . . even though many of them have been dead for years!

1. **Abbott and Costello** The classic comedy team whose films inspired Jerry Seinfeld's vision of *Seinfeld*'s New York City.

2. **Fatty Arbuckle** The 300-pound slapstick comic of the Silent Era who was accused of a rape/murder and ultimately acquitted. However, his films were shunned and he couldn't get work as an actor after the trial. He had a second career as a director working under the name of "William Goodrich."

3. **Brigitte Bardot** The legendary sex symbol turned animal activist.

4. **Charles Bronson** The taciturn action star who became a cult figure as the revenge-seeking hero of the *Death Wish* series.

5. **Marilyn Chambers** The Ivory Soap pitch girl who turned porn star.

6. **Jackie Chan** The martial arts maniac whose movies are clever, action-packed, and loads of fun. And Chan does all his own stunts, too!

7. **Cheech and Chong** The seventies comedy duo who created the pop culture archetype of the stoner—the perpetually stoned (and often paranoid) hippies who were into smoking weed, listening to music, and satisfying their munchies. ("Dave's not here.")

8. **James Dean** The ultimate teen outcast who died in his twenties after a career consisting of three memorable films, *East of Eden* (1955), *Rebel Without a Cause* (1955), and *Giant* (1956).

9. **Divine** The cross-dressing obese star of several John Waters films, Divine (real name Harris Milstead) had to be seen to be believed. Her most notorious on-screen stunt was to actually eat doggy doo-doo, fresh from the pooch's butt.

10. **W. C. Fields** He reportedly hated kids and definitely liked to drink. This was an irresistible, and extremely funny, persona.

11. **Long John Holmes** The seventies porn star with a fifteen-inch penis. He died of AIDS.

12. **Traci Lords** Buxom blond porn actress who made dozens of X-rated features while underaged and later moved into mainstream movie work.

13. **Linda Lovelace** Star of the seminal seventies porno film *Deep Throat.* Lovelace later claimed that she was coerced into making the movie and she became an anti-porn crusader.

14. **Jayne Mansfield** The forerunner of such modern sex symbols as Anna Nicole Smith, Pamela Anderson, and other actresses who are known more for their mammoth mammaries than for their thespian talents. Mansfield (who actually was extremely intelligent) died young when she was beheaded in an automobile accident, which only added to her cult status. (Bizarre deaths have a way of doing that. Cases in point: Jim Morrison and Kurt Cobain.)

15. **The Marx Brothers** The Marx Brothers and the Three Stooges are two of the most gifted comedy teams in the history of entertain-

ment. To this day, some of the lines from the Marx Brothers' movies are as funny as they were when the films were first released in the 1930s. Groucho wore a painted mustache and no one said a word about it; Harpo never spoke professionally and blew a horn instead; and one of the brothers of the Jewish comedy troupe (Chico) was faux Italian. How can you not love these guys?

16. **Marilyn Monroe** The quintessential sex symbol of the 20th century who committed suicide at the age of 36 . . . or did she?

17. **Monty Python** The irreverent British comedy troupe famous for their seventies series, *Monty Python's Flying Circus.*

18. **Bettie Page** A fifties sex symbol known as the Queen of the Pinups. Bettie Page dabbled in S&M and her bondage pictures and steamy short films made her a huge star with a rabid following.

19. **Elvis Presley** The King. As Eddie Murphy has said, Elvis was so popular, they let him make movies even though he couldn't act. (Eddie does this hilarious bit about Presley being instructed to sing all his lines: "Hey, Elvis, we gotta win this race! Elvis (singing): "We gotta win this race . . .")

20. **Roy Rogers** One of the most popular and best-known cowboy stars of all time. Roy, his wife Dale, and, of course, his horse Trigger (Roy had him stuffed after his death) have been and continue to be household names.

21. **Seka** The blond bombshell porn star of the seventies who once explained her enormous appeal to men as "blond hair and big tits."

22. **Shirley Temple** The adorable child star with a mop of curly hair who starred in a series of enormously popular films in the 1930s.

23. **The Three Stooges** Nyuk, nyuk, nyuk.

The "Abbott and Costello" Movie List

1. *One Night in the Tropics* (1940)
2. *Buck Privates* (1941)
3. *Hold That Ghost* (1941)
4. *In the Navy* (1941)
5. *Keep 'Em Flying* (1941)
6. *Lost in a Harem* (1944)
7. *Abbott and Costello in Hollywood* (1945)
8. *Here Come the Co-Eds* (1945)
9. *The Naughty Nineties* (1945)
10. *Buck Privates Come Home* (1947)
11. *Abbott and Costello Meet Frankenstein* (1948)
12. *Mexican Hayride* (1948)
13. *The Noose Hangs High* (1948)
14. *Abbott and Costello Meet the Killer, Boris Karloff* (1949)
15. *Africa Screams* (1949)
16. *Abbott and Costello in the Foreign Legion* (1950)
17. *Comin' Round the Mountain* (1951)
18. *Abbott and Costello Meet the Invisible Man* (1951)
19. *Abbott and Costello Meet Captain Kidd* (1952)
20. *Abbott and Costello Meet Dr. Jekyll and Mr. Hyde* (1952)
21. *Lost in Alaska* (1952)
22. *Abbott and Costello Go to Mars* (1953)
23. *Abbott and Costello Meet the Keystone Cops* (1954)
24. *Abbott and Costello Meet the Mummy* (1955)
25. *Dance With Me Henry* (1956)

For Your Consideration . . .

THE "B" LIST

Kevin Bacon *A Few Good Men* (1992); *Murder in the First* (1995)
Alec Baldwin *Glengarry Glen Ross* (1992); *Malice* (1993)
Fairuza Balk *Gas Food Lodging* (1992); *American History X* (1998)
Anne Bancroft *Fatso* (1980); *Agnes of God* (1985)
Antonio Banderas *Philadelphia* (1993); *The Mask of Zorro* (1998)
Ellen Barkin *Sea of Love* (1989); *Switch* (1991)
Drew Barrymore *Boys on the Side* (1994); *The Wedding Singer* (1997)
Kim Basinger *9-1/2 Weeks* (1986); *L.A. Confidential* (1997)
Angela Bassett *What's Love Got to Do With It?* (1993); *Waiting to Exhale* (1995)
Kathy Bates *Misery* (1990); *Primary Colors* (1998)
Warren Beatty *Reds* (1981); *Bulworth* (1998)
Annette Bening *The Grifters* (1990); *The American President* (1995)
Tom Berenger *The Big Chill* (1983); *Major League* (1989)
Candice Bergen *Carnal Knowledge* (1971); *Gandhi* (1982)
Elizabeth Berkley *Showgirls* (1995); *The Real Blonde* (1997)
Sandra Bernhard *King of Comedy* (1982); *The Late Shift* (1996)
Juliette Binoche *The Unbearable Lightness of Being* (1988); *The English Patient* (1996)
Helena Bonham Carter *A Room With a View* (1986); *Howards End* (1992)
Lorraine Bracco *GoodFellas* (1990); *The Sopranos* (1999)
Matthew Broderick *Ferris Bueller's Day Off* (1986); *The Cable Guy* (1996)
Albert Brooks *Broadcast News* (1987); *Defending Your Life* (1991)
Sandra Bullock *Speed* (1994); *A Time to Kill* (1996)
Steve Buscemi *Reservoir Dogs* (1992); *Fargo* (1996)

- -

Rumor has it that this is how Pez started

At the 1937 Oscar ceremony, an Academy Award was presented to ventriloquist Edgar Bergen's wooden dummy, Charlie McCarthy. In honor of Charlie's "anatomy," his Oscar was made of wood and had a movable mouth.

- -

The 20 Top-Grossing Films

$600,743,440.	*Titanic* (1997)
$461,000,000.	*Star Wars* (1977)
$399,800,000.	*E. T. The Extra-Terrestrial* (1982)
$337,832,005.	*Jurassic Park* (1993)
$329,650,110.	*Forrest Gump* (1994)
$312,900,000.	*The Lion King* (1994)
$309,100,000.	*Return of the Jedi* (1983)
$306,169,272.	*Independence Day* (1996)
$290,200,000.	*The Empire Strikes Back* (1980)
$285,015,670.	*Home Alone* (1990)
$251,188,924.	*Batman* (1989)
$242,400,000.	*Raiders of the Lost Ark* (1981)
$238,600,000.	*Ghostbusters* (1984)
$217,350,219.	*Aladdin* (1992)
$216,105,000.	*Jaws* (1975)
$208,200,000.	*Back to the Future* (1985)
$204,446,562.	*Terminator 2: Judgment Day* (1991)
$201,551,346.	*Armageddon* (1998)
$191,773,049.	*Toy Story* (1995)
$176,800,000.	*Top Gun* (1986)
$171,188,895.	*Rain Man* (1988)
$167,738,493.	*Three Men and a Baby* (1987)
$153,100,000.	*Grease* (1978)
$144,105,000.	*The Sting* (1973)
$134,594,000.	*The Godfather* (1972)
$119,500,000.	*Blazing Saddles* (1974)
$117,235,000.	*Rocky* (1976)
$106,300,000.	*Kramer vs. Kramer* (1979)
$105,263,000.	*Love Story* (1970)
$ 68,421,000.	*Billy Jack* (1971)

NOTE: Total box-office gross of the number 1 films of the past nineteen years: $7,068,270,985.00 ($353,413,549.25 per film average gross).
(Source: Exhibitor Relations)

The 100 Most Influential People in the History of the Movies

Someone once asked me if my dream was to live on in the hearts of my people, and I said I would like to live on in my apartment.

—WOODY ALLEN

This list is taken from *The Film 100: A Ranking of the Most Influential People in the History of the Movies* by Scott Smith (Citadel Press, 1998). Smith is editor of *Filmbreak* magazine and the creator of the "Film 100" Web site, the genesis of his important book.

The Film 100 offers detailed biographical profiles of the one hundred people he considers the most influential in the world of film. The following list does not attempt to duplicate his highly regarded efforts. Instead, it provides, at a glance, the luminaries—the actors, writers, directors, inventors, and others—who were responsible for the development of the movie as we know and love it today. It is an introduction of sorts to Scott Smith's book and Web site. (This list also provides, at a glance, the distribution of directors, writers, actors, and other film personnel, in order of their importance in the field. Personally, I find it fascinating that Smith ranked renowned directors Francis Ford Coppola and Martin Scorsese *below* actors Robert De Niro and Clark Gable. And does John Wayne *really* deserve to be ranked at number 11? I'm not sure I agree with some of the choices, but I find it interesting to consider the reasons why he assigned the specific rankings that he did.)

If you'd like to know even more about why the people on this list "made the grade," so to speak, then check out a copy of Scott Smith's book.

1. **William Kennedy Laurie Dickson** (1860–1935) The engineer and inventor most responsible for the development of the equipment that would record and preserve the moving image.

2. **Edwin S. Porter** (1869–1941) Editor, director, producer

3. **Charlie Chaplin** (1889–1977) Director, actor, writer

4. **Mary Pickford** (1893–1979) Actress

5. **Orson Welles** (1915–1985) Director, writer, actor; responsible for *Citizen Kane*

6. **Alfred Hitchcock** (1899–1980) Director

7. **Walt Disney** (1901–1966) Director, producer; founder of the Disneyland/World theme park empire

8. **D. W. Griffith** (1875–1948) Director

9. **Will Hays** (1879–1954) Creator of the industry's censoring Hays Code

10. **Thomas Edison** (1847–1931) Inventor

11. **John Wayne** (1907–1979) Actor

12. **J. R. Bray** (1879–1978) Animated cartoon producer

13. **Billy Bitzer** (1872–1944) Seminal cameraman

14. **Jesse Lasky** (1880–1958) Producer

15. **George Eastman** (1854–1932) Inventor

16. **Sergei Eisenstein** (1898–1948) Director

17. **Andre Bazin** (1918–1958) Film theorist

18. **Irving Thalberg** (1899–1936) Producer

19. **Thomas Ince** (1882–1924) Producer

20. **Marlon Brando** (1924–) Actor, director

21. **Louis B. Mayer** (1885–1957) Producer

22. **Greta Garbo** (1905–1990) Actress

23. **Robert Flaherty** (1884–1951) Father of the documentary

24. **Lon Chaney** (1883–1930) Actor

25. **Anita Loos** (1893–1981) Writer

26. **George Méliès** (1861–1938) Producer

27. **Adolph Zukor** (1873–1976) Producer

28. **John Gilbert** (1895–1936) Actor

29. **Max Fleischer** (1883–1972) Animator

30. **John Ford** (1895–1973) Director

31. **William Fox** (1879–1952) Producer

32. **George Lucas** (1944–) Director, writer, producer

33. **Linwood Gale Dunn** (1904–) Inventor of the optical printer

34. **Eadweard Muybridge** (1830–1904) Photographer, inventor

35. **Katharine Hepburn** (1907–) Actress

36. **Winsor McCay** (1867–1934) Animator

37. **Stanley Kubrick** (1928–1999) Director, writer

38. **Buster Keaton** (1895–1966) Actor

39. **James Agee** (1909–1955) Film critic

40. **Fritz Lang** (1890–1976) Director

41. **Marcus Loew** (1870–1927) Producer, founder of theater chain

42. **Cedric Gibbons** (1893–1960) Art director

43. **James Cagney** (1899–1986) Actor

44. **Ben Hecht** (1894–1964) Writer

45. **Ingmar Bergman** (1918–) Director, writer

46. **Humphrey Bogart** (1899–1957) Actor

47. **Leon Schlesinger** (1884–1949) Producer

48. **Louella Parsons** (1881–1972) Hollywood columnist

49. **Roger Corman** (1926–) Director, producer

50. **Edith Head** (1898–1981) Costume designer

51. **Bernard Herrmann** (1911–1975) Composer

52. **Gary Cooper** (1901–1961) Actor

53. **Mike Todd** (1907–1958) Producer

54. **Ernst Lubitsch** (1892–1947) Director

55. **Sidney Poitier** (1924–) Actor, director

56. **Saul Bass** (1920–1996) Titles sequence designer

57. **Billy Wilder** (1906–) Director

58. **Bette Davis** (1908–1989) Actress

59. **Erich Von Stroheim** (1885–1957) Director, actor

60. **Max Factor** (1872–1938) Makeup artist and innovator

61. **Auguste and Louis Lumière** (Auguste, 1862–1954; Louis, 1864–1948) Inventors of the movie projector

62. **Woody Allen** (1935–) Director, writer, actor

63. **Clark Gable** (1901–1960) Actor

64. **David O. Selznick** (1902–1965) Producer

65. **Gregg Toland** (1904–1948) Cinematographer

66. **Lillian Gish** (1896–1993) Actress

67. **William Cameron Menzies** (1896–1957) Art director

68. **Lucille Ball** (1911–1989) Actress

69. **Samuel Rothafel** (1882–1936) Theater designer

70. **Akira Kurosawa** (1910–1998) Director

71. **Marilyn Monroe** (1926–1962) Actress

72. **Vittorio De Sica** (1901–1974) Director, actor

73. **Natalie Kalmus** (1892–1965) Perfected the Technicolor process

74. **Gene Siskel & Roger Ebert** (Siskel, 1946–1999; Ebert, 1942–) Influential movie critics

75. **Willis O'Brien** (1896–1962) Animator and model innovator

76. **Shirley Temple** (1928–) Actress

77. **Yakima Canutt** (1895–1986) Stuntman

78. **Sam Peckinpah** (1925–1984) Director

79. **Jackie Coogan** (1914–1984) Actor

80. **Federico Fellini** (1920–1993) Director

81. **Leni Riefenstahl** (1902–) Director

82. **Steven Spielberg** (1947–) Director, producer

83. **Sam Warner** (1888–1927) Added sound to movies; one of the groundbreaking Warner brothers

84. **Jean-Luc Godard** (1930–) Director

85. **Robert De Niro** (1943–) Actor

86. **Fred Astaire** (1899–1987) Actor

87. **Francis Ford Coppola** (1939–) Director, writer, producer; responsible for *The Godfather* movies

88. **Ted Turner** (1938–) Movie investor and mogul, infamous movie colorizer

89. **Clint Eastwood** (1930–) Actor, director

90. **Dalton Trumbo** (1905–1976) Writer

91. **Dennis Hopper** (1936–) Actor

92. **Richard Hollingshead** (1900–1975) Invented the drive-in theater

93. **Melvin Van Peebles** (1932–) Actor

94. **John Chambers** (1922–) Legendary horror film makeup artist

95. **Mack Sennett** (1880–1960) Producer

96. **Martin Scorsese** (1942–) Director, writer, producer

97. **Karl Struss** (1886–1981) Cinematographer

98. **Busby Berkeley** (1895–1976) Choreographer

99. **John Hubley** (1914–1977) Animator

100. **John Cassavetes** (1929–1989) Actor

For Your Consideration . . .

The "C" List

James Caan *The Godfather* (1972); *Misery* (1990)
Nicolas Cage *Guarding Tess* (1994); *Leaving Las Vegas* (1995)
Michael Caine *Educating Rita* (1983); *Hannah and Her Sisters* (1986)
Neve Campbell *Scream* (1996); *Wild Things* (1998)
John Candy *Splash* (1984); *Planes, Trains & Automobiles* (1987)

Kate Capshaw *Indiana Jones and the Temple of Doom* (1984); *Just Cause* (1994)

Art Carney *Harry and Tonto* (1974); *Firestarter* (1984)

Jim Carrey *Liar Liar* (1996); *The Truman Show* (1998)

Dana Carvey *Wayne's World* (1992); *The Road to Wellville* (1994)

Phoebe Cates *Fast Times at Ridgemont High* (1982); *Bodies, Rest & Motion* (1993)

Chevy Chase *National Lampoon's Vacation* (1983); *National Lampoon's Christmas Vacation* (1989)

Don Cheadle *Boogie Nights* (1997); *Bulworth* (1998)

Cher *The Witches of Eastwick* (1987); *Moonstruck* (1987)

George Clooney *From Dusk Till Dawn* (1995); *The Perfect Storm* (2000)

Glenn Close *The Big Chill* (1983); *Fatal Attraction* (1987)

Jennifer Connelly *The Hot Spot* (1990); *Inventing the Abbotts* (1997)

Sean Connery *Goldfinger* (1964); *Just Cause* (1994)

Harry Connick Jr. *Little Man Tate* (1991); *Copycat* (1995)

Kevin Costner *JFK* (1991); *Tin Cup* (1996)

Courteney Cox *Ace Ventura: Pet Detective* (1993); *Scream* (1996)

Tom Cruise *A Few Good Men* (1992); *Jerry Maguire* (1996)

Billy Crystal *When Harry Met Sally . . .* (1989); *Mr. Saturday Night* (1992)

Macauley Culkin *Home Alone* (1990); *The Good Son* (1993)

Jamie Lee Curtis *Halloween* (1978); *True Lies* (1994)

Joan Cusack *Broadcast News* (1987); *In and Out* (1997)

John Cusack *Say Anything* (1989); *The Grifters* (1990)

He arrived in a chauffeur-driven tank

At the 1942 Oscar ceremony, Frank Capra gave the Best Director Award to William Wyler for *Mrs. Miniver.* Capra, a colonel in the U.S. Army at the time, was on leave and appeared at the Academy Award ceremony in uniform.

Woody Allen's 10 Best Movies (So Far)

1. ***Manhattan*** (1979) *"When it comes to relationships with women, I'm the winner of the August Strindberg Award."*

   I not only consider this to be Woody Allen's best film to date, I also believe it belongs on the short list of the greatest American films of all time, along with, yes, *Citizen Kane, Casablanca, The Godfather, Gone With the Wind, Schindler's List,* and a handful of others. Absolutely *everything* works here: the script (by Woody and Marshall Brickman); Gordon Willis's incredible cinematography; the casting; the performances (including wonderful work by Diane Keaton, Mariel Hemingway, Michael Murphy, Meryl Streep, Wallace Shawn, and Anne Byrne); the music (by Gershwin, of course), and Woody's inspired direction (just the park bench scene alone is worth the price of admission). I feel that *Manhattan* is what *Annie Hall* aspired to be, and so far, Woody has yet to top himself. *Manhattan* is funny, sad, provocative, inspiring, intelligent, and evocative, and every frame of the film is so beautifully composed, each could be blown up and framed as an example of magnificent black-and-white photographs of New York. The film also has cameos by Karen Allen (in a blond wig!), Mark Linn-Baker, and David Rasche.

2. ***Crimes and Misdemeanors*** (1989) This brilliant film is a dark meditation on the nature of morality, responsibility, and ultimate salvation. It poses a profound question: If you completely get away with a murder on Earth, and you don't believe in a judgmental God or even life after death, haven't you, in essence, been exonerated of all responsiblity for your sin, since you cannot be punished by a deity in which you have no faith? Yikes. What a question, eh? Martin Landau plays a doctor who is faced with this conundrum after he has his troublesome mistress (Anjelica Huston) killed and the crime is never traced back to him. Woody's writing and directing in this is so good, it's transcendent . . . it is truly art in one of its most sub-

lime manifestations. But since this is, after all, a Woody Allen movie, let us also not overlook the comedic elements of *Crimes and Misdemeanors,* mainly evinced through Alan Alda's character, a creator of sitcoms who is shallow, pompous, and utterly obnoxious to both Woody's character, and to us viewers as well. This great film should be seen more than once to fully experience the depth of Woody's writing, the nuances of the performances, and the sheer beauty of the cinematography.

The other winners . . .

3. *Hannah and Her Sisters* (1986) If Woody had not made *Manhattan* or *Crimes and Misdemeanors,* this would have been his masterpiece. Consistently brilliant throughout.

4. *Annie Hall* (1977) A classic that created and defined a new genre. (As well as turning women's fashions on their ear.)

5. *Sleeper* (1973) The movie that gave us the Orgasmatron (no, they're not on the market yet), as well as putting a completely new spin on the old "slipping on a banana peel" gag. (If you've seen *Sleeper,* you know the scene I'm referring to. If you haven't, go rent it. Now.)

6. *Husbands and Wives* (1992) Handheld cameras and marital angst with the quintessential Woody Allen touch.

7. *Mighty Aphrodite* (1996) The Woody Allen movie that won Mira Sorvino an Academy Award. One of his best.

8. *Stardust Memories* (1980) An autobiographical masterpiece inspired by Fellini's *8-1/2. Stardust Memories* also contains one of my favorite Woody jokes: At one point, Charlotte Rampling's character, Dorrie, tells Sandy (Woody) he smells nice. She says, "That aftershave. It just made my whole childhood come back in a sudden Proustian rush." Sandy tells her, "That's 'cause I'm wearing *Proustian Rush* by Chanel. It's reduced. I got a vat of it."

9. *Broadway Danny Rose* (1984) A wonderfully entertaining movie in which Woody plays Danny Rose, a hapless schlemiel in "theatrical management" who gets a shot at the big time when the career of one of his clients, Lou Canova, starts to take off. Hilarious.

10. *Interiors* (1978) *Hannah and Her Sisters: The Dark Side.* A family is in trouble, and *Interiors* shows how three complex and disparate women try to cope with their obsessive, suicidal mother. Brooding, intense . . . and pure poetry.

Joe Pesci's Greatest Role

GoodFellas
(1990)

His performance as wiseguy Tommy DeVito in Martin Scorsese's mob masterpiece *GoodFellas* may be Pesci's finest work as an actor to date. Tommy is the role Pesci was born to play and nowhere is this more evident than in his "What do you mean I'm funny?" scene with Ray Liotta (real-life Henry Hill) in Sonny's Bamboo Lounge.

Tommy is telling everyone at his table the story of when he was picked up for questioning for a bank job in Secaucus, New Jersey. When asked by the cops what he was going to tell them about the robbery, Tommy replies, "I'll tell you something. Go fuck your mother."

Tommy takes a beating for this and when he comes around, he sees the same cop standing in front of him. Like a seasoned Catskill emcee, Tommy finishes the story: "He says, 'Oh, what do you want to tell me now, tough guy?' I said, 'Ming, what are you doing here? I thought I told you to go fuck your mother?'" This story has the whole table in stitches and Henry Hill then makes the innocent comment, "You're a pisser, you know? Really funny. Really funny."

This remark sets Tommy off: "What do you mean I'm funny?" he asks Henry.

And then the atmosphere gets tense.

Henry does his best to assure Tommy that he meant no disrespect, but Tommy is having none of it: "I'm funny how? I mean, funny, like I'm a clown? I amuse you? I make you laugh? I'm here to fucking amuse you? What do you mean funny? Funny how? How am I funny? . . . What the fuck is so funny about me?"

Throughout the exchange with Liotta, Pesci literally becomes Tommy DeVito. It is one of the most compelling, believable performances ever committed to celluloid and is one of Pesci's all-time greatest scenes.

There are many other great award-caliber Pesci moments in *Good-Fellas,* including the two card game scenes during which he shoots Spider in the foot ("Don't make a big thing out of it, Spider! You little prick!"); and the scene in the bar on Queens Boulevard when Tommy tries to defend his honor against a disrespectful Billy Batts and ends up whacking him ("Sometimes you don't sound like you're kidding, you know. There's a lot of people around, you know?"). A personal favorite is the dining room scene with Tommy's mother (played by Martin Scorsese's mom), Jimmy (Robert De Niro), and Henry after they kill Batts. I especially like the moment when Tommy tells his mother that he needs to borrow a huge carving knife but that he'll bring it back. Why does he need it? He hit a deer and he's got to cut the hoof out of the front grill of the car: "Ma, it's a sin. You gonna leave it there?"

Ultimately, the character of Tommy DeVito is a tragic figure in *GoodFellas.* His life's dream was to become a made man, but when he killed Billy Batts—already made—he made a horrible mistake. Wiseguys who are not made men cannot whack a made man. Tommy ends up getting whacked himself in an empty garage. And as Henry Hill tells us later, "They even shot Tommy in the face so his mother couldn't give him an open coffin at the funeral."

■ ■ ■ ■ ■ ■ ■ ■ ■ ■ ■ ■ ■ ■ ■ ■ ■

Because of the movies I make, they think of me as difficult and angry. I *am* difficult and angry.

Martin Scorsese
Us, March 1998

■ ■ ■ ■ ■ ■ ■ ■ ■ ■ ■ ■ ■ ■ ■ ■ ■

The "Movies That Have Something to Do With Food or Have Food in Their Title" List

Titles notwithstanding, not all of these movies are about food . . . *9-1/2 Weeks* being a perfect example!

1. *Babette's Feast* (1987)
2. *Bananas* (1971)
3. *Big Night* (1995)
4. *The Coca-Cola Kid* (1984)
5. *The Cook, The Thief, His Wife & Her Lover* (1990)
6. *Crackers* (1984)
7. *Diner* (1982)
8. *Do the Right Thing* (1989)
9. *Duck Soup* (1933)
10. *Eat a Bowl of Tea* (1989)
11. *Eat and Run* (1986)
12. *Eat Drink Man Woman* (1994)
13. *Eat the Peach* (1986)
14. *Eating* (1990)
15. *Food of the Gods* (1976)
16. *The Fortune Cookie* (1966)
17. *Good Burger* (1997)
18. *Hamburger . . . The Motion Picture* (1986)
19. *Hot Chocolate* (1992)
20. *Hot Dog . . . The Movie!* (1983)
21. *Like Water for Chocolate* (1993)
22. *Mystic Pizza* (1988)

23. *9-1/2 Weeks* (1986)

24. *Six Pack* (1982)

25. *Soul Food* (1997)

26. *Sour Grapes* (1998)

27. *Soylent Green* (1973)

28. *The Spitfire Grill* (1995)

29. *Tom Jones* (1963)

30. *Watermelon Man* (1970)

31. *The Watermelon Woman* (1997)

32. *White Lightning* (1973)

33. *Wild Strawberries* (1957)

34. *Who Is Killing the Great Chefs of Europe?* (1978)

35. *Willy Wonka and the Chocolate Factory* (1971)

For Your Consideration . . .

THE "D" LIST

Willem Dafoe *Platoon* (1986); *Born on the Fourth of July* (1989)
Matt Damon *Good Will Hunting* (1997); *Saving Private Ryan* (1998)
Claire Danes *Little Women* (1994); *John Grisham's The Rainmaker* (1997)
Beverly D'Angelo *National Lampoon's Vacation* (1983); *American History X* (1998)
Rodney Dangerfield *Back to School* (1986); *Natural Born Killers* (1994)
Jeff Daniels *Terms of Endearment* (1983); *Dumb & Dumber* (1994)
Ted Danson *Three Men and a Baby* (1987); *Made in America* (1993)
Tony Danza *Illtown* (1996); *Twelve Angry Men* (1997)
Geena Davis *Thelma & Louise* (1991); *A League of Their Own* (1992)
Robert De Niro *Raging Bull* (1980); *Casino* (1995)
Dana Delany *Housesitter* (1992); *Live Nude Girls* (1995)
Dom DeLuise *The End* (1978); *Fatso* (1980)
Rebecca DeMornay *Risky Business* (1983); *The Hand That Rocks the Cradle* (1992)

Johnny Depp *What's Eating Gilbert Grape* (1993); *Donnie Brasco* (1996)
Laura Dern *Blue Velvet* (1986); *Rambling Rose* (1991)
Danny DeVito *Tin Men* (1987); *John Grisham's The Rainmaker* (1997)
Cameron Diaz *My Best Friend's Wedding* (1997); *There's Something About Mary* (1998)
Leonardo DiCaprio *What's Eating Gilbert Grape* (1993); *Titanic* (1997)
Matt Dillon *Singles* (1992); *There's Something About Mary* (1998)
Michael Douglas *Wall Street* (1987); *Falling Down* (1993)
Robert Downey Jr. *Natural Born Killers* (1994); *Home for the Holidays* (1995)
Richard Dreyfuss *Tin Men* (1987); *Mr. Holland's Opus* (1995)
Minnie Driver *Circle of Friends* (1994); *Good Will Hunting* (1997)
David Duchovny *The Rapture* (1991); *Kalifornia* (1993)
Robert Duvall *The Godfather 1902–1959: The Complete Epic* (1981); *The Apostle* (1997)
Shelley Duvall *The Shining* (1980); *Popeye* (1980)

- - - - - - - - - - - - - - - - - - -

The movie stars thought it was confetti

The 1948 Academy Award ceremony was held on Thursday, March 24, a few days after spring had sprung. The night of the Oscars it snowed in Hollywood.

- - - - - - - - - - - - - - - - - - -

73 Movies Starring the Stars of *Friends*

. . . the one with the movie listing . . .

The cast of *Friends* burst onto the pop culture landscape in 1995 like a supernova suddenly appearing in the evening sky. The show's three actors and three actresses were all good-looking, charismatic, engaging, and genuinely appealing, and when those priceless personality pluses were combined with sharp, hilarious writing, strong storylines, and top-notch directing, the result was the most popular and successful sitcom in years.

Most of the cast members had been around the showbiz block a few times, having appeared in sitcoms, movies, and other vehicles, none of which, however, made any of them a household name (except maybe for Courteney Cox, who had the most impressive résumé of the bunch, including a long stint on *Family Ties* as Michael J. Fox's girlfriend, plus roles in several movies).

Since *Friends* has been on the air, the cast has consistently also worked in films. This list looks at their big-screen work, from pre-*Friends,* through today.

JENNIFER ANISTON
"Rachel Greene"

1. *Leprechaun* (1993)
2. *She's the One* (1996)
3. *Picture Perfect* (1997)
4. *'Til There Was You* (1997)
5. *The Object of My Affection* (1998)
6. *Dream for an Insomniac* (1998)
7. *Waiting for Woody* (1998)
8. *The Thin Pink Line* (1998)
9. *Office Space* (1999)
10. *The Iron Giant* (1999)
11. *Time of Our Lives* (2000)
12. *Rock Star* (2001)

COURTENEY COX [ARQUETTE]
"Monica Geller"

1. *Masters of the Universe* (1987)
2. *Down Twisted* (1987)
3. *Cocoon: The Return* (1988)
4. *Shaking the Tree* (1990)
5. *Mr. Destiny* (1990)
6. *Blue Desert* (1991)
7. *The Opposite Sex and How to Live With Them* (1992)
8. *Ace Ventura: Pet Detective* (1994)
9. *Scream* (1996)
10. *Scream 2* (1997)
11. *Commandments* (1997)
12. *The Runner* (1999)
13. *Scream 3* (2000)
14. *The Shrink Is In* (2000)
15. *Alien Love Triangle* (2000)
16. *3,000 Miles to Graceland* (2001)

LISA KUDROW
"Phoebe Buffay"

1. *L.A. on $5 a Day* (1989)
2. *The Unborn* (1991)
3. *Dance With Death* (1991)
4. *In the Heat of Passion* (1992)
5. *In the Heat of Passion II: Unfaithful* (1994)
6. *The Crazysitter* (1995)
7. *Mother* (1996)
8. *Hacks* (1997)
9. *Clockwatchers* (1997)
10. *Romy and Michele's High School Reunion* (1997)
11. *The Opposite of Sex* (1998)
12. *Analyze This* (1999)
13. *Hanging Up* (2000)
14. *Lucky Numbers* (2000)
15. *Marci X* (2001)
16. *All Over the Guy* (2001)

MATT LeBLANC
"Joey Tribbiani"

1. *The Killing Box* (1993)
2. *Lookin' Italian* (1994)
3. *Ed* (1996)
4. *Lost in Space* (1998)
5. *Charlie's Angels* (2000)
6. *All the Queen's Men* (2001)

MATTHEW PERRY
"Chandler Bing"

1. *A Night in the Life of Jimmy Reardon* (1988)
2. *She's Out of Control* (1989)
3. *Getting In* (1994)
4. *Fools Rush In* (1997)
5. *Almost Heroes* (1998)
6. *Three to Tango* (1999)
7. *The Whole Nine Yards* (2000)
8. *The Kid* (2000)
9. *Servicing Sara* (2001)

DAVID SCHWIMMER
"Ross Geller"

1. *Flight of the Intruder* (1990)
2. *Crossing the Bridge* (1992)
3. *The Waiter* (1993)
4. *Twenty Bucks* (1993)
5. *Wolf* (1994)
6. *The Pallbearer* (1996)
7. *Breast Men* (1997) (HBO)
8. *Kissing a Fool* (1998)
9. *Six Days, Seven Nights* (1998)
10. *Apt Pupil* (1998)
11. *The Thin Pink Line* (1998)
12. *All the Rage* (1999)
13. *Love & Sex* (2000)
14. *Picking up the Pieces* (2000)

Success in show business depends on your ability to make and keep friends.

Sophie Tucker

The "Movies Based on TV Shows" List

Lately, TV has been looked to more and more as a source for movie ideas. This is not always a good thing . . . no matter how good the source show was.

But when a movie based on a TV show *does* work (*Beavis and Butthead Do America, The Fugitive, Mission: Impossible, Wayne's World* and many of the *Star Trek* movies rise immediately to the surface) the results are often unforgettable.

The Addams Family (1991); *Addams Family Values* (1993)
Alien Nation: Dark Horizon (1994)
The Avengers (1998)
Batman (1989); *Batman Returns* (1992); *Batman Forever* (1995); *Batman and Robin* (1997)
Baywatch the Movie: Forbidden Paradise (1995)
Bean (1997)
Beavis and Butt-Head Do America (1996)
The Beverly Hillbillies (1993)
The Blues Brothers (1980); *Blues Brothers 2000* (1998)
Boris and Natasha: The Movie (1992)
The Brady Bunch Movie (1995); *A Very Brady Sequel* (1996)
Car 54, Where Are You? (1994)
The Coneheads (1993)
Dennis the Menace (1993, 1998 [sequel])
Dragnet (1954, 1968, 1987)
The Flintstones (1994, 2000 [sequel])
The Fugitive (1993)
George of the Jungle (1997, 2001 [sequel])
Here Come the Nelsons [*The Adventures of Ozzie & Harriet*] (1952)
It's Pat: The Movie (1994)
Jetsons: The Movie (1990)
Leave It to Beaver (1997)
The Life of Riley (1948)
The Lone Ranger (1956)
The Long, Long Trailer [*I Love Lucy*] (1954)
Lost in Space (1998)
Maverick (1994)
McHale's Navy (1997)
Mission: Impossible (1996)
A Night at the Roxbury (1998)
Our Miss Brooks (1956)
The Adventures of Rocky and Bullwinkle (2000)
The Saint (1997)
Sgt. Bilko (1995)
Star Trek: The Motion Picture (1980); *Star Trek 2: The Wrath of Khan* (1982); *Star Trek 3: The Search for Spock* (1984); *Star Trek 4: The Voyage Home* (1986); *Star Trek 5: The Final Frontier* (1989); *Star*

Trek 6: The Undiscovered Country (1991); *Star Trek: Generations* (1994); *Star Trek: First Contact* (1996); *Star Trek: Insurrection* (1999)
Stuart Saves His Family (1994)
Twin Peaks: Fire Walk With Me (1992)
The Untouchables (1987)
Wayne's World (1992); *Wayne's World 2* (1993)
The X-Files Movie (1998)

For Your Consideration . . .

THE "E" LIST

Clint Eastwood *Unforgiven* (1992); *In the Line of Fire* (1993)
Anthony Edwards *Top Gun* (1986); *In Cold Blood* (1996)
Hector Elizondo *The Flamingo Kid* (1984); *Nothing in Common* (1986)
Chris Elliott *Groundhog Day* (1993); *There's Something About Mary* (1998)
Cary Elwes *Twister* (1996); *Kiss the Girls* (1997)
Emilio Estevez *Repo Man* (1983); *The Breakfast Club* (1985)

- - - - - - - - - - - - -

Show people have always been so cutting-edge liberal, haven't they?

When Hattie McDaniel won a Best Supporting Actress Oscar at the 1939 ceremony for her performance as Mammy in *Gone With the Wind,* she had to give a speech written for her by the studio in which she promised to be a "credit" to her race. McDaniel was the first African American to win an Academy Award and the first to attend an Oscar banquet. A week after she won this award for her brilliant work in the Civil War epic, *Daily Variety* wrote: "In addition to her ability as an actress, Hattie McDaniel could pose as an ad for Aunt Jemima."

- - - - - - - - - - - - -

86 Horror and Science Fiction Series

Horror and science fiction are to Hollywood what cheese pizza and meatball subs are to an Italian pizzeria: staples.

Oh, sure, the pizzeria owner may occasionally branch out into Hawaiian pizza (yuk) and Texas Bar-B-Q night, but there sure as hell had better be cheese pizza and meatball subs on the menu at all times.

Horror and science fiction are two of the most popular genres of movies, and each year's releases from Hollywood include a goodly sum of slasher flicks, alien epics, and monster movies.

Sure, they're often mindless entertainments providing vicarious thrills, but they're a great way to spend a couple of hours. It's like riding a roller-coaster: You feel like you're falling off a building, but you're safely strapped into the car. While watching a horror movie, you get to experience what it might feel like to be chased by a maniacal killer or be trapped in a coffin—(underwater, of course)—but the reality is that you're safe and sound in front of the movie or TV screen and you can control the chills and thrills.

This chapter looks first at *The Monsters*—the most important and most successful horror and sci-fi series of the past forty years—followed by a rundown of some of the lesser-known, but nevertheless unquestionably successful series. (Ever heard of the *Witchcraft* series? No? Well, since 1988 there have been nine individual *Witchcraft* movies—the original and an astonishing eight sequels. Somebody's watching this stuff and this chapter is for all those gorehounds out there . . . you know who you are.)

The Monsters

ALIEN

Monstrous, parasitical alien creatures with acid for blood are discovered during a routine mission by earthling salvage freighters. Mayhem ensues for hundreds of years (and three sequels). A classic series.

★ *Alien* (1979); *Aliens* (1986); *Alien 3* (1992); *Alien: Resurrection* (1997).

AMERICAN WEREWOLF

An American college student is bitten by a werewolf and tries to avoid transforming into one, while his dead friend (in increasingly disgusting stages of decomposition) offers advice from beyond. The first is a cult classic; the second, 15 years later, more a remake than a sequel. Great fun, with great special effects.

★ *An American Werewolf in London* (1981); *An American Werewolf in Paris* (1997).

THE AMITYVILLE HORROR

There's a house in Amityville, Long Island and it's haunted, see. And it remains haunted for several movies. That's about the gist of it. Some of these are good; some ain't . . . but the hits just keep on coming!

★ *The Amityville Horror* (1979); *Amityville II: The Possession* (1982); *Amityville 3: The Demon* (1983); *Amityville 4: The Evil Escapes* (1989); *The Amityville Curse* (1990); *Amityville 1992: It's About Time* (1992); *Amityville: A New Generation* (1993); *Amityville Dollhouse* (1996).

CANDYMAN

A graduate student comes upon the vengeful spirit of the lynched son of a slave who has come back to our reality with a hook and an attitude. Based on the stories of Clive Barker.

★ *Candyman* (1992); *Candyman 2: Farewell to the Flesh* (1994); *Candyman III* (1999).

CHILD'S PLAY

Chucky the doll is home to the spirit of a dead serial killer who uses him to continue his murderous rampage (and also as a means to try and somehow come back to life). Great, great fun, even if occasionally really, really stupid.

★ *Child's Play* (1988); *Child's Play 2* (1990); *Child's Play 3* (1991); *Child's Play 4: Bride of Chucky* (1998); *Child's Play 5: Son of Chucky* (2000).

CHILDREN OF THE CORN

The first film in this series is based on a chilling *Night Shift* short story by Stephen King about a group of young children in Nebraska who sacrifice their parents to "He Who Walks Between the Rows," a demonic Corn God who demands blood sacrifices on a regular basis. The three sequels are other writers' expansions of this tale and are not based on any of King's writings. The first is probably the best of the bunch.

★ *Children of the Corn* (1984); *Children of the Corn 2: The Final Sacrifice* (1992); *Children of the Corn 3: Urban Harvest* (1995); *Children of the Corn 4: The Gathering* (1996).

C. H. U. D.

C. H. U. D. stands for Cannibalistic Humanoid Underground Dwellers and this grisly series is about these always-hungry creeps who use the streets of New York as an all-you-can-eat buffet.

★ *C. H. U. D.* (1984); *C. H. U. D. 2: Bud the Chud* (1989).

CREEPSHOW

These anthology films (five short horror tales in the first one; three in the second) are Stephen King and director George Romero's tribute to E.C. Comics. In fact, the original film was "comic book-ized" (instead of novelized) and published as an oversized, garishly drawn and colored, full-blown trade paperback comic book (which is now a sought-after collectible to King fans). The first film (especially the "Jordy Verrill" segment which starred King himself) is campier than the second; both are a lot of fun to watch.

★ *Creepshow* (1982); *Creepshow 2* (1987).

CRITTERS

Critters are really "Krites," little alien creatures with rows of razor-sharp teeth and a voracious passion for flesh—especially human flesh. At the beginning of the series, a group of Krites escape from a prison transport, steal a ship and head for Earth, pursued by bounty hunters who can assume human form. The Krites end up in a small town called Grover's Bend where they immediately begin wreaking havoc and killing and eating people. The Krites are marvelous creations, sort of like alien "Gremlins," but a lot meaner and nastier. Overall, this is a rare example of a decent horror series that has a terrific (and sarcastic) sense of humor.

★ *Critters* (1986); *Critters 2: The Main Course* (1988); *Critters 3* (1991); *Critters 4* (1991).

THE CROW

This fantasy/horror series is based on the popular comic strip of the same name and is about a guy who comes back to life a year after his death to avenge his and his girlfriend's murders. Star Brandon Lee was accidentally killed during the making of *The Crow,* but computer trickery and stunt doubles allowed the producers to complete the film. The sequel is not as good as the first film.

★ *The Crow* (1993); *The Crow 2: City of Angels* (1996).

DARKMAN

Another horror series based on a comic strip. Darkman is a disfigured scientist who experiments with cloning body parts and "liquid skin" left for dead by a corrupt politician. One movie guide described this series as "exquisitely violent." Darkman Liam Neeson turned his mutant reins over to Arnold Vosloo for Parts 2 and 3 (both of which were straight-to-video releases).

★ *Darkman* (1990); *Darkman 2: The Return of Durant* (1994); *Darkman 3: Die Darkman Die* (1995).

THE EVIL DEAD

Make sure you hold on to something solid when you sit down to watch this series. Made with almost no budget at all, the plot of *The Evil Dead* is simple: Five young people in a cabin in the woods awaken demonic forces that want to possess them. They, of course, would prefer that that not happen, and thus the battle begins. Writer/director Sam Raimi was a mere college lad when he filmed the initial one and what he lacked in funds he more than made up for in cinematic style and bravado. The camera work and effects in this movie are incredible. We rush through the woods and feel as though we are certainly going to crash into a tree. We see demons that are beyond grotesque and that convince us that if we ever did see a real demon, this is what they would look like. *The Evil Dead* was followed by two sequels, both of which are actually better than the first. (Much of the improvement is due to bigger budgets.)

★ *The Evil Dead* (1983); *Evil Dead 2: Dead By Dawn* (1987); *Army of Darkness* (1993).

THE EXORCIST

One of the best horror tales of all time, the first film in this series is an undeniable classic. Certain moments from *The Exorcist* (Regan's rotating head, the pea-soup vomit scene, the crucifix masturbation scene, the Coca-Cola/pubic hair scene, etc.) have become part of the pop culture zeitgeist. Part 2 is ridiculous; Part 3, a little better, but neither even come close to the original.

★ *The Exorcist* (1973, 2000 ["Director's Cut" re-release); *The Exorcist 2: The Heretic* (1977); *The Exorcist 3: Legion* (1990).

THE FLY

The 1986 remake of the 1958 classic (itself a terrific film) is the one to watch. The amazing Jeff Goldblum stars as Seth Brundle, the scientist who ends up genetically combining himself with a housefly. He is undeniably brilliant. The other performances are superb (Geena Davis costars) and the script and direction by horror maven David Cronenberg are unparalleled. The 1989 sequel, written by Mick Garris and starring Eric Stoltz doesn't come close to Cronenberg's, but in all fairness, what could?

★ *The Fly* (1958); *The Fly* (1986); *The Fly II* (1989).

FRIDAY THE 13TH

The first film in this series is the granddaddy of the naked-dead-teens-in-the-woods slasher movies, and over the years, the inimitable Jason Voorhees has become one of the three most important unkillable killers in the horror movie genre, (the other two being, of course, Michael Myers from the *Halloween* series, and the lovable Freddy Kreuger from the *Nightmare on Elm Street* series). For the most part, the *Friday the 13th* movies are fairly unremarkable, but undeniably entertaining and well-produced. As with many of the series approaching double-digits in their number of offerings, some of the *Fridays* are terrific; some are almost unwatchable.

★ *Friday the 13th* (1980); *Friday the 13th, Part II* (1981); *Friday the 13th, Part III* (1982); *Friday the 13th: The Final Chapter* (1984);

Friday the 13th, Part V: A New Beginning (1985); *Friday the 13th, Part VI: Jason Lives* (1986); *Friday the 13th, Part VII: The New Blood* (1988); *Friday the 13th, Part VIII: Jason Takes Manhattan* (1989); *Jason Goes to Hell: The Final Friday* (1993); *Freddy vs. Jason* (1998).

FROM DUSK TILL DAWN

Quentin Tarantino scripted the first film in this series (which stars George Clooney, Harvey Keitel, Tarantino, Juliette Lewis, Salma Hayek, and Kelly Preston) when he was a video store clerk and when he sold it, he used the money to make *Reservoir Dogs.* That lineage alone makes this worth watching, wouldn't you say? George Clooney plays an ex-con who must wage war against vampires who have made a Mexican biker bar their lair. The second half of the first movie (which is directed by Robert *"El Mariachi"* Rodriguez) is the battle between Clooney and company and the vampires. This sequence is ultraviolent, meticulously staged, and a joy to behold (if you're a horror buff, that is). The second movie pales in comparison.

★ *From Dusk Till Dawn* (1995); *From Dusk Till Dawn 2: Texas Blood Money* (1998).

GREMLINS

The *Gremlins* series is a cinematic home run for Joe Dante and executive producer Steven Spielberg It is exciting, scary, funny, and endlessly entertaining. Rand Peltzer, an inept inventor; buys his son, Billy, an adorable Mogwai—a strange little creature from antiquity that looks like a teddy bear, is highly intelligent, and has a somewhat "schizophrenic" genetic identity—as a Christmas present. Billy promises to obey the very important "rules" regarding its care, but of course, the rules inevitably get broken, and that's when the real "fun" begins. The Mogwai reproduce as vicious little Gremlins who immediately go about trashing the hell out of Billy's beloved hometown, and doing away with its citizenry. It is up to Billy and his charming girlfriend Kate (Phoebe Cates), to exterminate the bad Mogwai and save the town from complete and total destruction. Both *Gremlins* movies have terrific casts and superb production values and special effects. (And in a flawless bit of casting, *Gremlins* boasts the hyperkinetic Howie Mandel as the voice of Gizmo the Mogwai.) The sequel is actually a little better than the excellent first movie. (And both flicks are jam-packed with movie references. How many can *you* find?).

★ *Gremlins* (1984); *Gremlins 2: The New Batch* (1990).

HALLOWEEN

As a young boy, Michael Myers murdered his sister on Halloween night because he saw her doing the nasty with her boyfriend. On Halloween night fifteen years later, he escapes his mental institution prison and heads straight back to the scene of the crime to kill all over again. The original *Halloween* has a foreboding and ominous tone that is very frightening and quite effective. The sequels don't even come close to the level of excellence of the first film and, except for *Halloween 3: Season of the Witch* (which has nothing to do with the original myth of Michael Myers), the others are all essentially about the unkillable Myers returning home to off a few more unwitting townfolk (usually none of whom will be back for the next installment in the series). This is one of the few horror franchises that were really successful, with a total gross (so far) of well over $200 million.

★ *Halloween* (1978); *Halloween II* (1981); *Halloween III: Season of the Witch* (1983); *Halloween 4: The Return of Michael Myers* (1988); *Halloween 5: The Revenge of Michael Myers* (1989); *Halloween 6: The Curse of Michael Myers* (1995); *Halloween: H20* (1998).

HANNIBAL LECTER

A brilliantly written, acted, and directed horror movie series, based on three equally superb novels by Thomas Harris (*Red Dragon, The Silence of the Lambs,* and *Hannibal*). Hannibal Lecter—Hannibal the Cannibal—is one of the most memorable human monsters in all of the horror universe. The movies are incredible—even though Hannibal has been played by two different actors, Brian Cox in *Manhunter*; Anthony Hopkins in *The Silence of the Lambs* (for which he won an Academy Award for Best Actor), and the recent *Hannibal. Lambs* also garnered Oscars for Jodie Foster, director Jonathan Demme, and as Best Picture. And all were well-deserved. In 1999, Harris released his third "Hannibal Lecter" novel, *Hannibal*.

★ *Manhunter* (1986); *The Silence of the Lambs* (1991); *Hannibal* (2001).

HELLRAISER

This Clive Barker series gave the world Pinhead, the grotesque and malevolent demon who is best remembered for the hundreds of pins sticking out of his face, and for his taste for torture, blood, and human body parts. The first two movies in the series are the most accessible (the plotline gets increasingly convoluted as the series progresses), although the grisly effects and graphic gore the series is known for is present in all four installments. The *Hellraiser* movies are the kinds of films people who are into horror adore. Others tend to flee the room.

★ *Hellraiser* (1987); *Hellbound: Hellraiser 2* (1988); *Hellraiser 3: Hell on Earth* (1992); *Hellraiser 4: Bloodline* (1995).

THE HOWLING

Werewolves are everywhere. Even in London. (Sorry.) And you better watch out you don't get bitten by one. That is essentially the plot of all the movies in this series. As is often the case, the first in the series is the best.

★ *The Howling* (1981); *The Howling 2: Your Sister Is a Werewolf* (1985); *The Howling 3* (1987); *The Howling 4: The Original Nightmare* (1988); *The Howling 5: The Rebirth* (1989); *The Howling 6: The Freaks* (1990); *The Howling: New Moon Rising* (1995).

I KNOW WHAT YOU DID LAST SUMMER

A group of teens cover up a fatal hit-and-run automobile accident and think they're in the clear, until they receive letters a year later which say . . . well, *you know* what they say! These two horror flicks are surprisingly effective and contain a self-referential sensibility that pays homage to—and makes fun of—horror movie traditions and scenarios, much the way *Scream* (1996) did, which makes sense since both were written by Kevin Williamson.

★ *I Know What You Did Last Summer* (1997); *I Still Know What You Did Last Summer* (1998).

NIGHT OF THE LIVING DEAD

The newly dead come alive and feed on the flesh of the living. Now we're talkin'! The first film of this horrific George Romero series is the best, even though it's in black-and-white and is the one with the lowest budget. *Night of the Living Dead* is the great granddaddy of all the zombie flicks to follow and is also memorable for graphic nudity, on-screen cannibalism (a little girl feasts on her mother in one of the movie's most unforgettable scenes), and for having a black lead . . . at a time when black males almost never were cast as the hero. The two sequels are good (and in color), but neither come close to the surreal horror of the first. A classic. If you're into horror, you must own at least the first film of this gruesome series.

★ *Night of the Living Dead* (1968); *Dawn of the Dead* (1979); *Day of the Dead* (1985); *Night of the Living Dead* (Remake, 1990).

A NIGHTMARE ON ELM STREET

One of the all time classic horror series, the *Nightmare on Elm Street* movies gave us that fabulous and irrepressible madman, the "Bastard Son of a Hundred Maniacs," the one, the only, FREDDY KREUGER! (Although when the series debuted, we didn't yet know that Freddy was the misbegotten offspring of a nun who had been raped by a hundred mental patients. We wouldn't find that out until Part 3, *The Dream Warriors*.) Freddy Kreuger is one of the most memorable characters in the horror universe. He is mean, violent, masochistic, sadistic, and heartless. But he is also poetic, sardonic, playful, and very funny.

In the first film of the series, we learn that some of the children who live on Elm Street are dreaming of a horribly disfigured man wearing a striped shirt and battered fedora. Oh yeah, and he has razor blades for fingers. They quickly learn that any violence Freddy commits against them in the dream world affects them in the waking world. Kids start dying, and it falls upon high schooler Nancy Thompson to figure out what's going on. Nancy's mother tells her the story of "Mr. Kreuger"; how he was a child molester who lived in the neighborhood and how, when the police did nothing to stop him, the parents of Elm Street took it upon themselves to get rid of Freddy once and for all. They burned him alive. But Freddy's "essence" (or putrid soul, if you like) survived and metamorphosed into a being that could do material damage in an immaterial world.

Nancy ends up going "womano a mano" with Freddy in a conflict that ends with her figuring out how to take away the Kreugster's power.

A Nightmare on Elm Street was written and directed by Wes Craven, and it is one of the best things he has ever done. Freddy Kreuger is an impeccably realized character and even Robert Englund, who plays Freddy, gives all the credit to Craven for the artistic success of the film and the character. The seven (at this writing) sequels to the first *Nightmare* are also quite good and I consider the entire series one of the most entertaining and well done in the horror movie genre. (The first *Nightmare* was also one of Johnny Depp's earliest film appearances.)

★ *A Nightmare on Elm Street* (1984); *A Nightmare on Elm Street 2: Freddy's Revenge* (1985); *A Nightmare on Elm Street 3: The Dream Warriors* (1987); *A Nightmare on Elm Street 4: The Dream Master* (1988); *Nightmare on Elm Street 5: The Dream Child* (1989); *Freddy's Dead: The Final Nightmare* (1991); *Wes Craven's New Nightmare* (1994); *Freddy vs. Jason* (1998).

THE OMEN

A U.S. ambassador to Great Britain (Gregory Peck, yet) inadvertently adopts Satan's son. And how was your day? This series, following on the heels of the popular *Rosemary's Baby* (1968) and *The Exorcist* movies, rightly can be considered a horror classic. *The Omen* itself contains two classic demonic execution scenes that have since been imitated in many other horror films. In one, a priest is speared to death by a lightning rod shot from a church steeple down into his body. He is left standing upright impaled through the chest with the rod planted in the ground. The other notable scene was quite shocking for its time. A character is decapitated by a huge pane of glass that slides off a truck and neatly takes his head off. We then get to see the head rolling merrily away. This scene alone is worth the price of admission (actually, the price of a rental these days).

★ *The Omen* (1976); *Damien: Omen II* (1978); *The Final Conflict* (1981); *Omen IV: The Awakening* (1992).

POLTERGEIST

Demonic spirits kidnap a little girl through her TV screen and hold her captive in a realm between heaven and hell. Her parents enlist the help of a psychic to rescue her; mayhem ensues. This enormously popular series (especially the first movie, which was written and produced by Steven Spielberg) spawned a cable TV series, and little Heather O'Rourke's "They're baaaack!" is now a pop culture catchphrase. But was the *Poltergeist* series cursed? Heather O'Rourke died suddenly four months before the release of the third installment; her costar Dominique Dunne (daughter of the noted author, Dominick Dunne) was murdered after the first film came out.

★ *Poltergeist* (1982); *Poltergeist 2: The Other Side* (1986); *Poltergeist 3* (1988); *Poltergeist: The Legacy* (Cable; 1996).

PSYCHO

The Alfred Hitchcock classic is ranked number 18 on the AFI's list of the 100 greatest American films of all time. A horror film in the AFI's top 20? *Psycho* must be pretty damn special to warrant that kind of praise   and it is. Shot in stark black-and-white, this haunting and grim tale of a mama's boy, his motel (which has peepholes in its walls), and his obsession with a female guest, is best remembered for its shower scene, which was a stunning manifestation of Hitchcock's genius with a camera. A few years back *Cinefantastique* magazine did a shot-by-shot deconstruction of the shower scene and we got to see just how meticulously structured the scene truly was. There is precisely one shot in the scene where the tip of the knife seems to be just touching Marion's belly, but it never actually pierces her skin. And yet, the overall effect of the scene is one of graphic and bloody violence. Hitchcock was especially inventive while shooting this scene. At one point in the scene, the camera points straight up at the showerhead as the water is flowing. Have you ever wondered how he was able to achieve that shot without getting the camera lens wet? A standard 50mm lens would have gotten soaked, so Hitchcock used a long lens and shot very tight, resulting in the water spraying past the lens, instead of on it. Also, *Psycho* was one of the first major films to use the legend of cannibalistic serial killer Ed Gein as part of its story [also see *The Texas Chainsaw Massacre*]. The Hitchcock movie is based on Robert Bloch's novel of the same name, which is loosely based on the Gein story. The three sequels (all with Anthony Perkins) and the 1998 remake are all well done, but not one approaches the original.

★ *Psycho* (1960); *Psycho 2* (1983); *Psycho 3* (1986); *Psycho 4: The Beginning* (1990); *Psycho* (remake, 1998).

SCANNERS

This is an entertaining science fiction/horror series about a group of telepaths who can use their powers to make people explode. The first film of the series boasts an exploding head scene that instantly made it a cult classic. The sequels are okay, but the first film—written and directed by the renowned David Cronenberg—has a dark quality to it that is quite effective.

★ *Scanners* (1981); *Scanners 2: The New Order* (1991); *Scanners 3: The Takeover* (1992); *Scanners: The Showdown* (1994).

SCREAM

Screenwriter Kevin Williamson grew up on eighties horror films, and in his *Scream* series, his characters know all the rules of the genre (and assume that we the viewers do, too). The way *Star Trek* fans knew that the crew member in the red shirt would be dead before the first commercial, Williamson's characters know that anyone who has sex in a horror movie usually ends up dead; and that anyone who says "I'll be right back" also often ends up dead. They also know that phone calls can be quite dangerous and in a perfect touch, the killer uses cell phones (which everyone has, of course) to terrorize his victims. Both *Screams* were directed by Wes *"Nightmare on Elm Street"* Craven and his willingness to play the clichés and mock a genre he helped create make for a genuinely entertaining, funny, scary, and smart horror series.

★ *Scream* (1996); *Scream 2* (1997); *Scream 3* (1999).

TERMINATOR

One of the all-time best (possibly *the* best) science fiction (with elements of horror) series ever committed to celluloid. First, Ahnuld is a *bad* Terminator, then he's a *good* Terminator . . . who knows what he'll be in the upcoming third installment? Great effects, powerful stories, and terrific performances all combine to create a sci-fi/horror classic.

★ *The Terminator* (1984); *Terminator 2: Judgment Day* (1991); *Terminator 3* (2002).

THE TEXAS CHAINSAW MASSACRE

Another classic series, although like *Night of the Living Dead,* the first film in the series is the most intense and most genuinely frightening. Based in part on the true story of cannibalistic serial killer Ed Gein, *Texas Chainsaw Massacre* was written and directed by Tobe Hooper, who would go on to *Salem's Lot* (1979), *Poltergeist* (1982), and the 1986 *Invaders From Mars* remake. *TCM* is the series that made chainsaws cool.

★ *The Texas Chainsaw Massacre* (1974); *The Texas Chainsaw Massacre 2* (1986); *Leatherface: The Texas Chainsaw Massacre III* (1989); *The Texas Chainsaw Massacre 4: The Next Generation* (1995).

Other notable horror and science fiction series

Alligator *Alligator* (1980); *Alligator 2: The Mutation* (1990)
Basket Case *Basket Case* (1982); *Basket Case 2* (1990); *Basket Case 3: The Progeny* (1992)
Beyond the Door *Beyond the Door* (1975); *Beyond the Door 2* (1979); *Beyond the Door 3* (1991)
Blade *Blade* (1998); *Blade 2* (2000)
Carrie *Carrie* (1976); *The Rage: Carrie 2* (1998)
The Curse *The Curse* (1987); *Curse 2: The Bite* (1988); *Curse 3: Blood Sacrifice* (1990); *Curse 4: The Ultimate Sacrifice* (1993)
Demons *Demons* (1986); *Demons 2* (1987)
The Dentist *The Dentist* (1996); *The Dentist 2* (1999)
The Gate *The Gate* (1987); *Gate 2* (1992)
Gates of Hell *Gates of Hell* (1983); *Gates of Hell 2: Dead Awakening* (1996)
Ghoulies *Ghoulies* (1984); *Ghoulies 2* (1987); *Ghoulies 3: Ghoulies Go to College* (1991); *Ghoulies 4* (1993)
The Hills Have Eyes *The Hills Have Eyes* (1977); *The Hills Have Eyes, Part 2* (1984)

The Hitchhiker *The Hitchhiker* (1985); *The Hitchhiker 2* (1985); *Hitchhiker 3* (1987); *Hitchhiker 4* (1987)

House *House* (1986); *House 2: The Second Story* (1987); *The Horror Show* (1989); *House 4: Home Deadly Home* (1991)

It's Alive *It's Alive* (1974); *It's Alive 2: It Lives Again* (1978); *It's Alive 3: Island of the Alive* (1987)

Killer Tomatoes *Attack of the Killer Tomatoes* (1977); *Return of the Killer Tomatoes* (1988); *Killer Tomatoes Strike Back* (1990); *Killer Tomatoes Eat France* (1991)

Lawnmower Man *The Lawnmower Man* (1992); *The Lawnmower Man 2: Beyond Cyberspace* (1995)

Leprechaun *Leprechaun* (1993); *Leprechaun 2* (1994); *Leprechaun 3* (1995); *Leprechaun 4: In Space* (1996)

Maniac Cop *Maniac Cop* (1988); *Maniac Cop 2* (1990); *Maniac Cop 3: Badge of Silence* (1993)

Mark of the Devil *Mark of the Devil* (1969); *Mark of the Devil 2* (1972)

Mirror, Mirror *Mirror, Mirror* (1990); *Mirror, Mirror 2: Raven Dance* (1994); *Mirror, Mirror 3: The Voyeur* (1996)

Mommy *Mommy* (1995); *Mommy 2: Mother's Day* (1996)

Night of the Demons *Night of the Demons* (1988); *Night of the Demons 2* (1994); *Night of the Demons 3* (1997)

976-Evil *976-EVIL* (1988); *976-EVIL 2: The Astral Factor* (1991)

Pet Sematary *Pet Sematary* (1989); *Pet Sematary 2* (1992)

Phantasm *Phantasm* (1979); *Phantasm II* (1988); *Phantasm III: Lord of the Dead* (1994)

Piranha *Piranha* (1978); *Piranha 2: The Spawning* (1982); *Piranha* (Remake, 1995)

Prom Night *Prom Night* (1980); *Hello Mary Lou: Prom Night II* (1987); *Prom Night III: The Last Kiss* (1989); *Prom Night IV: Deliver Us From Evil* (1991)

Pumpkinhead *Pumpkinhead* (1988); *Pumpkinhead 2: Blood Wings* (1994)

Psycho Cop *Psycho Cop* (1988); *Psycho Cop 2* (1994)

Puppet Master *Puppet Master* (1989); *Puppet Master 2* (1990); *Puppet Master 3: Toulon's Revenge* (1990); *Puppet Master 4* (1993); *Puppet Master 5: The Final Chapter* (1994)

Re-Animator *Re-Animator* (1985); *Bride of Re-Animator* (1990)

The Return of the Living Dead *The Return of the Living Dead* (1985); *Return of the Living Dead 2* (1988); *Return of the Living Dead 3* (1993)

Saturday the 14th *Saturday the 14th* (1981); *Saturday the 14th Strikes Back* (1988)

Silent Night, Deadly Night *Silent Night, Deadly Night* (1984); *Silent Night, Deadly Night, Part 2* (1987); *Silent Night, Deadly Night III: Better Watch Out!* (1989); *Silent Night, Deadly Night 4: Initiation* (1990); *Silent Night, Deadly Night 5: The Toymaker* (1991)

Sleepaway Camp *Sleepaway Camp* (1983); *Sleepaway Camp 2: Unhappy Campers* (1988); *Sleepaway Camp 3: Teenage Wasteland* (1989)

Slumber Party Massacre *The Slumber Party Massacre* (1982); *Slumber Party Massacre 2* (1987); *Slumber Party Massacre 3* (1990)

Sometimes They Come Back *Sometimes They Come Back* (1991); *Sometimes They Come Back . . . Again* (1996); *Sometimes They Come Back . . . For More* (1998)

Sorority House Massacre *Sorority House Massacre* (1986); *Sorority House Massacre 2: Nighty Nightmare* (1992)

The Stepfather *The Stepfather* (1987); *Stepfather II: Make Room for Daddy* (1989); *Stepfather III: Father's Day* (1992)

Things *Things* (1993); *Things 2* (1997)

To Die For *To Die For* (1989); *To Die For 2: Son of Darkness* (1991)

Toxic Avenger *The Toxic Avenger* (1986); *The Toxic Avenger, Part 2* (1989); *The Toxic Avenger, Part 3: The Last Temptation of Toxie* (1989)

Tremors *Tremors* (1989); *Tremors 2: Aftershocks* (1996)

Troll *Troll* (1986); *Troll 2* (1992)

The Unborn *The Unborn* (1991); *The Unborn 2* (1992)

The Unnamable *The Unnamable* (1988); *The Unnamable 2: The Statement of Randolph Carter* (1992)

Warlock *Warlock* (1991); *Warlock: The Armageddon* (1993); *Warlock III* (1999)

Watchers *Watchers* (1988); *Watchers 2* (1990); *Watchers 3* (1994); *Watchers Reborn* (1998)

Wishmaster *Wishmaster* (1997); *Wishmaster 2* (1999)

Witchboard *Witchboard* (1987); *Witchboard 2: The Devil's Doorway* (1993); *Witchboard 3: The Possession* (1995)

Witchcraft *Witchcraft* (1988); *Witchcraft 2: The Temptress* (1990); *Witchcraft 3: The Kiss of Death* (1990); *Witchcraft 4: Virgin Heart* (1992); *Witchcraft 5: Dance With the Devil* (1992); *Witchcraft 6: The Devil's Mistress* (1994); *Witchcraft 7: Judgment Hour* (1995); *Witchcraft 8: Salem's Ghost* (1995); *Witchcraft 9: Bitter Flesh* (1996)

Xtro *Xtro* (1983); *Xtro 2: The Second Encounter* (1991); *Xtro 3: Watch the Skies* (1995)

- - - - - - - - - - - - - - - -

My grandmother said I was the devil's spawn, that I was Satan. Because I talked back, I never did what I was told. I really should have had more respect for the teachers I had. It was my insecurity.

Sandra Bullock
Movieline, April 1999

- - - - - - - - - - - - - - - -

155 Hollywood Deaths

You may not recognize many of the names on this list (maybe you will) but what they all have in common is that they were all part of the Hollywood community. Some died "regular" deaths; some died odd deaths.

Reading through this necrography, some intriguing questions come to mind. Why do so many Hollywood celebrities fall out of windows? Why is ALS (Lou Gehrig's disease) seemingly more prevalent among celebrities than the general population (or is it)? Why do so many actors die from melanoma, one of the most easily cured cancers? And why do so many actors die from accidents during filming?

Riddle these riddles what you will. And even if these deaths *are* outside of the statistical norm, we can still nevertheless be fairly certain that most "civilians" (non-showbiz folk, that is) will probably *not* die by impaling themselves on a sword after falling from a horse during the filming of a battle scene.

Thank God for small favors, eh?

★ In 1918, actor **Ruth Darling Franklin** died when she was crushed by an automobile while waiting for a streetcar.

★ In 1918, actor **Franklin Ritchie** died when he was crushed by an overturned automobile in Los Angeles.

★ In 1920, actor **Omer Locklear** died in a plane crash in Los Angeles during the filming of a movie.

★ In 1923, actor **Martha Mansfield** died from burns when her dress accidentally ignited on location of a movie in San Antonio.

★ In 1923, actor **Inda Palmer**'s skeleton was found five months after her mysterious and unexplained death.

★ In 1924, actor **Kate Lester** died when her studio dressing gown caught fire from a gas stove explosion on a movie set in London.

★ In 1926, actor **Paul Humphrey** died when dynamite exploded prematurely during filming in San Diego.

★ In 1926, actor **Barbara LaMarr**, foreshadowing Karen Carpenter's death fifty-seven years later, died at the age of twenty-nine from "overdieting."

★ In 1927, actor **Isadora Duncan** was strangled in France when her scarf caught in the rear wheel of her car and choked her to death.

★ In 1928, actor **Holbrook Blinn** died when he fell off a horse in Crota, New York.

★ In 1928, actor **Frank Currier** died from blood poisoning after he slammed his finger in a car door and became severely infected.

★ In 1929, actor **Paul Leni** died from blood poisoning in Hollywood from a neglected ulcerated tooth.

★ In 1930, the official cause of actor **William Courtleigh Sr.**'s death was "indigestion."

★ In 1931, actor **Ullrich Haupt** died when he was mistakenly shot during a deer hunting trip near Santa Maria, California.

★ In 1931, actor **Alexander G. Penrod** died in a ship explosion while filming on location in the Antarctic Ocean.

★ In 1931, actor **George Westmore** committed suicide by swallowing bichloride of mercury—which took three full days to kill him.

★ In 1932, actor **Peg Entwistle** committed suicide by leaping from the "Hollywood" sign in the Hollywood Hills. (It is not known which letter she chose to jump from.)

★ In 1933, actor **Roy "Skeeter Bill" Robbins** died when he was hit by a truck in Georgia while cleaning snow off his car.

★ In 1934, actor **Eugenie Besserer** died in Los Angeles from a massive heart attack while planning her fiftieth wedding anniversary celebration.

★ In 1934, the official cause of actor **Emile Chautard**'s death was "organic trouble."

★ In 1934, actor **Russ Columbo** was accidentally shot to death by a friend while he was examining a pistol.

★ In 1935, actor **Gordon Westcott** was killed when he fell from his horse during a polo game.

★ In 1936, the official cause of actor **William Ingersoll**'s death was "acute indigestion."

★ In 1936, actor **Marilyn Miller** died from toxemia (blood poisoning) from a sinus infection.

★ In 1936, actor **James Murray** drowned when he accidentally fell off a pier in New York City.

★ In 1937, actor **Snitz Edwards** died from arthritis.

★ In 1937, actor **Jean Harlow** died of kidney disease.

★ In 1937, comedian and actor **Ted Healy** died from injuries sustained during a fight in a bar in Los Angeles.

★ In 1938, actor **Florence Lawrence** committed suicide in Beverly Hills by swallowing a mixture of cough syrup and ant paste.

★ In 1939, actor **Vsevolod Meyerhold** was tortured to death by Stalin's secret police on false charges of treason.

★ In 1939, actor **Helen Ware** died from a throat infection.

★ In 1940, actor **Hal Walters** was killed by a German bomb in England during a World War II air raid.

★ In 1941, actor **Bill Meade** died when he fell off a horse during filming in Hollywood and impaled himself on a sword.

★ In 1941, actor **Walther Ruttman** was killed as he was filming a newsreel about the Eastern Front during World War II.

★ In 1942, actor **Phillips Holmes** died in an air collision of two Royal Canadian Air Force planes near Armstrong, Ontario.

★ In 1942, actor **Buck Jones** was burned to death while trying to rescue people trapped in a nightclub fire in Boston.

★ In 1943, actor **Harry Bauer** died of unknown causes after being interrogated by the Gestapo in Paris.

★ In 1943, actor **Leslie Howard** died when a passenger plane he was flying in was shot down by a Nazi fighter over the Bay of Biscay, and later was reportedly revealed to be on a spy mission.

★ In 1943, actor **Charles Ray** died from a throat infection caused by an infected tooth.

★ In 1943, actor **Conrad Veidt** died from a massive heart attack while playing golf in Hollywood.

★ In 1943, journalist **Alexander Woollcott** died from a heart attack during a CBS broadcast in New York.

★ In 1944, actor **Kurt Gerron** was executed in Auschwitz.

★ In 1944, bandleader **Glenn Miller** died when his RAF plane went down on its way across the English Channel.

★ In 1944, actor **Lee B. Powell** was killed in action in the South Pacific during World War II.

★ In 1944, actor **Richard Purcell** died from a massive heart attack while playing golf in Hollywood.

★ In 1944, actor **Edward Fielding** died from a massive heart attack while mowing his lawn in Beverly Hills.

★ In 1945, actor **Robert "Wheezer" Hutchins** died in Army training camp accident during World War II.

★ In 1945, actor **Addison "Jack" Randall** was killed when he fell from his horse during filming in Canoga Park, California.

★ In 1945, actor **Lizzi Waldmüller** was killed during an air raid in Vienna.

★ In 1946, actor **Russell Gleason** died when he accidentally fell from a fourth floor hotel window in New York City.

★ In 1946, entertainer **Lionel Royce** died from a massive heart attack in Manila as he was entertaining the troops with the USO.

★ In 1947, actor **Will Fyffe** died when he accidentally fell from a hotel window in St. Andrews, Scotland.

★ In 1948, actor **Solomon Mikhoels** was killed when Stalin ordered him to be run over by a truck.

★ In 1949, actor **Owen Davis Jr.** drowned when he accidentally fell off a sloop in Long Island Sound.

★ In 1949, musician **Huddie "Leadbelly" Ledbetter** died from amytrophic lateral sclerosis (Lou Gehrig's disease).

★ In 1950, actor **Humphrey Jennings** died when he accidentally fell off a cliff on the Greek island of Poros.

★ In 1951, actor **Warner Baxter** died in Beverly Hills from pneumonia following a lobotomy performed to alleviate pain.

★ In 1952, actor **Richard Rober** died in California when he accidentally drove his car off an embankment due to heavy fog.

★ In 1953, actor **Lewis Stone** died in Los Angeles from a massive heart attack as he was chasing three teenage vandals.

★ In 1957, actor **Lois Austin** died from "cachexia," which is defined as a state of general ill health, emaciation, and malnutrition.

★ In 1957, director **James Whale** died in Hollywood when he accidentally fell into his empty swimming pool.

★ In 1958, actor **Fred Kennedy** died from a broken neck when he fell from his horse during filming in Louisiana.

★ In 1959, actor **Carl "Alfalfa" Switzer** was shot to death in Sepulveda, California, during an argument over a $50 debt.

★ In 1961, actor **Alan Marshal** died when he had a massive heart attack during a live performance of the play *Sextette* in Chicago.

★ In 1962, actor **Robert Emmett O'Connor** died in Hollywood from burns when a cigarette he was smoking ignited his clothing.

★ In 1964, singer **Sam Cooke** was shot to death by a motel manager as he was chasing a girl (who apparently did not want to be caught by Cooke).

★ In 1965, actor **Clara Bow** died from a heart attack in West Los Angeles as she was watching a movie on TV.

★ In 1965, actor **Linda Darnell** died as a result of burns from a fire while smoking in bed.

★ In 1965, actor **Paul Mantz** died when an unreliable replacement aircraft he was a passenger on crashed en route to a film set in California.

★ In 1966, actor **Pat O'Malley** died in Van Nuys, California, while he was calmly eating dinner.

★ In 1967, actor **Françoise Dorléac** died in Nice, France, when her car skidded on a wet road and then burst into flames.

★ In 1967, actor **Nelson Eddy** died from a stroke while performing live onstage in Miami Beach.

★ In 1968, actor **Albert Dekker** was found dead in his bathtub in Hollywood outfitted in full S & M gear.

★ In 1969, actor **Salvatore Baccaloni** died when a number of his organs "deteriorated."

★ In 1969, actor **Robert "Bo" Bolger** was killed in a skydiving accident in Oceanside, California.

★ In 1969, actor **Sharon Tate** was killed in Bel Air, California, by members of the Charles Manson cult.

★ In 1970, actor/photographer **Sean Flynn** was reported missing in Cambodia and presumed dead.

★ In 1970, actor **Frank Silvera** was accidentally electrocuted in his home in Pasadena.

★ In 1971, actor **David Burns** died from a massive heart attack while performing live onstage in Philadelphia.

★ In 1972, actor **Janet Munro** choked to death in London while drinking tea.

★ In 1973, musician **Jim Croce** died in a plane crash during takeoff from Natchitoches Municipal Airport in Louisiana.

★ In 1973, actor **Ken Maynard** was found dead of malnutrition in his trailer in Woodland Hills, California.

★ In 1975, actor **Cass Daley** died when her neck was pierced by broken glass when she fell in her home in Hollywood.

★ In 1975, actor **Mark Frechette** was crushed to death by a barbell while serving time in prison.

★ In 1975, actor **Roy Roberts** died suddenly after complaining of a pain in his back.

★ In 1976, actor **Sal Mineo** was murdered.

★ In 1978, actor **Bob Crane** was murdered.

★ In 1980, actor **Charles McGraw** died from injuries sustained when he fell through a glass shower door in his home in Studio City, California.

★ In 1982, actor **Renee Shinn Chen** was killed by a helicopter rotor while filming the *Twilight Zone* movie in the Sangus Desert in California.

★ In 1982, actor **Vic Morrow** also was beheaded by a helicopter rotor while filming the *Twilight Zone* movie in the Sangus Desert in California.

★ In 1983, actor **Ray Vitte** died when he stopped breathing after being forcibly restrained and arrested by the police in Los Angeles.

★ In 1983, playwright **Tennessee Williams** choked to death on a plastic bottle cap in New York City.

★ In 1985, actor **Steve Weston** died from injuries he sustained when he fell off the roof of his house in Toronto.

★ In 1986, director **Otto Preminger** died from Alzheimer's disease.

★ In 1987, actor **Rita Hayworth** died from Alzheimer's disease.

★ In 1987, actor **Vic Magnotta** drowned during the filming of a car stunt in Hoboken, New Jersey.

★ In 1987, actor **Dean Paul Martin Jr.** (Dean's son) died when his F-4C Phantom-II jet crashed during a training flight.

★ In 1987, actor **Dick Shawn** died after he had a heart attack while performing onstage in San Diego.

★ In 1988, actor **Chet Baker** died when he accidentally fell from a second-floor window in Amsterdam.

★ In 1988, ten-year-old actor **Judith Barsi** was shot to death by her father in Los Angeles.

★ In 1988, actor **John Carradine** died from a heart attack after much "strenuous" stair climbing in Milan.

★ In 1988, actor **Dennis Day** died from amyotrophic lateral sclerosis (Lou Gehrig's disease).

★ In 1988, actor **Harry Hope** died from a heart attack after playing basketball in Hollywood.

★ In 1988, actor **Ralph Meeker** died from Alzheimer's disease.

★ In 1989, actor **Pitt Herbert** died from amyotrophic lateral sclerosis (Lou Gehrig's disease).

★ In 1989, actor **Robert Webber** died from amytrophic lateral sclerosis (Lou Gehrig's disease).

★ In 1990, actor **Jay C. Currin** died from injuries sustained from a fifty-five-foot fall while filming in Malibu.

★ In 1990, actor **Jerome Schnur** died from melanoma (skin cancer), one of the most easily cured cancers.

★ In 1990, musician **Stevie Ray Vaughn** died in a helicopter crash.

★ In 1990, actor **David White** died from a heart attack after he was run over by an automobile in Hollywood.

★ In 1991, actor **Michael Colvin** died after suffering a head injury on a film set.

★ In 1991, actor **Redd Foxx** died from a massive heart attack in Hollywood during rehearsal for a new TV show.

★ In 1992, twenty-year-old actor **Micky Hays** died from progeria, an extremely rare genetic disease that causes its victims to age at four to five times the normal rate.

★ In 1992, musician **Jeff Porcaro** died from a toxic allergic reaction to pesticides.

★ In 1992, British actor **Sylvia Syms** had a fatal heart attack while performing onstage in London.

★ In 1993, actor **Duncan Gibbins** died from burns while trying to rescue his cat from a fire in Malibu.

★ In 1993, actor **Patience Jarvis** died from melanoma.

★ In 1993, actor **Brandon Lee** (Bruce's son) was killed when he was accidentally struck by a .44 caliber bullet while filming in Wilmington, North Carolina.

★ In 1993, actor **Dieter Plage** died in an airplane crash while filming in the Sumatra rain forest.

★ In 1993, actor **Tim "Tip" Tipping** died during the reenactment of a skydiving accident for British television.

★ In 1994, actor **Iris Adrian** died of complications from injuries sustained in an earthquake in Northridge, California.

★ In 1994, actor **Vasek Simek** died from a massive heart attack during a performance at the Croatian National Theater in Zagreb.

★ In 1994, actor **Frank Wells** died in a helicopter crash in central Nevada.

★ In 1994, actor **Dennis Wolfberg** died from melanoma.

★ In 1995, the body of director **Al Adamson** was found buried under his house in Indio, California.

★ In 1995, actor **Paul Eddington** died from melanoma.

★ In 1995, actor **Butterfly McQueen** died from burns she sustained while lighting a kerosene heater at her home in Augusta, Georgia.

★ In 1995, popcorn magnate and TV spokesman **Orville Redenbacher** died from a heart attack while soaking in his whirlpool spa.

★ In 1996, actor **Beth Amos** died suddenly while attending a performance at a theater.

★ In 1996, actor **Deedie Ball** died from a massive heart attack while playing the piano in a stage play in San Luis Obispo, California.

★ In 1996, actor **Ralston Hill** died suddenly during rehearsal for an upcoming play at the Paper Mill Playhouse in New Jersey.

★ In 1996, actor **Tom Mees** accidentally drowned in his neighbor's pool in Southington, Connecticut.

★ In 1996, actor **Jack O'Hara** perished in the TWA Flight 800 crash off the coast of Long Island, New York.

★ In 1996, actor **Haing Ngor** was murdered.

★ In 1996, actor **Kenneth Keith Steadman** was killed in a dune buggy accident while filming on location forty miles east of Los Angeles.

★ In 1997, theater owner **Laurence Austin** was shot to death in the lobby of his silent movie theater in Los Angeles.

★ In 1997, musician and actor **John Denver** died when the plane he was piloting crashed in California.

★ In 1997, actor **Allan Francovich** died from heart failure while going through United States Customs in Houston.

★ In 1997, studio magnate **Jeffrey L. Selznick** suffered a fatal heart attack during a business meeting in Los Angeles.

★ In 1997, actor **Jon Stone** died from amyotrophic lateral sclerosis (Lou Gehrig's disease).

★ In 1998, musician and actor **Sonny Bono** died in a skiing accident at the Heavenly Ski Resort at Lake Tahoe.

★ In 1998, actor **Phil Hartman** was shot to death at his home in Encino, California, by his troubled wife Brynn, who then committed suicide.

★ In 1998, actor **Theresa Merritt** died from melanoma.

★ In 1999, movie critic **Gene Siskel** died following surgery to remove a brain tumor.

★ In 1999, renowned director **Stanley Kubrick** died from "natural causes."

★ In 1999, actor **DeForest Kelley**—Dr. McCoy on *Star Trek*—died from stomach cancer.

★ In 1999, **John F. Kennedy Jr.** died when his small plane crashed into Long Island Sound.

★ In 1999, writer **Everett Greenbaum**, who used his brain to write some of the most memorable TV shows ever aired (including *The Andy Griffth Show* and *M*A*S*H*) died from brain cancer.

★ In 1999, actor **Sylvia Sidney**, famous for smoking a cigarette in *Beetlejuice* and exhaling the smoke through a slit in her throat— died from throat cancer.

★ In 1999, **Nerine Shatner**, wife of *Star Trek*'s James "Captain Kirk" Shatner, accidentally drowned in their pool.

★ In 2000, magician **Doug Henning** died from lung cancer.

★ In 2000, percussionist **Tito Puente** died from complications during heart surgery.

★ In 2000, writer, comedian, actor, and songwriter **Steve Allen** died of a heart attack several hours after a car accident.

★ In 2000, actor **Gwen Verdon** died of heart failure in her sleep.

★ In 2000, musician **Victor Borge** died of heart failure in his sleep.

★ In 2001, actor **Carroll O'Connor** died of a heart attack.

★ In 2001, actor **Jack Lemmon** died of complications from cancer.

For Your Consideration . . .

THE "F" LIST

Dennis Farina *Manhunter* (1986); *Get Shorty* (1995)
Chris Farley *Wayne's World 2* (1993); *Tommy Boy* (1995)
Mia Farrow *Rosemary's Baby* (1968); *Hannah and Her Sisters* (1986)
Sally Field *Norma Rae* (1979); *Forrest Gump* (1994)
Linda Fiorentino *The Last Seduction* (1994); *Men in Black* (1997)
Laurence Fishburne *Boyz 'N the Hood* (1991); *Just Cause* (1994)
Carrie Fisher The *Star Wars* series (1977–1983); *When Harry Met Sally . . .* (1989)
Louise Fletcher *One Flew Over the Cuckoo's Nest* (1975); *Brainstorm* (1983)
Bridget Fonda *Single White Female* (1992); *Point of No Return* (1993)
Jane Fonda *Coming Home* (1978); *Agnes of God* (1985)
Peter Fonda *Easy Rider* (1969); *Ulee's Gold* (1997)
Harrison Ford The *Star Wars* series (1977–1983); *The Fugitive* (1993)
Jodie Foster *The Accused* (1988); *The Silence of the Lambs* (1991)

Michael J. Fox The *Back to the Future* series (1985–1990); *Doc Holly-wood* (1991)
Vivica A. Fox *Independence Day* (1996); *Soul Food* (1997)
Brendan Fraser *Encino Man* (1992); *With Honors* (1994)
Morgan Freeman *Driving Miss Daisy* (1989); *The Shawshank Redemption* (1994)
Edward Furlong *Terminator 2: Judgment Day* (1991); *American History X* (1998)

Rumor has it that the laughter was loudest in France

Oldsmobile sponsored the 1955 Oscar ceremony and milked their sponsorship for all it was worth. They ran commercials lasting 2 minutes and 45 seconds, but insisted they were not commercials, but "intermissions." After one of these marathon ads, host Jerry Lewis got a huge laugh by ad-libbing, "And now, a brief word from the Academy." During another Olds commercial, Lewis brought out a chair and sat down center stage until the ad ended. The audience loved the bit, but the at-home TV audience did not get to see it: Jerry removed the chair before they returned to the live broadcast.

17 Questions With Director Mick Garris

I think everybody talks about every film that's going to be made as a huge hit. That's one of the things I actually like about the film business—there's this eternal hope.
—LIAM NEESON, *PLAYBOY*, NOVEMBER 1996

Mick Garris is the talented director and writer of such films as *Critters 2: The Main Course* (1988), *Psycho IV: The Beginning* (1991, made for cable), and *Virtual Obsession* (1998, made for TV) as well as being one of the few directors (Frank Darabont is another) who has "specialized," so to speak, in adapting Stephen King novels for the screen—both in the form of TV miniseries and as feature films.

Mick directed the feature film *Stephen King's Sleepwalkers,* as well as the miniseries *Stephen King's The Stand* and *Stephen King's The Shining.* He has also directed episodes of Steven Spielberg's TV series, *Amazing Stories,* and the series, *Tales From the Crypt* and *Freddy's Nightmares,* as well as the King segment ("Chattery Teeth") of the movie *Quicksilver Highway,* which is set in the desert. (Mick talks about his attraction to what he calls "desert noir" in this interview.)

Mick is an amiable guy with a punishing schedule who nevertheless made himself immediately available to me for this interview. [NOTE: This interview was conducted in two parts, the first, in the summer of 1994, and the conclusion, in the spring of 1999, thus, my question about *Stephen King's Desperation.* By the time this interview sees print, though, things may have changed, but I include his response to chronicle the status of the movie at the time of the interview.]

Stephen Spignesi: Lately, you're probably asked this question most often: What is the status of your movie adaptation of Stephen King's novel *Desperation* and what can you tell us about the script, cast, release date, King's involvement, etc.?

Mick Garris: At this stage, *Desperation* is in a kind of limbo. King has written the script, which is wonderful, but as of now, there are no actors attached. With any luck, this will change and I'll keep you posted.

SS: Personally, I think *Desperation* is brilliant and one of King's best. What attracted you to it and tipped the scales for you as a directing project? With all of the King novel and story film rights still available, why *Desperation?*

MG: I love the elements of fear and faith and family all rolled up in one apocalyptic tale. These worked so well in *The Stand* and in the *Desperation* novel, I knew I wanted to attack the novel with feature film resources. I've always been drawn to desert noir, and this one is as noir as noir gets. The combination of humanity and supernatural horror is what makes King King. It's incredibly scary, but has human conflicts and "Big Issues" throughout. Though I am not religious, I find it an interesting canvas. And of course, the opportunity to work with King is one I would never want to pass up. There's no more fun than working with Steve on a film. And, by the way, there aren't very many King story rights available anymore.

SS: How difficult is it to summon up the self-confidence necessary to take charge of a set and the making of a film? It has to be daunting to have everyone turning to you for answers. How do you stay focused? Could you discuss the mindset of a director?

MG: Taking charge of the set and surrounding situations are all part of the job directing.

You're there to answer any of the questions that come up from any department, and if you're not prepared to give guidance to those who request it (and they request it several times a minute, it seems), you'll have a tough time not being run over by the steam-powered train that is production.

Obviously, the more you work, the more you learn, and the more confident you should become, but to me, the main job of the director is to find, encourage, and allow the best people to do their best work.

It certainly can be daunting (particularly if your script is 460 pages long, like *The Stand*), but again, that's why you're there: to direct it.

Almost everything changes during production, and gives you punches you must roll with: the weather isn't what was scripted, a location owner changes his mind and decides not to let you shoot at his property the night before you're scheduled and you've got to find a totally new location; an actor is ill; you're running too long and scenes are either cut or combined; you can't have a crane or a dolly or a Steadicam you planned on using; etc.

I always shot-list the coming week's work every weekend (I usually don't storyboard, other than for action and FX scenes, anymore), but you have to remain flexible, and that shot-list is an important game plan.

You know you're never going to follow it to the letter, but just planning it makes you feel ready, feel prepared.

SS: With your busy directing schedule and all that it entails, do you deliberately work on other private creative projects that have nothing to do with your project at hand, or do you completely immerse yourself in the movie and not even think about anything else? Could you talk about your *artistic* mindset during the production of a film? Do you force yourself to sublimate the urge to paint, sketch, compose, write poetry, whatever . . . and if so is it because you feel it might hurt your focus? Or do you indulge these impulses, thinking you might gain some insight into a scene or a character through the "back door," so to speak?

MG: When I'm shooting, there really isn't much time for other creative endeavors. The same goes for postproduction. But I do like to write occasional short fiction (some of which has been published). I sketch once in a while, and my wife Cynthia gave me a Stratocaster and small amp, which I love to bash around on and embarrass myself with. I was a singer in a band for years before working in film, and I've been pulling together old tapes of the band and burning "Best of" CDs. The outside creative impulses are indulged between productions, not during. Production really is an all-encompassing process, with really long hours, and homework on the weekends. It's exhausting, frankly. There are only so many hours in the day, and for me it's best to keep focused on the work at hand.

SS: Were you a big King fan prior to *Sleepwalkers* or was it more of a casual following of his work? Do you have a favorite King book? Favorite King film? Of the King film adaptations you've seen, which do you think is the most successful?

MG: I've always been a huge King fan, now even more than ever. My favorite novels of his would have to be *The Stand, Salem's Lot, The Shining,* and *Gerald's Game.* I think the best King movies would have to be *Stand by Me, The Dead Zone, Misery,* and *Carrie.* Those were all terrific adaptations. The *Pet Sematary* script, which I met with Paramount about, was a wonderful screenplay. I like the movie, too, but it is missing the very high level of emotion and passion that was in both the book and King's screenplay.

SS: The scene in *Sleepwalkers* where Mädchen Amick ("Tanya") dances by herself in the theater lobby is really quite engaging and very charming. How did that scene come about? Was it in the original script or was it developed during shooting? Could you talk about directorial spontaneity and how willing you might be to make last-minute changes on the set?

MG: I'm a big believer in spontaneity on the set, as long as it fits within the structure of the film—and as long as it is *better* than what it scripted. Sometimes it's as simple as words that fit an actor's mouth better than the scripted dialogue; other times it's something like the scene you mention from *Sleepwalkers.*

First, King *had* scripted the scene and the song. He had written a moment of Tanya being caught up in the tune on her Walkman that culminated in her being startled and embarrassed by Charles (Brian Krause). But I thought we could stretch it out so that the audience could get as caught up in it as she was, forget about the world outside for a few moments, and be thrown off-guard. I wanted to make a little jump happen.

We built upon Madchen's talent as a dancer as well as her sweetness. I had a Steadicam operator on a crane outside the theater. He was brought down to the ground, and then walked into the theater and followed her. We kept each take running for the full length of the song, getting more and more mobile as it carried on, getting excited by the music and by her dance. We knew we'd have to cut into the shots to tighten and emphasize, but the long unbroken shots were really quite exciting.

SS: Do you like cats? What was it like working with an army of kitties on *Sleepwalkers?*

MG: I love animals, and the cats in *Sleepwalkers* performed amazingly well. We really had very few problems with them. The dog in *The Stand,* however, is another story completely.

SS: Did Stephen King offer any advice regarding your direction of either *Sleepwalkers* or *The Stand* or did he keep a hands-off attitude? Just how involved was he with the final results in the case of both films?

MG: Though King and I spoke a lot over the phone during the pre-production of *Sleepwalkers,* I never met him until he shot his cameo in the film. And once shooting began, we didn't have time to be in touch until postproduction. He was sent dailies as a courtesy, but was not heavily involved. On *The Stand,* however, he was quite involved, more than on any other production. And of course, I welcomed it. You'd be a fool not to. But he was quite respectful of my role as director. We have a Mutual Respect and Admiration Society going, I guess.

SS: Norman's mother was a real piece of work and your movie, *Psycho IV: The Beginning,* does a good job of helping us understand why Norman Bates turned out the way he did. How much of the legend (the three Robert Bloch novels and the three films) did you delve into for the making of this film? Or did you just work with Stefano's script and not worry about history or subtext?

MG: Sure, I studied the *Psycho* canon heavily before starting *Psycho IV: The Beginning.*

I'd seen *Psycho* many times since I saw it the first time at the drive-in with my family in 1961 (I was nine years old). I also saw the other sequels in theaters at the time of their release and watched them again on video.

I'd read the original novel and Bloch's own sequel, *Psycho II* (which was unrelated to the films). I don't think the third novel had been published at the time we were developing the film.

Of course, our film paid most attention to the films, since that is what the audience was most familiar with, but that history was very important to us.

Hitchcock's assistant director on *Psycho,* Hilton Green, was our executive producer; we had Anthony Perkins; we used several of the same set pieces and props; and we also used the Bernard Herrmann music (I'll never understand why nobody did that before).

Though we tried specifically not to emulate Hitchcock's style, it was important to respect the history.

SS: In 1994, the last time we spoke, the last movie you had rented was *Red Rock West;* the last book you had read was Jim Thompson's *A Swell Looking Babe;* your favorite directors were Billy Wilder and Preston Sturges; your favorite horror film was *Psycho;* your favorite monster movie was *The Fly;* and (perhaps most important) your favorite pizza was plain cheese. Could you update these please?

MG: The last movie I rented was the remake of *Carnival of Souls,* which we only got a few minutes into before regrettably giving up. The last book I read was, coincidentally, Stephen King's *The Girl Who Loved Tom Gordon.* Wilder and Sturges remain my favorite directors, though there are plenty of others right up close, including Steven Spielberg, Martin Scorsese, Frank Capra, David Cronenberg, and dozens of others. *The Fly* is still up there, sharing space with *King Kong, Bride of Frankenstein,* and another handful or so.

As for my pizza choice, I'll still take the plain cheese, but I won't complain if you sneak a few pepperoni slices in there, too.

SS: Play along here: If you had *all* the money in the world, could get film rights to *any* work in existence, and could have *any* cast you wanted, what would your ultimate fantasy project be?

MG: My fantasy project would have nothing to do with lots of money, a big budget, or a favorite novel. If I could make any movie I wanted, it would probably be a small-scale original screenplay of my own, something not effects oriented, something that plays on a more intimate, human scale.

I've been allowed to direct King's screenplays of my two favorites of his novels: it doesn't get any better than that. But an original script of mine called *Jimmy Miracle* would probably be the one I most want to see made. I wrote it immediately after we made *The Stand.* I also wrote a remake of *The Uninvited* for me to direct at Universal last year, but with their state of affairs, it crashed and burned. We're looking for another home for it. But that's another of my favorite projects.

SS: Who's the first person you'd thank if you won a Best Director Oscar?

MG: The likelihood of my ever being nominated for an Oscar is so remote that it has never crossed my mind. However, if I ever get a *Fangoria* award, I'd have to thank three: Steve King, Steven Spielberg, and my wife Cynthia. And probably not in that order.

SS: What is the most prevalent and pervasive misconception about Hollywood and the movie business?

MG: There are so many misconceptions about Hollywood that are prevalent that I don't think I could just name one. Here are a few:

The glamour is way out of proportion to the reality; it exists, and in a big way, but the making of a movie is the last place you'll find it.

There are thousands of noncreative, anticreative scum in this business, but you don't have to work with them. I've had very few dealings with that type.

Movies and TV don't make teenagers into killers; the fucking guns in their hands do. I know very few people who do drugs in this business.

And gorgeous actresses seldom offer sexual favors to miniseries directors.

SS: You've done TV series ("Freddy's Nightmares," "Tales from the Crypt," "Amazing Stories"); TV miniseries (*The Stand, The Shining*); TV movies (*Virtual Obsession, The Judge*); and you've done feature films (*Critters 2, Sleepwalkers*). As they say in essay questions, could you compare and contrast the two mediums and also tell us whether you prefer working on TV productions or features?

MG: There are advantages and disadvantages to features and television. The great thing about television is its insatiable maw. They have to keep making shows to fill the time between their commercials, so when they want to make a show, it generally gets made. And it can reach an enormous potential audience, all in a single sitting.

Unfortunately, the resources are more frugal than in features; you usually have a ridiculously accelerated delivery schedule, and a very tight budget. For instance, I just finished doing a pilot for DreamWorks and NBC that, despite its load of visual effects, was delivered *two-and-a-half weeks* after we wrapped production.

Though the means are usually greater on features, it seems there is a gauntlet of executives whose job is to either *not* make the movie, or at least lift their legs and leave their yellow stain on it.

Because so much more money is at stake, it is harder to get a project off the ground, and they are not led by schedule as much as television. The bigger budget actually makes the studios produce homogenized, safe films. And the independents are all being gobbled up by the majors, and making less adventurous choices. They're applying their own formulas to try for another *Four Wed-*

dings and a Funeral, another *Crying Game,* another whatever-was-successful-before.

SS: You've acted in *The Stand, The Quick and the Dead, The Stupids,* and *The Shining.* Any plans for more thespian work?

MG: I'm ready whenever I might be called (he said humbly).

SS: How much interaction with Michael Jackson did you have when you worked on *Ghosts?* If you did spend time with him, are there any impressions of him that come to mind?

MG: I spent a lot of time with Michael, and I like him a lot. He's enormously talented and gifted. Most surprising to people might be how bright and funny he is. He has a great sense of humor, and thinks very quickly. And the guy just drips ideas. I think there was a lot of money-grubbing going on behind the so-called scandal, and it had a lot more to do with a payout than anything else. It's a shame.

I was always fascinated by people like Orson Welles or Charlie Chaplin. Their whole lives are completely buried.

Magician David Blaine
TV Guide, April 10, 1999

. . . to ashes: 66 Movie Stars and Celebrities Who Were Cremated

Cremains—the cremated remains of a human body; a.k.a., the ashes—weigh an average of nine pounds.

This list looks at the careers and cremations of 513 pounds of Hollywood movie stars and other celebrities, starting with the most recent.

2000

Faron Young The beloved star of the Grand Ole Opry committed suicide with a shotgun because of depression over health and financial troubles. His ashes were scattered over Old Hickory Lake in Tennessee.

1999

Sir Dirk Bogarde The popular British actor (*The Password Is Courage*, 1962, and others) died of a heart attack at his home in London. His ashes were scattered somewhere in France.

Wilt Chamberlain The only professional basketball player to score 100 points in a single game died of heart failure.

DeForest Kelley The popular star of *Star Trek* (Dr. "Bones" McCoy) died after a long battle with stomach cancer. His ashes were scattered in the Pacific Ocean.

John F. Kennedy Jr. The son of President John Kennedy died when his small plane crashed into Long Island Sound. His ashes were scattered in the Sound off the coast of Martha's Vineyard.

Curtis Mayfield The popular musician and composer of "Superfly" died of complications from quadraplegia and diabetes. His ashes were given to his family.

Gary Morton The ashes of this respected producer, who was Lucille Ball's second husband, were given to his family.

Dana Plato The star of *Diff'rent Strokes* died of a drug overdose in what is believed to have been a suicide. Her ashes were given to her family.

Gene Rayburn The ashes of this popular host of TV's *The Match Game* were spread over his daughter's garden.

Dusty Springfield The British singer died of breast cancer and her ashes were spead somewhere in Ireland.

David Strickland The costar of TV's *Suddenly Susan* commtted suicide by hanging and his ashes were given to his family.

1998

Phil Hartman The popular and talented *Saturday Night Live* star and movie star. Hartman was murdered by his wife, Brynn Hartman, who then committed suicide. Hartman's ashes were scatted over Emerald Bay, California.

1997

Robert Mitchum The rugged actor who starred in dozens of movies from 1943 through 1995, including *Night of the Hunter* and *Ryan's Daughter.* Mitchum died of emphysema and lung cancer. His ashes were scattered at sea off the California coast.

Alvy Moore The charismatic character actor who made his film debut in the 1954 Marlon Brando biker flick *The Wild One* but who was best known for his role as the bumbling "Hank Kimball" on TV's *Green Acres.* Moore died of heart failure at his home in Palm Desert, California.

1996

Tupac Shakur The enormously popular rap star who was murdered in a drive-by shooting in Las Vegas.

Gene Kelly The legendary song and dance man who starred in *Anchors Aweigh* (1945); *On the Town* (1949); *Singin' in the Rain* (1952), and many other huge hits. Kelly died in his sleep after two strokes. His ashes were returned to his family.

1995

Jerry Garcia The founder and beloved leader of the seminal folk-rock group The Grateful Dead. Garcia died of a heart attack at a drug treatment facility. His ashes were scattered in the Ganges River in India.

Gale Gordon The superb character actor best known for playing Lucy's stuffy boss Mr. Mooney on *The Lucy Show*. Gordon died of cancer. His ashes were given to his sister in Arizona.

Elizabeth Montgomery The lovely actress who played Samantha Stevens on the hugely popular supernatural sitcom *Bewitched*. Montgomery died of cancer after surgery to remove a tumor.

1994

Kurt Cobain The brilliant leader and singer/songwriter of the groundbreaking rock group Nirvana. Cobain was married to Hole leader Courtney Love and he committed suicide with a shotgun. His ashes were given to his wife.

Claude Akins The talented actor who made his screen debut in the 1953 classic *From Here to Eternity* and who also did TV work, most notably appearing as Sheriff Elroy P. Lobo in the late seventies sitcom *B.J. and the Bear*. The character of Lobo was spun off and given his own series, *Lobo*, in 1979. Akins died of cancer.

1993

Vincent Price The legendary star of many classic horror flicks including *House of Wax* and *The Tingler*. Price died of lung cancer.

George McFarland The actor who played "Spanky" of *The Little Rascals*. McFarland died of unknown causes at a hospital in Texas. His ashes were given to his family.

Don Ameche The debonair actor of the thirties and forties who was introduced to a new generation of movie fans when he costarred with Ralph Bellamy in the Eddie Murphy/Dan Aykroyd hit comedy *Trading Places* in 1983, and made a huge comeback in the touching 1985 Ron Howard comedy/drama *Cocoon*. Ameche died of prostate cancer.

Bill Bixby The engaging actor and director best known for playing "Mr. Eddie's father" Tom Corbett on the popular early seventies sitcom *The Courtship of Eddie's Father,* and his most famous role, as Uncle Martin the Martian's nephew Tim O'Hara on *My Favorite Martian.* Bixby also played David Banner, the scientist who transformed into "The Incredible Hulk" (played by Lou Ferrigno) from 1978 through 1982 on the TV series of the same name, and later in four theatrical movies based on the character. Bixby died of prostate cancer and his ashes were scattered on the grounds of his estate in Maui.

1992

Anthony Perkins The gifted character actor who starred in *Psycho* and dozens of other movies. Perkins died of complications from AIDS.

1991

Jean Arthur The talented actress best known for her starring role in the classic 1938 Frank Capra film adaptation of *You Can't Take It With You.* Arthur also had her own sitcom, *The Jean Arthur Show,* on CBS in 1966. Arthur died of a heart attack following a paralyzing stroke. Her ashes were scattered at sea off Point Lobos, California.

1990

Greta Garbo The notoriously private actress known for her classic roles in *Mata Hari* (1932), *Grand Hotel* (1932), *Anna Karenina* (1935), *Camille* (1935), and, of course, *Ninotchka* (1939). Garbo died of undisclosed causes in New York and her ashes were given to her niece Gray Reisfield.

Barbara Stanwyck The regal actress who appeared in almost four dozen movies including *Stella Dallas* (1937), *Titanic* (1953), and *The Thorn Birds* (1983) during her five-decade career that began in the thirties, but who was probably best known for her role as matriarch Victoria Barkely on the popular sixties Western series *The Big Valley.* Stanwyck died of congestive heart failure and her ashes were scattered over Lone Pine, California.

Alan Hale Jr. The burly character actor (look-alike son of actor Alan Hale) who appeared in two dozen movies, including *The Spirit of West Point* (1947) and *Young at Heart* (1954), but who is remembered most for playing The Skipper on the enormously popular sixties sitcom *Gilligan's Island.* Hale died of cancer of the thymus and, appropriately, his ashes were scattered at sea. (By the way, did you know that The Skipper actually had a real name on the series? It was Jonas Grumby.)

1986

Desi Arnaz He loved Lucy! Desi—"Ricky Ricardo"—died of lung cancer. His ashes were scattered privately.

Cary Grant The debonair leading man who starred in many Hollywood classics, including *The Philadelphia Story* (1940), *To Catch a Thief* (1955), and *North by Northwest* (1959). Grant died of a massive stroke.

1985

Rock Hudson The handsome actor who starred in such Hollywood classics as *Giant* (1956), *Pillow Talk* (1959), and *Ice Station Zebra* (1968). The once-studio-wed Hudson hid his homosexuality from his fans for decades until he was diagnosed with AIDS and he then publicly admitted he was gay. Hudson died from complications from the disease and his ashes were scattered at sea.

Margaret Hamilton The beloved character actress who was never able to distance herself from her most famous role, that of the Wicked Witch of the West in the 1939 classic, *The Wizard of Oz.* Hamilton died of a heart attack. Her ashes were scattered over her hometown of Amenia, New York.

1984

Peter Lawford The debonair British actor who was part of the "Rat Pack," which also included as members Frank Sinatra, Joey Bishop, Sammy Davis Jr., and Dean Martin. Lawford was at one point married to Pat Kennedy, sister of President Kennedy. His many credits include *Easter Parade* (1948), *Oceans 11* (1960), and *The Longest Day* (1962).

Lawford died of cardiac arrest and liver and kidney disease. His ashes were scattered at sea.

Marvin Gaye The talented R&B singer with a silky voice known for such huge hits as "Sexual Healing" and "What's Goin' On?" Gaye was shot to death by his father in anger. His ashes were scattered at sea.

1982

Paul Lynde The acerbic comic actor who appeared in movies—most memorably *Bye Bye Birdie* (1963) and *The Glass Bottom Boat* (1966)— but who was best known for being the "center square" on the daytime version of the long-running game show *The Hollywood Squares.* Lynde died of a heart attack and prostate cancer. His ashes were buried in Mount Vernon, Ohio.

Jack Albertson The curmudgeonly Oscar-winning actor who appeared in movies but was best known for his portrayal of Ed Brown ("The Man") opposite Freddie Prinze on the seventies sitcom *Chico and the Man.* Albertson died of cancer and his ashes were scattered at sea.

Ingrid Bergman The stunningly beautiful actress who starred in such Hollywood classics as *Intermezzo* (1939), *Gaslight* (1944), *Notorious* (1946), *Indiscreet* (1958), *Autumn Sonata* (1978), and, most memorably, *Casablanca* (1942). Bergman died of breast cancer and her ashes were scattered off the coast of Sweden.

1981

William Holden The talented light-comedian-turned-rugged-actor who starred in such powerful films as *Sunset Boulevard* (1950), *Stalag 17* (1953), *Picnic* (1955), *The Bridges at Toko-Ri* (1955), *The Bridge on the River Kwai* (1957), *The Wild Bunch* (1969), and *Network* (1976). Holden died from massive blood loss after his head was cut during a fall in Santa Monica.

1980

Steve McQueen The macho actor who starred in many action thrillers including *The Great Escape* (1963), *The Thomas Crown Affair* (1968),

Bullitt (1968), *The Getaway* (1972), *Papillon* (1973), and *The Towering Inferno* (1974). McQueen, who then was married to actress Ali McGraw, died from a heart attack following cancer surgery. His ashes were scattered in Santa Paula Valley, California.

John Lennon Beatle. John Lennon was assassinated by an insane fan outside the Dakota Arms in New York City. His ashes were given to his wife, Yoko Ono.

John Bonham The drummer for the legendary and seminal heavy metal group Led Zeppelin. Bonham choked to death after drinking forty shots of vodka.

Jay Silverheels The character actor best known for playing the Lone Ranger's faithful companion Tonto on TV's *The Lone Ranger* from 1949 until the show went off the air in 1957. His last role was in the 1973 Burt Reynolds western *The Man Who Loved Cat Dancing*. Silverheels died of complications from pneumonia. His ashes were returned to his birthplace in Ontario, Canada.

Alfred Hitchcock The legendary, innovative director of such brilliant thrillers as *Spellbound* (1945), *Rear Window* (1954), *Vertigo* (1958), *Psycho* (1960), and *The Birds* (1963). Hitchcock died of a heart attack and his ashes were scattered privately.

1979

Zeppo Marx The "romantic" Marx Brother. Zeppo died of cancer and his ashes were scattered at sea.

Vivian Vance The beloved actress who became famous playing Ethel Mertz opposite Lucille "Lucy Ricardo" Ball on *I Love Lucy*. Vance died of cancer.

Ted Cassidy The tall, hulking actor best known for his portrayal of the Addams Family butler Lurch ("You rang?") in both the sixties TV series and the 1979 movie *Halloween With the Addams Family*. Cassidy died during heart surgery. His ashes were buried in the front lawn of his home.

Richard Rodgers The legendary composer known for such classic film scores as *Oklahoma!* (1955), *The King and I* (1956), *Carousel* (1956),

South Pacific (1958), *Flower Drum Song* (1961), and, most memorably, *The Sound of Music* (1965). Rodgers died of cancer and his ashes were scattered privately.

1978

Ed Wood The low-budget director of really terrible movies such as *Plan 9 From Outer Space* and *Glen or Glenda?*, films that now, ironically, boast huge cult followings. Wood died from a heart attack triggered by acute alcoholism. His ashes were scattered at sea.

1977

Howard Hawks The seminal director of such Hollywood classics as *Bringing Up Baby* (1938), *To Have and Have Not* (1944), *The Big Sleep* (1946), *Gentlemen Prefer Blondes* (1953), and *Rio Bravo* (1959). Hawks died in his sleep following a fall that resulted in a concussion. His ashes were scattered privately.

Andy Devine The humorous, tubby character actor best known for his work in Westerns from the thirties through the sixties, including *Stagecoach* (1939), *The Man Who Shot Liberty Valance* (1962), and *How the West Was Won* (1963). Devine died from leukemia and diabetes and his ashes were scattered at sea.

1976

Anissa Jones The charming child actor who played "Buffy" on the popular sixties sitcom *Family Affair*. Jones died from an overdose of Quaaludes and alcohol. Her ashes were scattered at sea.

1974

Cliff Arquette The comic actor best known for his alter ego "Charley Weaver." "Charley" was a regular on both *The Jack Paar Show* from 1958 through 1962 and the 1968 daytime version of *The Hollywood Squares*. (He was Rosanna Arquette's grandpa.) Arquette died of a heart attack and his ashes were scattered by the Telophase Society.

Bud Abbott One half of the legendary comedy team Abbott and Costello. Abbott died of cancer and his ashes were scattered in the Pacific Ocean.

1973

Wally Cox The popular comic actor who starred as "Mr. Peepers" in the fifties sitcom and who went on to become a regular on the daytime version of *The Hollywood Squares.* He also appeared in movies during his career, including *State Fair* (1962) and *The One and Only, Genuine, Original Family Band* (1968). Cox died of a heart attack and his ashes were scattered in the Atlantic Ocean.

Veronica Lake The forties Hollywood sex symbol best known for her starring roles in *Sullivan's Travels* (1941) and *This Gun for Hire* (1942). Lake died of acute hepatitis and her ashes were scattered at sea in the U.S. Virgin Islands.

1971

Bennett Cerf The writer and raconteur known for many popular books of humor and satire and also for being a regular on the popular CBS game show *What's My Line?* from 1961 to 1967. Cerf died of a heart attack and his ashes were scattered on the grounds of his home in Mt. Kisco, New York.

1970

Janis Joplin The groundbreaking blues singer best known for her work with her band Big Brother and the Holding Company. Joplin died from an overdose of heroin. Her ashes were scattered along the coast of northern California.

Inger Stevens The pretty blond actress who became best known for her role as "Katy Holstrum" on the sixties sitcom *The Farmer's Daughter.* Stevens died en route to the hospital after an overdose of barbiturates. Her ashes were scattered at sea.

1969

Boris Karloff The legendary star of dozens of classic horror flicks, including *Frankenstein* (1931), *The Mummy* (1932), *The Body Snatchers* (1945), *Corridors of Blood* (1958), and *Cauldron of Blood* (1967). Karloff died in England of a respiratory disease and his ashes were interred in the Garden of Remembrance in Guildford, Surrey.

1967

Woody Guthrie The popular folk singer best known for his anthem-like song "This Land Is Your Land." The father of actor and singer/songwriter Arlo Guthrie died after a thirteen-year battle with Huntington's chorea, a degenerative, genetic, muscular and neurological disease. Guthrie's ashes were cast into the ocean off Coney Island, New York.

1950

Walter Huston The noted actor who embarked on a career spanning six decades with his role as the outlaw leader in one of the first talking Westerns, the 1929 classic *The Virginian,* directed by Victor Fleming. Huston played opposite Gary Cooper and the movie was responsible for the oft-repeated line, "If you want to call me that, smile." Huston died of an aneurysm and he was cremated at the Chapel of the Pines in Los Angeles. His ashes were given to his family.

George Bernard Shaw The renowned British playwright who cowrote the screenplay for the 1938 film adaptation of his best-known play *Pygmalion.* (The play was made into a musical comedy and then adapted for the screen again in 1964 as *My Fair Lady.*) Shaw died in England from a bladder disease and from injuries sustained in a fall. His ashes were scattered in his garden.

1946

H. G. Wells The legendary British science fiction writer whose stories were adapted into many popular films, including *The War of the Worlds*

(1953), *The Time Machine* (1960), *The Island of Dr. Moreau* (1933, 1977, 1996), and *The Invisible Man* (1933). Wells died of liver cancer and his ashes were scattered in the English Channel.

1933

Roscoe "Fatty" Arbuckle The portly actor best known for starring in Charlie Chaplin's 1914 *Keystone Comedies* and Mack Sennett's *Comedies* in 1915 and 1916. Arbuckle, who at one point was embroiled in a sex scandal, died of a heart attack. His ashes were scattered at sea.

- - - - - - - - - - - - - -

Hollywood is a dreary industrial town controlled by hoodlums of enormous wealth, the ethical sense of a pack of jackals, and taste so degraded that it befouled everything it touched.

Humorist and writer S. J. Perelman

- - - - - - - - - - - - - -

For Your Consideration . . .

THE "G" LIST

Andy Garcia *Hero* (1992); *Desperate Measures* (1998)

Janeane Garofalo *The Truth About Cats and Dogs* (1996); *Romy and Michele's High School Reunion* (1997)

Teri Garr *Tootsie* (1982); *Mr. Mom* (1983)

Richard Gere *An Officer and a Gentleman* (1982); *Pretty Woman* (1990)

Gina Gershon *Showgirls* (1995); *Bound* (1996)

Mel Gibson *Lethal Weapon* (1987); *Ransom* (1996)

Jackie Gleason *The Hustler* (1961); *Nothing in Common* (1986)

Scott Glenn *The Right Stuff* (1983); *The Silence of the Lambs* (1991)

Crispin Glover *What's Eating Gilbert Grape* (1993); *The People vs. Larry Flynt* (1996)

Danny Glover *Lethal Weapon* (1987); *John Grisham's The Rainmaker* (1997)

Whoopi Goldberg *Ghost* (1990); *Sister Act* (1992)

Jeff Goldblum *The Big Chill* (1983); *The Fly* (1986)

Cuba Gooding Jr. *Jerry Maguire* (1996); *As Good As It Gets* (1997)

John Goodman *Raising Arizona* (1987); *Punchline* (1988)

Elliott Gould *M*A*S*H* (1970); *American History X* (1998)

Heather Graham *Boogie Nights* (1997); *Two Guys and a Girl* (1998)

Hugh Grant *Four Weddings and a Funeral* (1994); *Nine Months* (1995)

Jennifer Grey *Ferris Bueller's Day Off* (1986); *Dirty Dancing* (1987)

Melanie Griffith *Something Wild* (1986); *Working Girl* (1988)

Charles Grodin *Midnight Run* (1988); *Dave* (1993)

And it's one less union job, too

The 1957 Oscar ceremony was the first year that presenters carried the all-important envelope with the winner's name in it with them to the podium, thereby retiring, once and for all, the melodramatic (and unnecessarily time-consuming) question, "May I have the envelope, please?"

The Feature Film Debuts of 30 Best Actor Academy Award Winners

This list (and the Best Actress Film Debut list) looks at the feature film credits of some of the Oscar winners. Many of these actors appeared in made-for-TV movies, miniseries, documentaries, and short films before scoring a theatrical feature, but we decided that even though their minor work is interesting as part of each actor's overall filmography, it is more interesting (and more entertaining) to take a look at the "real" movies in which these guys (and gals) got their thespian feet wet. (NOTE: The film in parentheses following the actor's name is the movie for which he won the Best Actor Oscar.)

1. **Nicolas Cage** (*Leaving Las Vegas,* 1995)
   Debut *Fast Times at Ridgemont High* (1982, as "Nicholas Coppola"), directed by Amy Heckerling; with Sean Penn, Jennifer Jason Leigh, Judge Reinhold, Ray Walston, Phoebe Cates.
   The full spectrum of high schoolers at a Southern California high school in the eighties party hearty, lose their virginity, work at All-American Burger, and generally try to graduate by doing as little real work as possible in this comedy classic. Cage plays burger flipper "Brad's Bud." (He changed his name to Cage after this movie.)

2. **Marlon Brando** (*The Godfather,* 1972)
   Debut *The Men* (1950), directed by Fred Zinnemann; with Teresa Wright, Everett Sloane, Jack Webb, Richard Erdman, Dorothy Tree, Howard St. John.
   Brando made an astonishing film debut in this earnest drama about a paralyzed World War II vet trying to adjust to life after the war, which he has to live in a wheelchair. An undeniable classic, and his performance as the paraplegic GI foretold what was to come in later roles.

3. **Yul Brynner** (*The King and I,* 1956)
   Debut *Port of New York* (1949), directed by Laslo Benedek; with Scott Brady, K. T. Stevens, Richard Rober.

This standard crime melodrama about a female drug smuggler (Stevens) who decides to rat on her colleagues (including leader Brynner) is notable for two things: its gritty and realistic New York locations, and the fact that this was one of the few times Yul Brynner appeared with a full head of hair!

4. **Art Carney** (*Harry and Tonto*, 1974)

   Debut *Pot O' Gold* (1941), directed by George Marshall; with James Stewart, Paulette Goddard, Horace Heidt, Charles Winninger, Mary Gordon.

   Jimmy Stewart is a harmonica player with Horace Heidt's orchestra who tries to get the band on his uncle's radio program. Carney has a small part as a radio announcer and this film has the notoriety of Stewart describing it as the worst film he ever made.

5. **Daniel Day-Lewis** (*My Left Foot*, 1989)

   Debut *Sunday, Bloody Sunday* (1971), directed by John Schlesinger; with Glenda Jackson, Peter Finch, Murray Head.

   The intense and complex story of a *menage à trois* involving a homosexual, a heterosexual, and a bisexual, none of which, though, were portrayed by Day-Lewis in his film debut. He played a car-vandalizing teenager in a brief scene.

6. **Robert De Niro** (*Raging Bull, 1980*)

   Debut *The Wedding Party* (1963, released in 1969), directed by Brian De Palma; with Jill Clayburgh, William Finley.

   Even though *Greetings* was released first, *The Wedding Party*, shot six years earlier, is the first time Robert De Niro appeared in a feature film. In this comedy (which was also director Brian De Palma's and star Jill Clayburgh's first film), De Niro plays Cecil, a friend of a confused bridegroom who tries to talk him out of getting married. De Niro's name was misspelled in the credits twice as "De Nero."

7. **Michael Douglas** (*Wall Street*, 1987)

   Debut *Hail, Hero!* (1969), directed by David Miller; with Arthur Kennedy, Teresa Wright, John Larch, Charles Drake, Deborah Winters, Peter Strauss.

   Douglas plays a young, angst-filled hippie who confronts his family about his negative feelings about the Vietnam War.

8. **Robert Duvall** (*Tender Mercies,* 1983)

Debut *To Kill a Mockingbird* (1962), directed by Robert Mulligan; with Gregory Peck, Brock Peters, Philip Alford, Mary Badham, Rosemary Murphy, William Windom.

Duvall makes an auspicious debut (he doesn't have one single line!) as the dimwitted, yet heroic Boo Radley in this brilliant drama about a Southern lawyer (Peck) who defends a black man charged with raping a white woman.

9. **Henry Fonda** (*On Golden Pond,* 1981)

Debut *The Farmer Takes a Wife* (1935), directed by Victor Fleming; with Janet Gaynor, Charles Bickford, Slim Summerville, Jane Withers.

Henry Fonda re-creates the role he played on stage in this charming romance, as a farmer who opposes the building of the Erie Canal and courts a boat cook as he struggles with the builders.

10. **Gene Hackman** (*The French Connection,* 1971)

Debut *Mad Dog Coll* (1961), directed by Burt Balaban; with John Davis Chandler, Brooke Hayward, Kay Doubleday, Jerry Orbach, Vincent Gardenia, Telly Savalas.

Hackman made his film debut in this minor crime drama about the career of the vicious gangland killer, Vincent "Mad Dog" Coll. Hackman played a cop (in an uncredited part).

11. **Tom Hanks** (*Philadelphia,* 1993; *Forrest Gump,* 1994)

Debut *He Knows You're Alone* (1980), directed by Armand Mastroianni; with Don Scardino, Caitlin O'Heaney, Tom Rolfing, Paul Gleason, Elizabeth Kemp, James Rebhorn.

A psychotic killer *really* wants to get married and in his quest for a bride, he terrorizes a bride-to-be and her bridal party.

12. **Dustin Hoffman** (*Rain Man,* 1988)

Debut *The Tiger Makes Out* (1967), directed by Arthur Hiller; with Eli Wallach, Anne Jackson, Bob Dishy, John Harkins, Charles Nelson Reilly.

A fanatical crusader against society's ills (Wallach) kidnaps a housewife (Jackson) in order to make a statement. Hoffman has a brief cameo.

13. **Anthony Hopkins** (*The Silence of the Lambs,* 1991)

Debut *The Lion in Winter* (1968), directed by Anthony

Harvey; with Peter O'Toole, Katharine Hepburn, Jane Merrow, Nigel Terry, Timothy Dalton.

Henry II and Eleanor of Aquitaine fight over which of their three sons should inherit the throne. Mom wants her favorite, Richard the Lionheart (Hopkins), to ascend to the throne; his brothers and the king have different ideas.

14. **William Hurt** (*Kiss of the Spider Woman*, 1985)
Debut *Altered States* (1980), directed by Ken Russell; with Blair Brown, Bob Balaban, Charles Haid, Dori Brenner, Drew Barrymore, John Larroquette.

Hurt plays Harvard scientist Eddie Jessup, a visionary who evolutionarily regresses himself with the help of some Mexican hallucinogenic drugs and an immersion tank. Havoc ensues. Hurt manifests the intensity he would bring to later roles, but the script is often a confusing mess.

15. **Jeremy Irons** (*Reversal of Fortune*, 1990)
Debut *Nijinsky* (1980), directed by Herbert Ross, with Alan Bates, George de la Peña, Leslie Browne, Alan Badel.

A somewhat unsuccessful biography of the homosexual ballet dancer and his fiery relationship with his mentor and lover Sergei Diaghilev. Irons plays *Ballet Russe* choreographer Mikhail Fokine.

16. **Ben Kingsley** (*Gandhi*, 1982)
Debut *Fear Is the Key* (1972, British), directed by Michael Tuchner; with Barry Newman, Suzy Kendall, John Vernon, Dolph Sweet.

This thriller, based on an Alistair MacLean novel, is about a man pushed to the limit pursuing stolen money and seeking revenge against the murders of his wife and child. Other than the 1973 British-TV film, *Hard Labour* (directed by Mike Leigh), after *Fear Is the Key*, Kingsley did not make another feature until *Gandhi*.

17. **Burt Lancaster** (*Elmer Gantry*, 1960)
Debut *The Killers* (1946), directed by Robert Siodmak; with Edmond O'Brien, Albert Dekker, Ava Gardner, Sam Levene, William Conrad, Charles McGraw, Virginia Christine.

In this marvelous film noir adaptation of an Ernest Hemingway story, Lancaster plays a dead man: He's an ex-boxer known as The Swede who is murdered in a contract hit. The killers spend the rest of the movie piecing together their target's life.

18. **Jack Lemmon** (*Save the Tiger*, 1973)

    Debut *It Should Happen to You* (1954), directed by George Cukor; with Judy Holliday, Peter Lawford, Michael O'Shea, Vaughn Taylor.

    In this charming comedy scripted by Garson Kanin, Judy Holliday plays an ambitious small-town girl who wants to become an actress and a model. She moves to New York and tries to gain attention by plastering her picture on a billboard. Lemmon is wonderful in his first film and Holliday is irresistible.

19. **Jack Nicholson** (*As Good As It Gets*, 1997)

    Debut *The Cry Baby Killer* (1958), directed by Jus Addis; with Harry Lauter, Carolyn Mitchell, Brett Halsey, Lynn Cartwright, Ed Nelson.

    A low-budget flick scripted by Roger Corman and the late Leo Gordon about a juvenile delinquent who panics and becomes the "cry baby" of the title when he thinks he's accidentally killed the two guys who beat him up.

20. **Paul Newman** (*The Color of Money*, 1986)

    Debut *The Silver Chalice* (1954), directed by Victor Saville; with Virginia Mayo, Pier Angeli, Jack Palance, Natalie Wood, Joseph Wiseman, Lorne Greene, E. G. Marshall.

    Newman plays a Greek sculptor in a mini-toga who designs the chalice from which Jesus will drink at the Last Supper. Newman was so humiliated by this debut that he later ran an ad (now legendary) in *Daily Variety*, in which he actually apologized for the film.

21. **Al Pacino** (*Scent of a Woman*, 1992)

    Debut *Me, Natalie* (1969), directed by Fred Coe; with Patty Duke, James Farentino.

    Patty Duke plays an ugly duckling who wants to feel pretty and get a guy. Pacino's only scene is at a dance about twenty minutes into the movie. Pacino asks Duke, "Wanna dance?" and then, "You have a nice body . . . do you put out?" After failing to score, he exits and his debut scene is over. To say the respected actor Alfredo Pacino would go on to bigger and better roles is something of an understatement!

22. **Gregory Peck** (*To Kill a Mockingbird*, 1962)

    Debut *Days of Glory* (1944), directed by Jacques Tourner; with

Tamara Toumanova, Alan Reed, Maria Palmer, Lowell Gilmore, Hugo Haas.

Peck (totally miscast) plays a Russian peasant bravely fighting the Nazis in this turgid war drama.

23. **Sidney Poitier** (*Lilies of the Field,* 1963)

Debut *No Way Out* (1950), directed by Joseph L. Mankiewicz; with Richard Widmark, Stephen McNally, Linda Darnell, Harry Bellaver, Stanley Ridges, Ruby Dee, Ossie Davis.

A black hospital intern (Poitier) tries to save the life of a white bigot (Bellaver) who was shot and ultimately dies. The racist's like-minded brother (Widmark) subsequently blames the doctor and seeks revenge.

24. **Cliff Robertson** (*Charly,* 1968)

Debut *Picnic* (1955), directed by Joshua Logan; with William Holden, Kim Novak, Rosalind Russell, Susan Strasberg, Arthur O'Connell, Betty Field, Verna Felton, Reta Shaw, Nick Adams, Phyllis Newman, Raymond Bailey.

This classic small-town drama, based on the play by William Inge, has Holden arriving in a Kansas burg and immediately falling for the young fianceé (Novak) of his old college buddy (Robertson).

25. **Geoffrey Rush** (*Shine,* 1996)

Debut *Hoodwink* (1981, Australian), directed by Claude Watham, with Judy Davis.

Many film sources cite *Shine* as Rush's film debut, but in 1981, he appeared as "Detective #1" in this very obscure Australian flick, described as a romantic crime story. Judy Davis also appeared in this impossible-to-find (in the U.S. anyway) movie, which is apparently not (yet?) available on video.

26. **Paul Scofield** (*A Man for All Seasons,* 1966)

Debut *That Lady* (1955), directed by Terence Young; with Olivia de Havilland, Gilbert Roland, Dennis Price, Christopher Lee.

Olivia de Havilland plays a widowed noblewoman in 16th century Spain in this bland costume drama.

27. **George C. Scott** (*Patton,* 1970)

Debut *The Hanging Tree* (1959), directed by Delmer Daves; with Gary Cooper, Maria Schell, Ben Piazza, Karl Malden, Karl Swenson, Virginia Gregg, King Donovan.

An offbeat yet well-crafted Western about a blind traveler (Schell) who is taken care of in a mining town by a frontier doctor (Cooper) with secrets from his past. When she is attacked by Malden, who subsequently is shot by Cooper, a lynch mob takes the good doctor out to "The Hanging Tree" of the title but he is rescued by Schell and a thief (Piazza) he himself earlier rescued from a mob. Scott has a minor role.

28. **Rod Steiger** (*In the Heat of the Night,* 1967)
     Debut *Teresa* (1951), directed by Fred Zinnemann; with Pier Angeli, John Ericson, Patricia Collinge, Richard Bishop, Peggy Ann Garner, Ralph Meeker, Bill Maudlin, Edward Binns.
     Ericson plays a World War II vet returning from Europe with an Italian bride and facing prejudice for marrying a foreigner. Steiger plays a psychiatrist.

29. **Jon Voight** (*Coming Home,* 1978)
     Debut *Hour of the Gun* (1967), directed by John Sturges; with James Garner, Jason Robards, Robert Ryan, Albert Salmi, Charles Aidman, William Windom, Frank Converse.
     This superb Western tells the story of what happens *after* the gunfight at the OK Corral and is, in fact, a sequel to director Sturges's 1957 epic *Gunfight at the OK Corral.* James Garner delivers a brilliant performance as an embittered Wyatt Earp, and today the film is considered a minor classic of the genre.

30. **John Wayne** (*True Grit,* 1969)
     Debut *Big Trail* (1930), directed by Raoul Walsh; with Marguerite Churchill, El Brendel, Tully Marshall, Tyrone Power Sr., Ward Bond, Helen Parrish.
     Even though he had had minor, uncredited parts in earlier films (including playing a football player in 1926 in *Brown of Harvard*), John Wayne's first feature film appearance was in *Big Trail.* The Duke plays a scout leading a wagon train across the frontier wilderness. The company encounters the usual perils of such endeavors, including Indians, rampaging herds of buffalo, and seemingly impassable terrain (as well as the occasional romantic predicament). This was one of the first films shot in 55mm wide-screen cinematography, although most theaters would not spend the money on the projection equipment necessary to show the film properly and the movie subsequently bombed at the box office.

The "Movies About Monkeys" List

These shining examples of simian cinema feature real monkeys, fake monkeys, robot monkeys, guys in monkey suits, and more. Banana, anyone?

King Kong (1933, 1976)

The Monster and the Girl (1941)

Monkey Business (1952)

King Kong vs. Godzilla (1963)

Monkey's Uncle (1965)

Monkeys, Go Home! (1966)

Planet of the Apes (1968)

Every Which Way But Loose (1978)

King of Kong Island (1978)

Any Which Way You Can (1980)

Trading Places (1983)

King Kong Lives (1986)

Monkey Shines (1988)

Monkey Boy (1990)

Monkey Trouble (1994)

Outbreak (1994)

Born to be Wild (1995)

Congo (1995)

Dunston Checks In (1995)

Ed (1996)

Buddy (1997)

George of the Jungle (1997)

For Your Consideration . . .

THE "H" LIST

Gene Hackman *Get Shorty* (1995); *The Birdcage* (1995)

Linda Hamilton *The Terminator* (1984); *Terminator 2 Judgment Day* (1991)

Tom Hanks *Philadelphia* (1993); *Forrest Gump* (1994)

Daryl Hannah *Splash* (1984); *Steel Magnolias* (1989)

Woody Harrelson *Natural Born Killers* (1994); *The People vs. Larry Flynt* (1996)

Ed Harris *Glengarry Glen Ross* (1992); *The Truman Show* (1998)

Richard Harris *A Man Called Horse* (1970); *Unforgiven* (1992)

Phil Hartman *Greedy* (1994); *Sgt. Bilko* (1995)

Rutger Hauer *Blade Runner* (1982); *The Hitcher* (1982)

Ethan Hawke *Dead Poets Society* (1989); *Gattaca* (1997)

Goldie Hawn *Private Benjamin* (1980); *The First Wives Club* (1996)

Salma Hayek *Fools Rush In* (1997); *54* (1998)

Anne Heche *Wag the Dog* (1997); *Six Days, Seven Nights* (1998)

Mariel Hemingway *Personal Best* (1982); *Star 80* (1983)

Barbara Hershey *Hannah and Her Sisters* (1986); *Tin Men* (1987)

Jennifer Love Hewitt *I Know What You Did Last Summer* (1997); *I Still Know What You Did Last Summer* (1998)

Judd Hirsch *Ordinary People* (1980); *Independence Day* (1996)

Dustin Hoffman *The Graduate* (1967); *Rain Man* (1988)

Lauren Holly *Dumb & Dumber* (1994); *Sabrina* (1995)

Anthony Hopkins *The Silence of the Lambs* (1991); *Amistad* (1997)

Dennis Hopper *Blue Velvet* (1986); *True Romance* (1993)

Whitney Houston *The Bodyguard* (1992); *The Preacher's Wife* (1996)

Tom Hulce *Amadeus* (1984); *Dominick & Eugene* (1988)

Helen Hunt *The Waterdance* (1991); *As Good As It Gets* (1997)

Bonnie Hunt *Jumanji* (1995); *Jerry Maguire* (1996)

Holly Hunter *Broadcast News* (1987); *The Piano* (1993)

William Hurt *The Big Chill* (1983); *The Doctor* (1991)

Anjelica Huston *Crimes & Misdemeanors* (1989); *The Grifters* (1990)

■ ■ ■ ■ ■ ■ ■ ■ ■ ■ ■ ■ ■ ■ ■ ■

It saved her from going door-to-door

At the 1951 Oscar ceremony, Debbie Reynolds, then a winsome nineteen-year-old and neither a nominee nor a presenter that year, attended the festivities clutching a handbag filled with Girl Scout cookies.

■ ■ ■ ■ ■ ■ ■ ■ ■ ■ ■ ■ ■ ■ ■ ■

64 Signs That *Saturday Night Live* Might Be Cursed

Live . . . from New York!

Can a TV show be cursed?

During its two-and-a-half decade run on NBC, the cast, hosts, and musical guests of *Saturday Night Live* have experienced untimely deaths, prison sentences, sex scandals, horrible diseases, mental illness, ugly divorces, legal troubles, drug problems, and financial ruin.

The following list illustrates that there could be a black cloud poised over Lorne Michael's beloved pet show and makes you wonder if the celebs who agree to appear on the show have even the remotest idea of what the SNL's denizens have experienced in the past twenty-five years.

The money's good, though.

Here is a rundown of *SNL*'s Catalog of Calamity. This list includes cast members, guest hosts, and musical guests. Cast members are in ALL CAPS.

JOHN BELUSHI died young of a heroin and cocaine drug overdose.

GILDA RADNER died young of ovarian cancer.

Michael O'Donoghue, one of the show's charter writers, died young of a massive stroke.

PHIL HARTMAN was shot to death by his wife, who then committed suicide.

Andy Kaufman died young of lung cancer.

Richard Pryor is now almost completely paralyzed from multiple sclerosis.

Dick Cavett has suffered from chronic depression and mental illness for decades.

Carly Simon had breast cancer.

Jodie Foster was stalked by an insane fan who attempted to assassinate President Reagan as a way to impress her.

Brian Wilson suffered from mental illness.

Frank Zappa died of prostate cancer.

Jackson Browne had troubles with the law and was allegedly physically abusive towards Daryl Hannah.

Hugh Hefner suffered a stroke.

Willie Nelson had serious problems with the IRS.

Billy Joel was embezzled by his manager and ended up divorced from model Christie Brinkley.

O. J. Simpson No explanation necessary.

The Grateful Dead Jerry Garcia had lifelong drug problems and died young from heart disease.

Rick Nelson died young in a plane crash.

Gary Busey was seriously injured in a motorcycle accident.

Margot Kidder suffered from mental illness.

James Taylor had drug and alcohol problems.

Kirk Douglas suffered a stroke.

Linda McCartney died young from breast cancer.

EDDIE MURPHY was caught in an allegedly illicit situation with a transvestite.

James Brown did time in prison.

Prince's infant son died mysteriously shortly after birth.

Rick James did time in prison.

John Cougar Mellencamp had a heart attack when he was quite young.

Elton John has had lifelong drug and alcohol problems as well as a failed marriage.

Olivia Newton-John had breast cancer.

Queen Lead singer **Freddie Mercury** died young from AIDS.

Drew Barrymore had drug and alcohol problems at a very young age.

Joan Rivers's husband committed suicide.

Brandon Tartikoff died young from cancer.

John Candy died young from heart disease.

Robin Williams has had drug and alcohol problems and a failed marriage.

Ringo Starr was almost killed in a car accident.

Christopher Reeve was paralyzed in a horse riding accident.

ROBERT DOWNEY JR. has had serious drug and alcohol problems and did time in prison.

Pee-wee Herman was busted for masturbating in public.

Sam Kinison died young in a car accident.

John Larroquette is an admitted alcoholic.

Garry Shandling was embezzled by his manager.

Sean Penn did time in prison.

The Rolling Stones Guitarist **Keith Richards** has had lifelong drug problems.

Tony Danza was almost killed in a skiing accident.

Ted Danson was responsible for a Friars Club racial scandal. (He wore blackface and told racial jokes.)

Rob Lowe was caught having sex with underaged girls when a homemade videotape he made of his dalliances was made public.

Eric Clapton's young son died falling out a window.

Alec Baldwin was sued for beating up a paparazzi photographer.

CHRIS FARLEY died young from a morphine and cocaine drug overdose.

JULIA SWEENEY had ovarian cancer.

Roseanne claims to suffer from multiple personality disorder and has had marriage and addiction troubles.

Michael Bolton was involved in a scandal involving his namesake charity.

Macaulay Culkin was involved in a parental custody scandal.

Nirvana Leader **Kurt Cobain** committed suicide.

Vanessa Williams lost her Miss America crown when nude lesbian photos of her were published in *Penthouse*.

Bobby Brown has had repeated trouble with the law.

NORM MACDONALD has been involved in live performance scandals in which he was accused of being drunk on stage and of not fulfilling his contract.

Christian Slater did time in prison.

Martin Lawrence has had drug and alcohol problems and troubles with the law.

Nancy Kerrigan had her knee smashed by an emissary of rival skater Tonya Harding.

Kelsey Grammer has had problems with alcohol and drugs and was involved in a serious car accident.

Pamela Anderson was abused by her husband, Mötley Crüe drummer **Tommy Lee,** who ended up in jail, and a hardcore videotape of them having sex was stolen from their home and made public. Reportedly, tens of thousands of copies of the tape now exist.

People Magazine's 25 Best and Worst Selling Covers

A review of *People* magazine's best- and worst-selling issues over the past twenty-five years provides a *dramatic* survey of popular culture during this period, as well as a crystal-clear illustration of what *People*'s readers are interested in.

Weddings, deaths, hunks, scandals, and babies?

Absolutely.

Astronauts, Supreme Court justices, politicians, financiers, radicals, hostages, child abuse, rape, and assisted suicide?

Absolutely . . . *no way.*

People acknowledges that 66 percent of their readers are of the female persuasion. Armchair sociologists can make of these findings what they will. Regardless, though, of the conclusions reached by pondering this chart, reading these cover topics is a fascinating exercise in nostalgia.

Year	Best-Selling Issue	Worst-Selling Issue
1974	The Johnny Carsons	J. Paul Getty
1975	Cher and Gregg Allman	Liv Ullmann
1976	Cher, Gregg Allman, Chastity, and Elijah Blue	Ronald and Nancy Reagan
1977	"Tony Orlando's Breakdown"	Julie Andrews

Year	Best-Selling Issue	Worst-Selling Issue
1978	Olivia Newton-John	Vice President and Mrs. Walter Mondale
1979	5th Anniversary Issue	Fleetwood Mac
1980	John Lennon 1940–1980: A Tribute	Paul Simon
1981	Behind the scenes of Princess Diana's wedding	Justice Sandra Day O'Connor
1982	Princess Grace 1929–1982: A Tribute	*Annie*
1983	Karen Carpenter's death	Astronaut Sally Ride
1984	Michael Jackson	"How to Make Your Kid a Star"
1985	"The Other Life of Rock Hudson"	Jacqueline Bisset and Alexander Godunov
1986	Princess Fergie's wedding	The raid on Libya
1987	"Naughty, Naughty: The Follies of Fergie and Di"	Michael Caine
1988	Burt Reynolds and Loni Anderson's wedding	"Our American Hostages"
1989	Lucy: 1911–1989	The death of Abbie Hoffman
1990	Patrick Swayze	"Raped on Campus"
1991	Jeffrey Dahmer	Richard Dreyfuss's wife's disease
1992	Princess Diana	"I helped my mother die."
1993	Julia Roberts and Lyle Lovett's wedding	Hillary Clinton's first 100 days
1994	The Nicole Simpson murders	Kelsey Grammer
1995	Susan Smith's ex-husband David	Larry Hagman
1996	Margaux Hemingway	Jackie Gleason and Audrey Meadows
1997	Goodbye, Diana	The fight against child abuse
1998	Barbra Streisand and James Brolin's wedding	Emmy's 50th birthday

■ ■ ■ ■ ■ ■ ■ ■ ■ ■ ■ ■ ■ ■ ■ ■

I heard [about Hollywood], "Your agent is never your friend." It's a complete and total fucking piece-of-shit lie. I also heard that all producers are scumbags. Also untrue of the producers I've worked with. So everybody was wrong. But my brother [actor Eric Roberts] told me something that *was* true: "You have to remember that this is show *business,* not show friendship."

Julia Roberts
Playboy, November 1991

■ ■ ■ ■ ■ ■ ■ ■ ■ ■ ■ ■ ■ ■ ■ ■

For Your Consideration . . .

The "I" List

Jeremy Irons *Dead Ringers* (1988); *Reversal of Fortune* (1990)
Amy Irving *The Competition* (1980); *Crossing Delancey* (1988)

■ ■ ■ ■ ■ ■ ■ ■ ■ ■ ■ ■ ■ ■ ■ ■

Yes, Mr. Tracy, we have.

At the 1958 Oscar ceremony, all Academy business was completed in record time: After Mitzi Gaynor closed the show with "There's No Business Like Show Business!" director Jerry Wald signaled to host Jerry Lewis that they still had an incredible *twenty minutes* of air time to fill. Jerry did his best to vamp and fill the time but those last twenty minutes were an unmitigated train wreck. First, the winners danced with each other on stage for a while; then Lewis ad-libbed some lame comedy bits; then he tried conducting the orchestra; and finally he picked up a trumpet (which he could not play) and began blowing off-key notes. That was the last straw: NBC pulled the plug on the broadcast and aired a short film on pistols for the remaining time. Spencer Tracy, watching the debacle at home on TV, was reported to exclaim, "My God, have we fallen to this?!"

■ ■ ■ ■ ■ ■ ■ ■ ■ ■ ■ ■ ■ ■ ■ ■

Money for Nothing: The Values of 223 Movie Stars' Signed Photos

Signed photos of movie stars are one of the most popular Hollywood collectibles and an entire industry exists to serve the wants of fans.

The selling prices of signed celebrity photos are an accurate indicator of the box office clout of the celeb in question as well as the rarity of the signed pictures themselves.

Some stars sign willingly and their autographs are plentiful; others do not sign that often and their John Hancocks are rare and, thus, expensive. Signed Marlon Brando photographs are dear; ol' Marl doesn't affix his moniker to pix that often.

$500	Marlon Brando		Meryl Streep
$250	Madonna		Jack Nicholson
$180	Barbra Streisand		Gillian Anderson
$120	Sean Connery		Eddie Murphy
$110	Julia Roberts		Clint Eastwood
$100	Paul Newman		Chris Farley
	Mel Gibson	$70	Val Kilmer
	Harrison Ford		Sylvester Stallone
$90	Christopher Reeve		Steven Spielberg
$85	Tom Hanks		Robert Redford
	Tom Cruise		Michael Keaton
	Robert De Niro		Kevin Spacey
	Demi Moore		Kate Winslet
$80	Michelle Pfeiffer		Johnny Depp
	Brad Pitt		Jessica Lange
	Arnold Schwarzenegger		Cameron Diaz
$75	Winona Ryder		Bruce Willis
	Sharon Stone		Billy Bob Thornton

	Anjelica Huston	Salma Hayek
$65	Meg Ryan	Rosie O'Donnell
	Leonardo DiCaprio	Pierce Brosnan
	Kyra Sedgwick	Nicolas Cage
	Holly Hunter	Matt Damon
	Alicia Silverstone	Lori Petty
$60	Will Smith	Lisa Kudrow
	Wesley Snipes	Kevin Costner
	Uma Thurman	Keanu Reeves
	Susan Sarandon	Juliette Lewis
	Sarah Michelle Gellar	Jennifer Love Hewitt
	Patrick Swayze	Jennifer Lopez
	Nicole Kidman	Goldie Hawn
	Molly Ringwald	Glenn Close
	Melanie Griffith	Emma Thompson
	Jodie Foster	Drew Barrymore
	Jim Carrey	David Duchovny
	Helen Hunt	Daryl Hannah
	George Clooney	Cuba Gooding Jr.
	Dustin Hoffman	Chris O'Donnell
$55	Sigourney Weaver	Burt Reynolds
	Liv Tyler	Antonio Banderas
	Linda Hamilton	Al Pacino
	Elisabeth Shue	Adam Sandler
	Diane Keaton	$45 Warren Beatty
	David Spade	Vanessa Williams
	Bill Paxton	Tom Berenger
$50	Woody Harrelson	Teri Hatcher
	Tommy Lee Jones	Téa Leoni
	Tim Allen	Steven Seagal
	Teri Garr	Sean Penn
	Sandra Bullock	Richard Gere
	Samuel L. Jackson	Matthew McConaughey

	Marisa Tomei	Kim Basinger
	Lauren Holly	Kelly Preston
	Kurt Russell	Judge Reinhold
	Kelly Lynch	Jennifer Aniston
	Julianne Moore	Jeff Bridges
	John Travolta	Jean-Claude Van Damme
	Halle Berry	Harry Connick Jr.
	Gwyneth Paltrow	Greg Kinnear
	Gary Oldman	Gene Hackman
	Elizabeth Hurley	Ellen Barkin
	Denzel Washington	Courteney Cox
	Dennis Hopper	Corbin Bernsen
	Courtney Love	Christina Ricci
	Claire Danes	Christian Slater
	Chris Rock	Chevy Chase
	Charlton Heston	Charles Bronson
	Bill Murray	Bridget Fonda
	Bette Midler	Billy Crystal
	Ashley Judd	Andy Garcia
	Anthony Hopkins	Alec Baldwin
	Annette Bening	$35 Woody Allen
	Anne Heche	Tom Selleck
$40	Spike Lee	Tim Robbins
	Rosie Perez	Sophia Loren
	Robin Williams	Sean Young
	Rebecca DeMornay	Sarah Jessica Parker
	Ray Liotta	Robert Duvall
	Nick Nolte	Richard Dreyfuss
	Mira Sorvino	René Russo
	Mike Myers	Peter Fonda
	Michael Douglas	Morgan Freeman
	Liam Neeson	Matthew Broderick
	Kirstie Alley	Kristy Swanson

	Kirk Douglas	Angela Bassett
	Kevin Bacon	Andie MacDowell
	Kathleen Turner	$25 Walter Matthau
	John Malkovich	Vivica A. Fox
	Joe Pesci	Tom Skerritt
	Joan Cusack	Sally Field
	Jeff Goldblum	Robin Givens
	Jamie Lee Curtis	Randy Quaid
	James Earl Jones	Phoebe Cates
	James Caan	Pam Grier
	Geena Davis	Lea Thompson
	Emilio Estevez	Jada Pinkett
	Danny Glover	Jack Lemmon
	Dana Carvey	Gary Busey
	Christina Applegate	Edward Burns
	Cher	Dudley Moore
	Charlie Sheen	Dennis Quaid
	Brooke Shields	Danny DeVito
	Ben Stiller	Chris Tucker
	Ann-Margret	Billy Zane
$30	Whoopi Goldberg	Ally Sheedy
	Neve Campbell	$20 William Baldwin
	Minnie Driver	Stephen Baldwin
	Edward Norton	Eric Roberts
	Dan Aykroyd	Ed Harris
	Ben Affleck	Daniel Baldwin
	Beau Bridges	Casey Affleck
	Anne Archer	

Source: *White's Guide to the Movies*

a.k.a.: The Real Names
of Hollywood Celebrities

What's in a name?

In Hollywood, a *lot* . . . but not everything.

It *used* to be that a name change was a must if you wanted to make it in Hollywood. If you really wanted to be in show business, you had to have a catchy name, one that was not too ethnic, and one that looked good on a marquee. Thus Edward Heimberger became Eddie Albert; Betty Jean Perske became Lauren Bacall; Anna Maria Italiano became Anne Bancroft; Doris von Kappelhoff became Doris Day; and Issur Demsky became Kirk Douglas.

Things are different today, to say the least.

Many actors and actresses now proudly use their real names, no matter how long (Mary Elizabeth Mastrantonio); how difficult to pronounce (Joaquin Phoenix—it's pronounced "wah-keen"); or how hard to spell (Nina Siemaszko).

But there are still hundreds and hundreds of movie stars, TV stars, and assorted other varieties of Hollywood celebrities (including directors, writers, musicians, comedians, etc.) who did change their name to something they believed to be more "fame-friendly," and this list looks at a bunch of them.

There are secrets revealed in this list.

For instance, did you know that comedian Redd Foxx's real name was John Sanford? Foxx's hit TV series was titled *Sanford and Son,* so we can make of that what we will!

Also, Diane Keaton's real name was Diane Hall and one of her all-time biggest hits was in Woody Allen's *Annie Hall,* which allegedly chronicled her and Woody's longtime romance.

Everyone knows the popular actor Michael Douglas. But did you know that if Michael Keaton had not changed his name when he entered show business, there would have been *two* actors named Michael Douglas? "Michael Douglas" was Keaton's real name before he changed it (in an example of Hollywood's seniority system: By the time Keaton made his film debut in 1982 with *Night Shift,* the original Michael Douglas had already done close to ten movies).

There is also revelation in the name change of the brilliantly talented actor Ben Kingsley. Have you ever wondered how he was able to seemingly inhabit the persona of Gandhi in the 1982 film? Kingsley's real name is Krishna Banji, and, thus, it can be concluded that the actor was able to draw on his (and Gandhi's, of course) heritage in his interpretaton of the role.

But this list is about those actors who have changed their names and before the list proper, we thought it would be interesting (and amusing) to take a look at what pop culture and the field of entertainment might look like if certain celebs had not assumed a new moniker on their way to fame and glory.

If certain celebs had not changed their names . . .

★ The credits of the popular seventies TV series *Charlie's Angels* would have looked a tad different. The show would have starred **Cheryl Stoppelmoor** instead of Cheryl Ladd.

★ *This Gun for Hire* would have starred **Constance Ockleman** instead of Veronica Lake.

★ Vegas audiences would have been watching the husband-and-wife team of **Sidney Leibowitz** and **Edith Gormezano** instead of Steve Lawrence and Eydie Gorme.

★ The classic Alfred Hitchcock chiller *Psycho* would have starred **Jeanette Morrison** instead of Janet Leigh.

★ The hit TV series *Barney Miller* would have starred **Harold Lipshitz** instead of Hal Linden.

★ *Frankenstein and The Mummy* would have starred **William Henry Pratt** instead of Boris Karloff.

★ The classic 1931 horror flick *Dracula* would have starred **Bela Blasko** instead of Bela Lugosi.

★ The hugely popular TV series *The Six Million Dollar Man* would have starred **Harvey Lee Yeary 2nd** instead of Lee Majors.

★ The exciting TV drama *The Streets of San Francisco* would have starred **Mladen Sekulovich** instead of Karl Malden.

★ The popular game show *The Hollywood Squares* would have been hosted by **Pierre LaCock** instead of Peter Marshall.

★ The hilarious movie *The Odd Couple* would have starred **Walter Matuschanskayasky** instead of Walter Matthau.

★ The thrilling movie *Bullitt* would have starred **Terence McQueen** insead of Steve McQueen.

★ The rock group Queen would have had as its lead singer **Frederick Bulsara** instead of Freddie Mercury.

★ *The Man With the X-Ray Eyes* would have starred **Reginald Truscott-Jones** instead of Ray Milland.

★ The classic 1971 folk-rock album *Blue* would have been written and recorded by **Roberta Joan Anderson** instead of Joni Mitchell.

Δ The hit fifties and sixties TV series *I've Got a Secret* would have starred **Thomas Garrison Morfit** instead of Garry Moore.

★ Thousands would have learned to ballroom dance at **The Moses Teichman Dance Studio** instead of The Arthur Murray Studio.

★ The sexy 1993 movie *Indecent Proposal* would have starred **Demi Guynes** instead of Demi Moore.

★ *The Graduate* would have been directed by **Michael Igor Peschowsky** instead of Mike Nichols.

★ The popular TV Western *Walker, Texas Ranger* would star **Carlos Ray** instead of Chuck Norris.

★ "Tie a Yellow Ribbon" would have been a huge hit for **Michael Cassavitis** & Dawn instead of Tony Orlando & Dawn.

★ "Here She Is, Miss America" would have been sung by **Bert Jacobson** instead of Bert Parks.

★ The Gibson Guitar Company would have manufactured their famous **Lester Polsfuss** guitar instead of the Les Paul.

★ *The Man in the Gray Flannel Suit* would have starred **Eldred Peck** instead of Gregory Peck.

★ The charming TV series *Hart to Hart* would have starred **Stefania Ferderkievicz** instead of Stefanie Powers.

★ The legendary film *Gone With the Wind* would have starred **William Gable** and **Vivien Hartley** instead of Clark Gable and Vivien Leigh.

★ The enormously popular TV series *The Odd Couple* would have starred **Leonard Rosenberg** instead of Tony Randall.

★ The beloved sixties TV series *The Donna Reed Show* would instead have been called *The Donna Mullenger Show.*

★ "Can we talk?" would have been the trademark line of **Joan Molinsky** instead of Joan Rivers.

★ *Double Indemnity* and *Key Largo* would have starred **Emmanuel Goldberg** instead of Edward G. Robinson.

★ Trigger would have been ridden by **Leonard Slye** instead of Roy Rogers.

★ The hit movie *Gentlemen Prefer Blondes* would have starred sex symbol **Ernestine Russell** instead of Jane Russell.

★ The wacky spy spoof TV series *Get Smart!* would have starred **Donald Yarmy** instead of Don Adams.

★ *Annie Hall* would have been written and directed by **Allen Konigsberg** instead of Woody Allen.

★ *The Soupy Sales Show* would have starred **Milton Hines** instead of Soupy Sales.

★ The second Darren on *Bewitched* would have been played by **Richard Cox** instead of Dick Sargent.

★ *Dr. Quinn, Medicine Woman* and *War and Remembrance* would have starred **Joyce Frankenberg** instead of Jane Seymour.

★ The Lone Ranger's faithful Indian companion Tonto would have been played by **Harold J. Smith** instead of Jay Silverheels.

★ *The Big Valley* would have starred **Ruby Stevens** as Victoria Barkley instead of Barbara Stanwyck.

★ *Make Room for Daddy* would have starred **Muzyad Yaghoob** instead of Danny Thomas.

★ The hilarious comedies *Young Frankenstein* and *Blazing Saddles* would have starred **Jerome Silberman** instead of Gene Wilder.

★ Fiery Latina Maria would have been played in *West Side Story* by **Natasha Gurdin** instead of Natalie Wood.

Another fascinating element of celebrity name changes is the actual way some of them modified their handle. Many kept their last names but came up with an extremely cool first name; while others kept their first names but opted for a hotter last name.

Here is a look at some new "First Namers":

Mary Elizabeth Spacek became *Sissy* Spacek; Mary Louise Streep became *Meryl* Streep; Alice Pons became *Lily* Pons; Marilyn Novak became *Kim* Novak; Maria Mercouri became *Melina* Mercouri; Margaret Kidder became *Margot* Kidder; Susan Weaver became *Sigourney* Weaver; Ethel Keeler became *Ruby* Keeler; James Hendrix became *Jimi* Hendrix; Ruth Grable became *Betty* Grable; Sari Gabor became *Zsa Zsa* Gabor (actually, Sari is a pretty cool first name, wonder why she changed it?); Anna Marie Duke became *Patty* Duke; Cornelius Chase became *Chevy* Chase; Salvatore Philip Bono became *Sonny* Bono (a name he kept even while serving in the United States Congress, an institution where the name "Salvatore Philip" might have garnered more respect); Elmore Torn became *Rip* Torn; Susan Weld became *Tuesday* Weld; Gretchen Young became *Loretta* Young (again, a perfectly cool first name changed to something a tad more stuffy); and, in what might be an example of the ultimate too-cool name change; Barbara Streisand became *Barbra* Streisand. I guess that extra "a" just aggravated the heck out of her, eh?

Then there are those who "reverse engineered" their family names, keeping their first (and sometimes middle) names but changing their last name to something more suitable for a marquee. Some examples:

Barbara Herzstein became Barbara Seagull and then Barbara *Hershey*; Joel Katz became Joel *Grey*; Greta Gustafsson became Greta *Garbo*; Joan de Havilland became Joan *Fontaine*; Phyllis Driver became Phyllis *Diller*; Diana Fluck became Diana *Dors* (big shock there, eh?); Thomas Cruise Mapother IV became Tom *Cruise*; Nicholas Coppola became Nicolas *Cage* (like Streisand, that extra letter in his first name must have really annoyed him!); Maria Calogeropoulos became Maria

Callas; Fannie Borach became Fanny *Brice*; David Hayward-Jones became David *Bowie*; Charles Buchinsky became Charles *Bronson*; Lionel Blythe became Lionel *Barrymore*; and Maude Kiskadden became Maude *Adams*.

What's in a name? Read through the following list of name changes and decide for yourself. But one thing's for certain: You'll never watch a John Wayne movie the same way again . . . now that you know that the rugged hero's real first name was Marion!

A

Don Adams = Donald James Yarmy
Maude Adams = Maude Kiskadden
Eddie Albert = Edward Albert Heimberger
Robert Alda = Alphonso Giuseppe Giovanni Roberto d'Abruzzo
Fred Allen = John Florence Sullivan
Gracie Allen = Grace Ethel Cecile Rosalie
Woody Allen = Allen Stewart Konigsberg
Don Ameche = Dominic Felix Amici
Julie Andrews = Julia Elizabeth Wells
Ann-Margret = Ann-Margret Olsson
Fatty Arbuckle = Roscoe Conklin Arbuckle
Eve Arden = Eunice Quedens
Desi Arnaz = Desiderio Alberto Arnaz y de Acma
James Arness = James King Aurness
Bea Arthur = Bernice Frankel
Jean Arthur = Gladys Georgianna Greene
Fred Astaire = Frederick Austerlitz
Frankie Avalon = Francis Thomas Avallone
Tex Avery = Frederick B. Avery

B

Lauren Bacall = Betty Jean Perske
Lucille Ball = Dianne Belmont
Kaye Ballard = Catherine Gloria Balotta
Anne Bancroft = Anna Maria Italiano

Theda Bara = Theodosio Goodman
Brigitte Bardot = Camille Javal
Orson Bean = Dallas Frederick Burroughs
Warren Beatty = Henry Warren Beatty
Pat Benatar = Patricia Andrzejewski
Tony Bennett = Anthony Dominick Benedetto
Jack Benny = Benjamin Kubelsky
Robby Benson = Robin David Seagal
Edgar Bergen = Edgar John Berggren
Busby Berkeley = William Berkeley Enos Jr.
Milton Berle = Milton Berlinger
Irving Berlin = Israel Isidore Baline
Sarah Bernhardt = Henrietta Rosine Bernard
Joey Bishop = Joseph Abraham Gottlieb
Amanda Blake = Beverly Louise Neill
Robert Blake = Michael James Vijencio Gubitosi
Ray Bolger – Raymond Wallace Bulcao
Bono = Paul Hewson
Sonny Bono = Salvatore Philip Bono
Pat Boone = Charles Eugene Patrick Boone
Shirley Booth = Thelma Booth Ford
Victor Borge = Borge Rosenbaum
David Bowie = David Robert Hayward-Jones
Fanny Brice = Fannie Borach
Charles Bronson = Charles Dennis Buchinsky
Albert Brooks = Albert Einstein
Mel Brooks = Melvin Kaminsky
Lenny Bruce = Leonard Alfred Schneider
Yul Brynner = Taidje Khan
Ellen Burstyn = Edna Rae Gilhooley
Richard Burton = Richard Walter Jenkins Jr.
Red Buttons = Aaron Chwatt

C

Nicolas Cage = Nicholas Coppola
Michael Caine = Maurice Joseph Micklewhite

Rory Calhoun = Francis Timothy Durgin
Maria Callas = Maria Sophie Cecilia Calogeropoulos
Eddie Cantor = Edward Israel Iskowitz
Yakima Canutt = Enos Edward Canutt
Capucine = Germaine Lefebvre
John Carradine = Richmond Reed Carradine
Diahann Carroll = Carol Diahann Johnson
Jeff Chandler = Ira Grossel
Cyd Charisse = Tula Ellice Finklea
Ray Charles = Ray Charles Robinson
Chevy Chase = Cornelius Crane Chase
Cher = Cherilyn Sarkisian LePierre
Patsy Cline = Virginia Patterson Hensley
Lee J. Cobb = Leo Jacoby
Claudette Colbert = Lily Claudette Chaucoin
Nat King Cole = Nathaniel Adams Coles
Perry Como = Pierino Roland Como
Chuck Connors = Kevin Joseph Connors
Robert Conrad = Conrad Robert Falk
Hans Conried = Frank Foster Conried
Alice Cooper = Vincent Furnier
Gary Cooper = Frank James Cooper
David Copperfield = David Seth Kotkin
Elvis Costello = Declan Patrick McManus
Lou Costello = Louis Francis Cristillo
Joan Crawford = Lucille Fay LeSeur
Hume Cronyn = Hume Cronyn Blake
Bing Crosby = Harry Lillis Crosby
Tom Cruise = Thomas Cruise Mapother IV
Robert Cummings = Charles Clarence Robert Orville Cummings
Curly of "The Three Stooges" = Jerome Lester Horwitz
Tony Curtis = Bernard Schwartz

D

Vic Damone = Vito Farinola
Rodney Dangerfield = Jacob Cohen
James Darren = James William Ercolani

Bobby Darin = Walden Robert Cassotto
Bette Davis = Ruth Elizabeth Davis
Dennis Day = Eugene Dennis McNulty
Doris Day = Doris Mary Anne von Kappelhoff
Yvonne DeCarlo = Peggy Yvonne Middleton
Sandra Dee = Alexandra Cymboliak Zuck
Dolores Del Rio = Lolita Dolores de Martinez
Bo Derek = Mary Cathleen Collins
Angie Dickinson = Angeline Brown
Marlene Dietrich = Maria Magdalene von Losch
Phyllis Diller = Phyllis Driver
Divine = Harris Glenn Milstead
Troy Donahue = Merle Johnson
Diana Dors = Diana Mary Fluck
Kirk Douglas = Issur Danielovitch Demsky
Melvyn Douglas = Melvyn Hesselberg
Patty Duke – Anna Marie Duke
Margaret Dumont = Daisy Margaret Baker
Deanna Durbin = Edna Mae Durbin
Bob Dylan = Robert Allen Zimmerman

E

Buddy Ebsen = Christian Rudolf Ebsen
Barbara Eden = Barbara Jean Huffman
Vince Edwards = Vincent Edward Zoine III
Duke Ellington = Edward Kennedy Ellington
Cass Elliot = Ellen Naomi Cohen

F

Fabian = Fabian Anthony Forte-Bonaparte
Fabio = Fabio Lanzoni
Nanette Fabray = Ruby Bernadette Nanette Theresa Fabares
Douglas Fairbanks Sr. = Douglas Elton Thomas Ullman
Morgan Fairchild = Patsy McClenny
James Farentino = Ferdinand Anthony Ferrandino

Mia Farrow = Maria de Lourdes Villiers
Farrah Fawcett = Mary Farrah Leni Fawcett
Alice Faye = Alice Jeanne Leppert
José Ferrer = José Vincente Ferrery de Otero y Cintron
Mel Ferrer = Melchior Gaston Ferrer
Totie Fields = Sophie Feldman
W. C. Fields = William Claude Dukenfield
Larry Fine of "The Three Stooges" = Louis Feinberg
Ian Fleming = Ian Mac Farlane
Henry Fonda = Henri Jaynes Fonda
Joan Fontaine = Joan de Beauvoir de Havilland
Dame Margot Fonteyn = Peggy Hookham
Glenn Ford = Gwyllyn Samuel Newton Ford
John Ford = Sean Aloysius O'Fearna
Mary Ford = Colleen Summers
Paul Ford = Paul Ford Weaver
John Forsythe = John Lincoln Freund
Jodie Foster = Ariane Alicia Christian Foster
Michael J. Fox = Michael Andrew Fox
Redd Foxx = John Elroy Sanford
Tony Franciosa = Anthony George Papaleo
Ann Francis = Frances S. Roberts
Arlene Francis = Arlene Francis Kazanjian
Connie Francis = Concetta Maria Rosa Franconero
Gert Froebe = Karl-Gerhard Frober

Clark Gable = William Clark Gable
Zsa Zsa Gabor = Sari Gabor
Greta Garbo = Greta Louisa Gustafsson
Andy Garcia = Andres Arturo Garcia-Menendez
Vincent Gardenia = Vincenzio Scognamiglio
John Garfield = Jacob Julius Garfinkle
Judy Garland = Frances Ethel Gumm
James Garner = James Scott Baumgarner
Crystal Gayle = Brenda Gayle Webb
Janet Gaynor = Laura Gainer

Mitzi Gaynor = Francesca Mitzi Marlene de Czanyi von Erber
Boy George = George Alan O'Dowd
Dorothy Gish = Dorothy Elizabeth de Guiche
Paulette Goddard = Pauline Marion Goddard
Whoopi Goldberg = Karen Johnson
Samuel Goldwyn = Samuel Goldfish
Ruth Gordon = Ruth Gordon Jones
Eydie Gorme = Edith Gormezano
Betty Grable = Ruth Elizabeth Grable
Stewart Granger = James Stewart-Lablache
Cary Grant = Archibald Alexander Leach
Lee Grant = Lyova Haskell Rosenthal
Peter Graves = Peter Aurness-Graves
Rocky Graziano = Thomas Rocco Barbella
Joel Grey = Joel Katz

H

Buddy Hackett = Leonard Hacker
Alan Hale = Rufus Alan McKanan
Hammer = Stanley Kirk Burrell
Jean Harlow = Harlean Carpenter
June Havoc = Ellen Evangeline Hovick
Sterling Hayden = Sterling Christian Relyea Walter
Helen Hayes = Helen Hayes Brown
Susan Hayward = Edythe Marreanner
Rita Hayworth = Margarita Carmen Cansino
Van Heflin = Emmett Evan Helfin Jr.
Jimi Hendrix = James Marshall Hendrix
Pee-wee Herman = Paul Reubenfeld
Barbara Hershey = Barbara Herzstein
William Holden = William Franklin Beedle Jr.
Billie Holiday = Eleanor Gough McKay
Earl Holliman = Anthony Earl Numkena
Buddy Holly = Charles Hardin Holly
Bob Hope = Leslie Townes Hope
Hedda Hopper = Elda Furry
Vladimir Horowitz = Vladimir Gorowicz

Harry Houdini = Ehrich Weiss
John Houseman = Jacques Haussmann
Rock Hudson = Roy Harold Scherer Jr.
Engelbert Humperdinck = Arnold George Dorsey
Kim Hunter = Janet Cole
Ross Hunter = Martin Fuss
Tab Hunter = Arthur Gelien
Mary Beth Hurt = Mary Beth Supinger
Walter Huston = Walter Houghston
Betty Hutton = Elizabeth Jane Thornburg
Jim Hutton = Dana James Hutton

I

Ice-T = Tracy Marrow
Vanilla Ice = Robert Van Winkle
Billy Idol = William Michael Broad
Burl Ives = Burl Icle Ivanhoe

J

David Janssen = David Harold Meyer
Claudia Jennings = Mimi Chesterton
Elton John = Reginald Kenneth Dwight
Van Johnson = Charles Van Dell-Johnson
Al Jolson = Asa Yoelson
Jennifer Jones = Phyllis Isley
Louis Jourdan = Louis Gendre
Raul Julia = Raul Rafael Carlos Julia y Arcelay

K

Ish Kabibble = Merwyn Bogue
Boris Karloff = William Henry Pratt
Danny Kaye = David Daniel Kominski
Elia Kazan = Elia Kazanjoglous

Stacy Keach = Walter Stacy Keach Jr.
Buster Keaton = Joseph Francis Keaton
Diane Keaton = Diane Hall
Michael Keaton = Michael Douglas
Howard Keel = Harold Leek
Ruby Keeler = Ethel Keeler
Brian Keith = Robert Brian Keith Jr.
Deborah Kerr = Deborah Kerr-Trimmer
Margot Kidder = Margaret Kidder
Carole King = Carole Klein
Ben Kingsley = Krishna Banji
Klaus Kinski = Nikolaus Gunther Nakszynski
Nastassja Kinski = Nastassja Nakszynski
Evel Knievel = Robert Craig
Ted Knight = Tadeus Wladyslaw Konopka

L

Cheryl Ladd = Cheryl Stoppelmoor
Bert Lahr = Irving Lahrheim
Frankie Laine = Frank Paul Lo Vecchio
Veronica Lake = Constance Ockleman
Hedy Lamarr = Hedwig Kiesler
Dorothy Lamour = Mary Leta Dorothy Stanton
Elsa Lanchester = Elizabeth Sullivan
Carole Landis = Frances Ridste
Michael Landon = Eugene Maurice Orowitz
Rocky Lane = Harry L. Albershart
Mario Lanza = Alfredo Arnold Cocozza
Stan Laurel = Arthur Stanley Jefferson
Piper Laurie = Rosetta Jacobs
Gertrude Lawrence = Alexandre Dagmar Lawrence-Klasen
Steve Lawrence = Sidney Leibowitz
Brenda Lee = Brenda Mae Tarpley
Bruce Lee = Li Yuen Kam
Dixie Lee = Wilma Wyatt
Gypsy Rose Lee = Rose Louise Hovick

Michelle Lee = Michelle Dusiak
Peggy Lee = Norma Egstrom
Janet Leigh = Jeanette Morrison
Vivien Leigh = Vivien Mary Hartley
Lotte Lenya = Karoline Blaumauer
Sheldon Leonard = Sheldon Leonard Bershad
Huey Lewis = Hugh Cregg
Jerry Lewis = Joseph Levitch
Ted Lewis = Theodore Leopold Friedman
Liberace = Wladziu Valentin Liberace
Hal Linden = Harold Lipshitz
Viveca Lindfors = Else Viveca Tortensdotter
Herbert Lom = Herbert Charles Angelo Kuchacevich
   ze Schluderpacheru
Carole Lombard = Jane Alice Peters
Julie London = Julie Peck
Jack Lord = John Joseph Ryan
Traci Lords = Nora Louise Kuzma
Sophia Loren = Sofia Scicolone
Peter Lorre = Laszlo Loewenstein
Myrna Loy = Myrna Williams
Clare Boothe Luce = Ann Clare Boothe
Bela Lugosi = Bela Lugosi Blasko

M

Moms Mabley = Loretta Mary Aiken
Gisele MacKenzie = Marie Marguerite Louise Gisele LaFleche
Shirley MacLaine = Shirley Maclean Beatty
Madonna = Madonna Louise Veronica Ciccone
Lee Majors = Harvey Lee Yeary 2nd
Karl Malden = Mladen Sekulovich
Dorothy Malone = Dorothy Maloney
Jayne Mansfield = Vera Jane Palmer
Rocky Marciano = Rocco Francis Marchegiano
Hugh Marlowe = Hugh Hipple

Peter Marshall = Pierre LaCock
Dean Martin = Dino Paul Crocetti
Ross Martin = Martin Rosenblatt
Tony Martin = Alvin Maris
Walter Matthau = Walter Matuschanskayasky
Fibber McGee = Jim Jordan
Molly McGee = Marion Jordan
Steve McQueen = Terence Stephen McQueen
Melina Mercouri = Maria Amalia Mercouri
Freddie Mercury = Frederick Bulsara
Burgess Meredith = Oliver Burgess
Ethel Merman = Ethel Zimmerman
Vera Miles = Vera Ralston
Ray Milland = Reginald Truscott-Jones
Carmen Miranda = Maria de Carmo Miranda de Cunha
Joni Mitchell = Roberta Joan Anderson
Moe Howard of "The Three Stooges" = Moses Horowitz
Marilyn Monroe = Norma Jean Mortenson
Yves Montand = Yvo Livi
Lola Montcz = Eliza Gilbert
Robert Montgomery = Henry Montgomery
Demi Moore = Demi Guynes
Garry Moore = Thomas Garrison Morfit
Harry Morgan = Harry Bratsburg
Henry Morgan = Henry Lerner von Ost Jr.
Zero Mostel = Samuel Joel Mostel
Mr. Green Jeans = Hugh Brannum
Arthur Murray = Moses Teichman

N

Gene Nelson = Gene Berg
Harriet Nelson = Harriet Louise Snyder
Ozzie Nelson = Oswald Nelson
Rick Nelson = Eric Hilliard Nelson
Mike Nichols = Michael Igor Peschowsky

Harry Nilsson = Harry Edward Nelson III
Chuck Norris = Carlos Ray
Kim Novak = Marilyn Novak

O

Merle Oberon = Estelle Merle O'Brien Thompson
Maureen O'Hara = Maureen Fitzsimons
Tony Orlando = Michael Anthony Orlando Cassavitis

P

Patti Page = Clara Ann Fowler
Jack Palance = Vladimir Palaniuk
Lilli Palmer = Lilli Peiser
Bert Parks = Bert Jacobson
Louella Parsons = Louella Oettinger
Les Paul = Lester Polsfuss
Minnie Pearl = Sarah Ophelia Colley Cannon
Gregory Peck = Eldred Gregory Peck
Bernadette Peters = Bernadette Lazzaro
Edith Piaf = Edith Gassion
Slim Pickens = Louis Bert Lindley
Mary Pickford = Gladys Mary Smith
Ezio Pinza = Fortunato Pinza
Lily Pons = Alice Josephine Pons
Stefanie Powers = Stefania Zofia Ferderkievicz
Paula Prentiss = Paula Ragusa
Robert Preston = Robert Preston Meservey
Prince = Prince Rogers Nelson
Freddie Prinze = Freddie Preutzel

R

George Raft = George Ranft
Dirk Rambo = Orman Ray Rambo

Sally Rand = Helen Gould Beck
Tony Randall = Leonard Rosenberg
Martha Raye = Margaret Yvonne Reed
Robert Redford = Charles Robert Redford Jr.
Donna Reed = Donna Belle Mullenger
Robert Reed = John Robert Rietz Jr.
Della Reese = Delloreese Patricia Early
George Reeves = George Besselo
Fernando Rey = Fernando Casado Arambillet
Debbie Reynolds = Marie Frances Reynolds
Buddy Rich = Bernard Rich
Tex Ritter = Maurice Woodward Ritter
Chita Rivera = Delores Conchita Figuero del Rivero
Geraldo Rivera = Miguel Rivera
Joan Rivers = Joan Sandra Molinsky
Jerome Robbins = Jerome Rabinowitz
Edward G. Robinson – Emmanuel Goldberg
Ginger Rogers = Virginia Katherine McMath
Roy Rogers = Leonard Slye
Mickey Rooney = Joe Yule Jr.
Mickey Rourke = Philip André Rourke
Jane Russell = Ernestine Jane Russell
Winona Ryder = Winona Laura Horowitz

S

Susan Saint James = Susan Miller
Soupy Sales = Milton Hines
Susan Sarandon = Susan Tomaling
Dick Sargent = Richard Cox
John Saxon = Carmen Orrico
Romy Schneider = Rosemarie Magdalena Albach-Retty
Mack Sennett = Mickall Sinott
Jane Seymour = Joyce Frankenberg
Omar Sharif = Michel Shalhouz
Artie Shaw = Arthur Ashawsky
Dick Shawn = Richard Schulefand

Norma Shearer = Edith Norma Fisher
Charlie Sheen = Carlos Irwin Estevez
Martin Sheen = Ramon Estevez
Shemp Howard of "The Three Stooges" = Samuel Horwitz
Sam Shepard = Samuel Shepard Rogers
Talia Shire = Talia Coppola
Dinah Shore = Frances (Fanny) Rose Shore
Sylvia Sidney = Sophia Kosow
Simone Signoret = Simone Kaminker
Beverly Sills = Belle Silverman
Jay Silverheels = Harold J. Smith
Phil Silvers = Phil Silversmith
Red Skelton = Richard Skelton
Suzanne Somers = Suzanne Mahoney
Elke Sommer = Elke Schletz
Jack Soo = Goro Suzuki
Ann Sothern = Harriette Lake
Sissy Spacek = Mary Elizabeth Spacek
Barbara Stanwyck = Ruby Stevens
Jean Stapleton = Jeanne Murray
Ringo Starr = Richard Starkey
Stepin Fetchit = Lincoln Perry
Cat Stevens = Stephen Demetri Georgiu
Connie Stevens = Concetta Ingolia
Stella Stevens = Estelle Eggleston
Jon Stewart = Jon Stewart Liebowitz
Sting = Gordon Matthew Sumner
Jill St. John = Jill Oppenheim
Gale Storm = Josephine Cottle
Dorothy R. Stratten = Dorothy Hoogstraten
Meryl Streep = Mary Louise Streep
Barbra Streisand = Barbara Streisand
Gloria Stuart = Gloria Stuart Finch
Preston Sturges = Edmond P. Biden
Donna Summers = LaDonna Gaines
Gloria Swanson = Gloria Swenson

T

Terry-Thomas = Thomas Terry Hoar-Stevens
Danny Thomas = Muzyad Yaghoob
Tiny Tim = Herbert Khaury
Rip Torn = Elmore Torn
Sophie Tucker = Sonia Kalish
Lana Turner = Julia Jean Mildred Frances Turner
Tina Turner = Annie Mae Bullock
Twiggy = Leslie Hornby
Conway Twitty = Harold Lloyd Jenkins

V

Roger Vadim = Roger Vadim Plemiannikow
Jerry Vale = Genaro Louis Vitaliano
Rudolph Valentino = Rudolfo Alfonzo Raffaelo Pierre Filbert
    Guglielmi di Valentina d'Antonguolla
Rudy Vallee = Hubert Prior Vallee
Frankie Valli = Frank Castelluccio
Jean-Claude Van Damme = Jean-Claude Van Varenberg
Mamie Van Doren = Joan Lucille Olander
Erich Von Stroheim = Hans Erich Maria Stroheim von Nordenwall
Max Von Sydow = Carl Von Sydow

W

Christopher Walken = Ronald Walken
Nancy Walker = Anna Myrtle Swoyer
Dinah Washington = Ruth Jones
John Wayne = Marion Michael Morrison
Doodles Weaver = Winstead Sheffield Glendenning Dixon Weaver
Sigourney Weaver = Susan Alexandra Weaver
Clifton Webb = Webb Parmalee Hollenbeck

Johnny Weissmuller = Peter John Weissmuller
Raquel Welch = Teresa Jo Tejada
Tuesday Weld = Susan Ker Weld
Orson Welles = George Orson Welles
Mae West = Mae Cohen
Cornel Wilde = Cornelius Louis Wilde
Gene Wilder = Jerome Silberman
Hank Williams Sr. = Hiram Williams
Shelley Winters = Shirley Schrift
Stevie Wonder = Stevland Morris
Natalie Wood = Natasha Gurdin
Jane Wyman = Sarah Jane Fulks
Ed Wynn = Isaiah Edwin Leopold

X

Malcolm X = Malcolm Little

Y

Gig Young = Byron Ellsworth Barr
Loretta Young = Gretchen Young

For Your Consideration . . .

THE "J" LIST

Samuel L. Jackson *Pulp Fiction* (1994); *Jackie Brown* (1997)
Don Johnson *The Hot Spot* (1990); *Tin Cup* (1996)
Angelina Jolie *Gia* (1998); *Girl, Interrupted* (2000)
Tommy Lee Jones *The Fugitive* (1993); *Men in Black* (1997)
Ashley Judd *Normal Life* (1996); *Kiss the Girls* (1997)

- - - - - - - - - - - - - - - - - - -
The "Free O.J." signs would come later

The 1961 ceremony was the first time protesters picketed the Oscars. The cause this April evening was equality for blacks in the film industry. Some of the signs read, "Film Equality for Negroes" and "All Negroes Want a Break."

- - - - - - - - - - - - - - - - - - -

127 Hollywood Suicides of the Past Fifty Years

Face downward lay the huddled suicides
Like litter that a riot leaves.
— WILLIAM PLOMER, "THE SILENT SUNDAY"
FROM *VISITING THE CAVES* (1936)

The vast majority of these 127 Hollyood suicides are not, to put it tactfully, household names. In fact, the average moviegoer will probably not recognize many of the people on this list.

But the relative anonymity of these poor souls might just be what make this list so interesting: The fact that these are almost all "unknowns" (with some notable exceptions) begs the question, Could these people have killed themselves because they did not become big stars in Hollywood? Do aspiring box-office stars invest so much of themselves in their goal of being a huge success in the movies that when they fail, they simply cannot go on living?

We can, of course, be certain that some of the people on this list committed suicide for reasons other than career failure. It's likely that some were terminally ill, mentally ill, or suffering through some other torment that they just couldn't take anymore.

Regarding the "footnoted" people listed here: See the footnotes at the conclusion of the list for a few details on these famous folk.

★ **Stanley Adams** (shot himself in 1977)

★ **Adrian** (1959; method not revealed)

★ **Chet Allen** (1984; method not revealed)

★ **Pier Angeli**[1] (1971; took an overdose of barbiturates)

★ **Pedro Armendariz Sr.** (1963; shot himself)

★ **Marion Aye** (1951; ingestion of poison)

★ **David Aylmer** (1964; method not revealed)

★ **Faith Bacon** (1956; method not revealed)

★ **Albert Bailey** (1952; method not revealed)

★ **Boris Barnet** (1965; method not revealed)

★ **Red Barry** (1980; shot himself)

★ **Barbara Bates** (1969; gas)

★ **David Begelman** (1995; shot himself)

★ **Brenda Benet** (1982; shot herself)

★ **Jill Bennett** (1990; method not revealed)

★ **Clara Blandick** (1962; took an overdose of pills and plastic bag suffocation)

★ **Bobby Bloom** (1974; shot himself or was possibly a murder victim)

★ **William Payne Bourne** (1972; shot himself)

★ **Charles Boyer**[2] (1978; took an overdose of Seconal)

★ **Barry Brown** (1978; self-inflicted wounds)

★ **Clyde Bruckman** (1955; shot himself)

★ **Donald Cammell** (1996; shot himself)

★ **Capucine** (1990; jumped from her eighth-floor apartment)

★ **James Cardwell** (1954; shot himself)

★ **Lynn Carver** (1955; method not revealed)

★ **Kurt Cobain**[3] (1994; shot himself)

★ **Ray Combs**[4] (1996; hanged himself)

★ **Darby Crash** (1980; massive heroin overdose)

★ **Howard Marion Crawford** (1969; took an overdose of sleeping pills)

★ **Dennis Crosby** (1991; shot himself)

★ **Lindsay Crosby** (1989; shot himself)

★ **Dorothy Dandridge**[5] (1965; took an overdose of Tofranil)

★ **Bella Darvi** (1971; asphyxiation by gas from stove)

★ **John Dodsworth** (1964; self-asphyxiation)

★ **Patric Doonan** (1958; gassed himself)

★ **Michael Dorris** (1997; method not revealed)

★ **Peter Duel** (1971; shot himself)

★ **John Paul Duffy** (1993; method not revealed)

★ **Ethyl Eichelberger** (1990; slashed wrists)

★ **Richard Farnsworth** (2000; shot himself)

★ **Andrea Feldman** (1972; jumped from fourteenth floor of 51 Fifth Avenue, in Manhattan)

★ **Ed Flanders** (1995; shot himself)

★ **Dudley Foster** (1973; hanged himself)

★ **Anton Furst** (1991; jumped from eighth level of parking garage)

★ **Judy Garland** (1969; took an overdose of sleeping pills)

★ **Dave Garroway**[6] (1982; shot himself)

★ **Kurt Gloor** (1997; method not revealed)

★ **Michael Goodliffe** (1976; jumped from a window in a London hospital)

★ Shauna Grant (1984; shot herself)

★ Gustav Grundgens (1963; method not revealed)

★ Ellen Gurin (1972; method not revealed)

★ Jonathan Hale (1966; shot himself)

★ Jon Hall (1979; shot himself)

★ Lillian Hall (1959; took an overdose of barbituates)

★ Gardner Halliday (1966; took an overdose of sleeping pills)

★ Rusty Hamer[7] (1990; shot himself)

★ Tony Hancock (1968; took an overdose of sleeping pills)

★ Brinn Hartman[8] (1998; shot herself)

★ Elizabeth Hartman[9] (1987; jumped from her fifth-floor apartment)

★ Phyllis Haver (1960; method not revealed)

★ Margaux Hemingway[10] (1996; took an overdose of phenobarbital)

★ Doug Henderson (1978; carbon monoxide poisoning)

★ Abbie Hoffman[11] (1989; massive drug overdose)

★ Judd Holdren (1974; shot himself)

★ Anthony Holland (1988; method not revealed)

★ Victoria Howden (1991; shot herself)

★ Paul C. Hurst (1953, method not revealed)

★ Phyllis Hyman (1995; took an overdose of pills)

★ Johnny Indrisano (1968; hanged himself)

★ William Inge[12] (1973; method not revealed)

★ Juzo Itamo (1997; jumped off an eight-story roof)

★ Rick Jason (2000; shot himself)

★ **Claude Jutra** (1986; drowning)

★ **Steven Keats** (1994; method not revealed)

★ **Terry Keegan** (1993; method not revealed)

★ **Megan Leigh** (1990; method not revealed)

★ **Ronald Lewis** (1982; took an overdose of sleeping pills)

★ **Joseph Massengale** (1983; shot himself)

★ **Maggie McNamara** (1978; took an overdose of pills)

★ **Bob Merrill** (1998; method not revealed)

★ **Charles B. Miller** (1955; shot himself)

★ **Milos Milos** (1966; shot himself)

★ **Miroslava** (1955; ingestion of poison)

★ **Marilyn Monroe**[13] (1962; drug overdose, questionable suicide)

★ **Ona Munson** (1955; took an overdose of sleeping pills)

★ **Murray Newey** (1998; method not revealed)

★ **Hugh O'Connor**[14] (1995; shot himself)

★ **Christine Pascal** (1996; jumped out a window in Paris)

★ **Luigi Pistilli** (1996; method not revealed)

★ **Ben Pollack** (1971; hanged himself)

★ **Suzy Prim** (1991; method not revealed)

★ **Freddie Prinze**[15] (1977; shot himself)

★ **Robert Pursell** (1982; hanged himself)

★ **Richard Quine** (1989; shot himself)

★ **David Rappaport** (1990; shot himself)

★ **George Reeves**[16] (1959; shot himself)

★ **Michael Reeves** (1969; took an overdose of sleeping pills)

★ **Rachel Roberts** (1980; took an overdose of barbiturates)

★ **Will Rogers Jr.**[17] (1993; shot himself)

★ **Richard "Dick" Rosson** (1953; carbon monoxide poisoning)

★ **David Salmi** (1990; shot himself)

★ **George Sanders** (1972; took an overdose of barbiturates)

★ **Steve Sanders** (1998; shot himself)

★ **Sybillie Schmitz** (1955; took an overdose of pills)

★ **Jean Seberg** (1979; drug overdose)

★ **Del Shannon**[18] (1990; method not revealed)

★ **Simone Silva** (1957; method not revealed)

★ **Georgia Skelton** (1976; shot herself)

★ **Walter Slezak** (1983; shot himself)

★ **Everett Sloane** (1965; took an overdose of sleeping pills)

★ **June Smaney** (1993; method not revealed)

★ **Pete Smith** (1979; jumped off the roof of his nursing home)

★ **Margaret Sullavan** (1960; took an overdose of sleeping pills)

★ **Carlos Thompson** (1990; shot himself)

★ **Sammee Tong** (1964; method not revealed)

★ **Helen Twelvetrees** (1958; took an overdose of sleeping pills)

★ **Philip Van Zandt** (1958; took an overdose of sleeping pills)

★ **Herve "Tattoo" Villechaize**[19] (1993; shot himself)

★ **Doodles Weaver** (1983; shot himself)

★ **Richard Webb** (1993; shot himself)

★ **Dick Wesson** (1979; shot himself)

★ **Paul Williams** (1973; method not revealed)

★ **Grant Withers** (1959; took an overdose of sleeping pills)

★ **Frank Wolff** (1971; slashed throat with safety razor)

★ **Duke York** (1952; shot himself)

★ **Faron Young** (1996; shot himself)

★ **Gig Young**[20] (1978; shot himself)

---

[1] Appeared in *The Silver Chalice* (1954) with Paul Newman.

[2] Very popular French actor.

[3] The brilliant leader of groundbreaking rock band Nirvana.

[4] Popular host of TV's *Family Feud*.

[5] Popular actress of the '40s and '50s.

[6] Popular newscaster, raconteur, and original host of NBC's *The Today Show* in the '50s.

[7] Played "Rusty Williams" (Danny's son) on *The Danny Thomas Show* from 1953–1971.

[8] Popular comedian and actor Phil Hartman's wife. (She killed Phil before shooting herself.)

[9] Actress who appeared in the 1966 classic *The Group*.

[10] Popular fashion model; Ernest Hemingway's granddaughter and actress Mariel Hemingway's sister.

[11] Outspoken 1960s radical and author of *Steal This Book!*

[12] Acclaimed playwright and Academy Award-winning screenwriter, author of *Splendor in the Grass* (1961).

[13] The twentieth century's quintessential sex symbol; to this day there are questions as to whether she actually committed suicide or was murdered.

[14] Carroll "Archie Bunker" O'Connor's adopted son; costar of his father's TV series, *In the Heat of the Night*.

[15] Popular 1970s comedian and star of the sitcom *Chico and the Man*. (His son Freddie Jr. is a gifted young actor who made his screen debut in the 1997 hit *I Know What You Did Last Summer*.)

[16] TV's Superman.

[17] The comedian's son.

18Popular songwriter. "Runaway" was his most successful and best-known hit.

19Became famous for his role as "Tattoo" on TV's *Fantasy Island* and his signature proclamation at the beginning of each show, "De plane! De plane!"

20Popular actor with a career spanning the forties (*Air Force,* 1943; *The Three Musketeers,* 1948) through the seventies (*Lovers and Other Strangers,* 1970; *Bring Me the Head of Alfredo Garcia,* 1974).

41 Directors Who Have Cameos in Their Own Movies

The Italians call it *boria*—which translates as arrogant self-conceit or runaway egotism.

Show business might be the only business in existence in which *boria* is not only a ubiquitous presence in everyone involved, but also actually encouraged.

The director is the God of the Set.

Directors are entrusted with millions of dollars and tons of equipment, not to mention fragile actors, and the title of Guardian of the Script. The buck stops with the director.

Some directors are not content to simply helm a movie from start to finish; some feel called to immortalize their reign by committing their visage to celluloid through the hoary, yet honorable device known as the cameo.

This list looks at 41 well-known directors who appear in one or more of their movies. Can you spot them?

1. **Jim Abrahams** One of the religious fanatics at the airport in *Airplane* (1980).

2. **Gillian Armstrong** A backup singer in *My Brilliant Career* (1979).

3. **John Badham** A room service waiter in *Point of No Return* (1993).

4. **James Cameron** His hands draw Rose in the parlor scene and he is glimpsed briefly in the third class party scene in *Titanic* (1998).

5. **Francis Ford Coppola** A documentary filmmaker in *Apocalypse Now* (1979).

6. **Wes Craven** A high school janitor in *Scream* (1996).

7. **David Cronenberg** The obstetrician who delivers the maggot baby in *The Fly* (1986).

8. **Mike Figgis** A mobster in *Leaving Las Vegas* (1995); a hotel clerk in *One Night Stand* (1997).

9. **Terry Gilliam** A pedestrian in *Brazil* (1985).

10. **George Roy Hill** The airplane pilot who crashes into the house in *The World According to Garp* (1982).

11. **Ron Howard** A sax player in *Night Shift* (1982).

12. **John Huston** A white-suited tourist in *The Treasure of the Sierra Madre* (1948).

13. **Peter Jackson** A bum in *Heavenly Creatures* (1994); the bearded guy Michael J. Fox bumps into in *The Frighteners* (1996).

14. **Lawrence Kasdan** A film producer in *Grand Canyon* (1991).

15. **Stephen King** The nerdy guy who is called an asshole by an ATM machine in *Maximum Overdrive* (1986).

16. **John Landis** King Kong (a.k.a. The Schlockthropolus) in *Schlock* (1971); a TV technician in *The Kentucky Fried Movie* (1977); a guy thrown through a window in *An American Werewolf in London* (1981); an Arab in pursuit of Jeff Goldblum in *Into the Night* (1985).

17. **David Lean** The man who calls out to Lawrence across the Suez Canal in *Lawrence of Arabia* (1962).

18. **Richard Lester** Seen on stage with the Beatles in the "Tell Me Why" segment of *A Hard Day's Night* (1964).

19. **Barry Levinson** A psychiatrist in *Rain Man* (1988); TV personality Dave Garroway in *Quiz Show* (1994)

20. **David Lynch** A radio operator in *Dune* (1984).

21. **Garry Marshall** A drummer in *Overboard* (1987).

22. **Paul Mazursky** A restaurant diner in *An Unmarried Woman* (1978); a party guest in *Tempest* (1982); in drag in *Moon over*

Parador (1988); an author on TV in *Scenes From a Mall* (1991).

23. **Frank Oz** A salesman in *Little Shop of Horrors* (1986).

24. **Jerry Paris** A police photographer in *Never a Dull Moment* (1968).

25. **Alan Parker** A visitor to the recording studio in *The Commitments* (1991); a film director in *Evita* (1996).

26. **Roman Polanski** A musical spoon player in *Repulsion* (1965); the hood who slashes Jack Nicholson's nose in *Chinatown* (1974).

27. **Sydney Pollack** The frustrated agent of Michael Dorsey (Dustin Hoffman) in *Tootsie* (1982).

28. **Carol Reed** The hand reaching up out of the sewer grate in *The Third Man* (1949).

29. **Rob Reiner** A helicopter pilot in *Misery* (1990).

30. **Ivan Reitman** The voice of the creature Zuul in *Ghostbusters* (1984).

31. **Ken Russell** A tour boat passenger in *Gothic* (1986).

32. **Martin Scorsese** A brothel customer in *Boxcar Bertha* (1972); the man who shoots Robert De Niro in *Mean Streets* (1973); the cuckolded husband in Travis's cab, and the man sitting on the steps outside the campaign headquarters in *Taxi Driver* (1976); a stagehand in *Raging Bull* (1980); a TV director in *The King of Comedy* (1983); a nightclub light operator in *After Hours* (1985); the man photographed with Nick Nolte in *New York Stories* (1989); a photographer in *The Age of Innocence* (1993).

33. **John Singleton** A mailman in *Boyz 'N the Hood* (1991).

34. **Charles Martin Smith** A high school teacher in *Trick or Treat* (1986).

35. **Kevin Smith** "Silent Bob" in *Clerks* (1994); *Mallrats* (1995); *Chasing Amy* (1997); and *Dogma* (1999).

36. **Mel Smith** A drunk in *The Tall Guy* (1989).

37. **Steven Spielberg** A voice on the Orca's radio in *Jaws* (1975); the flesh-pulling hands in *Poltergeist* (1982); a tourist in *Indiana Jones and the Temple of Doom* (1984); seen on CNN in *The Lost World: Jurassic Park* (1997).

38. **Oliver Stone** A TV reporter in *Born on the Fourth of July* (1989); a film instructor in *The Doors* (1991); a military officer in *Platoon* (1986); a stockbroker in *Wall Street* (1987).

39. **Quentin Tarantino** One of the reservoir dogs in *Reservoir Dogs* (1992); Jimmy (who buys expensive coffee) in *Pulp Fiction* (1994).

40. **John Waters** A psychiatrist in *Hairspray* (1988); seen in a portrait in *Serial Mom* (1994).

41. **The Zucker Brothers** Air traffic controllers in *Airplane* (1980).

Hollywood always had a streak of the totalitarian in just about every-thing it did.

Shirley MacLaine

----

40 Alfred Hitchcock Cameos

1. *The Birds* (1963) Hitch is seen exiting the pet shop as Tippi Hendren enters. He is walking two white dogs, his own Sealyham terriers, Geoffrey and Stanley.

2. *Blackmail* (1929) Hitch is seen in a coat and hat, with a briefcase on his lap, being bothered by a little boy as he tries to read a book in a subway car. (Hitch uses the book to swat at the annoying little brat.)

3. *Dial M for Murder* (1954) Hitch is seen about thirteen minutes into the movie in a class reunion photo held by Ray Milland.

4. *Easy Virtue* (1927) Hitch is seen walking past a tennis court carrying a walking stick.

5. *Family Plot* (1976) Hitch is seen only in silhouette through the door of the office of Registrar of Births and Deaths, obtaining copies of death certificates at approximately forty-one minutes into the movie.

6. *Foreign Correspondent* (1940) Hitch is seen walking past Joel McCrea early in the movie shortly after McCrea leaves his hotel. Hitch is wearing a hat and coat and reading a newspaper.

7. *Frenzy* (1972) Hitch is seen at three minutes into the movie standing in the center of a crowd wearing a bowler hat. He is the only character not applauding the speaker.

8. *I Confess* (1953) Hitch is seen shortly after the opening credits in silhouette crossing the top of a staircase.

9. *Jamaica Inn* (1939) Hitch is seen in costume in this movie, wearing a top hat and waistcoat,

10. *The Lady Vanishes* (1938) Hitch is seen at the end of the movie in Victoria Station smoking a cigarette and wearing a black coat.

11. *Lifeboat* (1944) Hitch is seen in a newspaper ad for the Reduco Obesity Slayer corset. Hitch is both the "Before" and "After" pictures.

12. *The Lodger* (1927) Hitch is seen twice in this movie. His first appearance is when he is seen sitting at a desk in the newsroom scene. His second appearance is in a crowd scene toward the end of the film as he watches an arrest being made.

13. *The Man Who Knew Too Much* (1956) Hitch is seen just before the murder, standing in a Moroccan marketplace with his back to the camera watching the acrobats perform.

14. *Marnie* (1964) Hitch is seen five minutes into the movie, entering from the left of a hotel corridor immediately after Tippi Hedren passes by.

15. *Mr. and Mrs. Smith* (1941) Hitch is seen about forty-eight minutes into the movie walking past Robert Montgomery in front of his building.

16. *Murder* (1930) Hitch is seen about an hour into the movie walking past the house where the murder was committed.

17. *North by Northwest* (1959) Hitch is seen missing a bus (the bus door is slammed in his face) during the opening credits sequence of the movie.

18. *Notorious* (1946) Hitch is seen about an hour into the film sipping champagne at a party at Claude Rains's mansion.

19. *The Paradine Case* (1948) Hitch is seen carrying a cello while walking through a door at England's Cumberland Station. (This was the first of Hitch's three "carrying a musical instrument" cameos.)

20. *Psycho* (1960) About four minutes into the movie, Hitch is seen through the window (wearing a cowboy hat) standing outside Janet Leigh's real estate office.

21. *Rear Window* (1954) Hitch is seen about a half hour into the movie winding a clock in the songwriter's apartment.

22. *Rebecca* (1940) Hitch is seen toward the end of the film walking by a phone booth, waiting for George Sanders to finish his call.

23. *Rope* (1948) Hitch is seen twice (sort of) in this movie. His first appearance is right after the opening credits when he is seen crossing the street. His second "appearance" is when his trademark sil-

houette image is seen from an apartment window on a neon sign, about fifty-five minutes into the movie.

24. *Sabotage* (1936) Hitch is seen buying a ticket at a box office.

25. *Saboteur* (1942) Hitch is seen about an hour into the movie, standing in front of Cut Rate Drugs in New York City as the saboteur's car stops.

26. *Shadow of a Doubt* (1943) Hitch is seen playing cards on the train to Santa Rosa, California. (He is holding a full house.)

27. *Spellbound* (1945) Hitch is seen exiting an elevator in the Empire Hotel. He is smoking a cigarette and carrying a violin case. (This was the second of Hitch's three "musical instrument" cameos.)

28. *Stage Fright* (1950) Hitch is seen walking past, and then turning to look at, Jane Wyman, who is in disguise as Marlene Dietrich's maid.

29. *Strangers on a Train* (1951) Hitch is seen at the beginning of the movie carrying a double bass and boarding a train as Farley Granger disembarks the train in his hometown. (This was the last of Hitch's three "musical instrument" cameos.)

30. *Suspicion* (1941) Hitch is seen about forty-five minutes into the movie mailing a letter at the village mailbox.

31. *The 39 Steps* (1935) Hitch is seen about seven minutes into the movie throwing away some litter as Robert Donat and Lucie Mannheim run from the theater.

32. *To Catch a Thief* (1955) Hitch is seen ten minutes into the film sitting on a bus to the left of star Cary Grant.

33. *Topaz* (1969) Hitch is seen about thirty minutes into the film being pushed in a wheelchair through an airport. He then gets up out of the wheelchair, shakes hands with a man, and exits the scene to the right.

34. *Torn Curtain* (1966) Hitch is seen sitting in the Hotel d'Angleterre lobby early in the film. He is holding a blonde baby who ends up peeing on him.

35. *The Trouble With Harry* (1955) Hitch is seen about twenty minutes into the film walking past the parked limousine of an old man who is looking at John Forsythe's outdoor painting exhibition.

36. *Under Capricorn* (1949) Hitch is seen twice in this movie. His first

appearance is about five minutes into the film when he is seen standing in the town square during a parade. He is wearing a blue coat and brown hat. His second appearance is about fifteen minutes into the film (ten minutes later) when he is seen as one of the three men standing on the steps of Government House.

37. *Vertigo* (1958) Hitch is seen about eleven minutes into the movie walking past a subway entrance wearing a gray suit.

38. *The Wrong Man* (1957) Hitch narrates the film's Prologue. (He is never actually seen in the movie.)

39. *Young and Innocent* (1937) Hitch is seen outside the courthouse holding a camera.

40. BONUS: The "Dip in the Pool" episode of *Alfred Hitchcock Presents* (1955–1961): In Hitch's only TV cameo (aside from all his show Introductions) Hitch is seen in this episode on the cover of a magazine that a passenger is reading.

For Your Consideration . . .

THE "K" LIST

Diane Keaton *Annie Hall* (1977); *Father of the Bride* (1991)
Michael Keaton *Gung Ho* (1985); *The Paper* (1994)
Harvey Keitel *The Piano* (1993); *Pulp Fiction* (1994)
Nicole Kidman *To Die For* (1995); *Eyes Wide Shut* (1999)
Val Kilmer *Top Gun* (1986); *The Doors* (1991)
Stephen King *Creepshow* (1982); *Maximum Overdrive* (1986)
Ben Kingsley *Gandhi* (1982); *Schindler's List* (1993)
Greg Kinnear *Sabrina* (1995); *As Good As It Gets* (1997)
Bruno Kirby *Good Morning, Vietnam* (1987); *When Harry Met Sally . . .* (1989)
Kevin Kline *Dave* (1993); *In and Out* (1997)
Kris Kristofferson *Alice Doesn't Live Here Anymore* (1974); *The Sailor Who Fell From Grace With the Sea* (1976)
Lisa Kudrow *Romy and Michele's High School Reunion* (1997); *The Opposite of Sex* (1998)

- - - - - - - - - - - - - - - - - - -

'Bout time

The 1970 Oscar ceremony was notable for its first public acknowl-
edgment of the impact of the Beatles on film music. Goldie Hawn
introduced a filmed musical salute to the Fabs and John, Paul,
George, and Ringo won Best Original Song Score that evening for
their *Let It Be* soundtrack.

- - - - - - - - - - - - - - - - - - -

People Magazine's 18 Beatles Covers, 1975–2000

The Beatles had been broken up for five years when *People* ran its first
Fab Four-related cover, a feature story in 1975 about Paul and Linda's
happy marriage, along with a look at Paul's successful solo career.

Over the next twenty-five years, *People* would return to the Beatles
a total of seventeen times: seven covers focusing on John, Yoko, and
Sean Lennon; four on Paul and Linda McCartney; three on Ringo Starr;
two on The Beatles as a group; and one on George Harrison.

A review of the *People* Beatles covers gives us an interesting per-
spective on how the Beatles were covered by the media from the time of
their breakup through the end of the century.

Interestingly, through the seventies and the eighties, a Beatles cover
story appeared on a fairly regular basis—say, every year or two. John's
assassination, George's work with Madonna, Ringo's rehab, and Linda's
death were all cover topics.

There were also several issues that looked at Yoko after John's
death—including cover stories about Albert Goldman's detestable biography of John and even stories about John's killer.

But then after the August 28, 1989, story about Ringo being "newly
sober," *People* did not do another Beatles cover story until Linda
McCartney's death in April 1998—nine years later.

Oddly, even the enormously successful Beatles *Anthology* project (in all its incarnations—miniseries, CDs, videotape, etc.) did not warrant a cover.

As John sang in "Not a Second Time," "I'm wondering why."

1. **April 21, 1975**
   Headline: "The McCartneys: Paul and Linda"
   Cover text: "My family is my life, then my music."
   Photo: Paul and Linda.

2. **April 5, 1976**
   Headline: "The Beatles"
   Cover text: "Will they sing again for $50 million?"
   Photo: A collage of an early photo of the Fabs, and four individual headshots of the individual Beatles.

3. **June 7, 1976**
   Headline: "Paul McCartney"
   Cover text: "His kids ask, 'What will Daddy do when he grows up?'"
   Photo: A smiling headshot of Paul.

4. **January 17, 1977**
   Headline: "Ringo"
   Cover text: "His tax exile, his new fiancée, his rap on a Beatle reunion"
   Photo: Ringo wearing a red hat.

5. **December 22, 1980**
   Headline: "John Lennon 1940–1980: A Tribute"
   Cover text: None.
   Photo: John and Yoko in a photo taken shortly before his death.

6. **January 12, 1981**
   Headline: "Yoko"
   Cover text: "How she is holding up."
   Photo: A headshot of Yoko in a gray cap.

7. **February 23, 1981**
   Headline: "Ringo"
   Cover text: "Talks movingly about John, the reunion that never was and his saving love for Barbara Bach"; "Plus an update on Paul, George and Yoko."

Photo: A photo of a bearded Ringo clad all in black being embraced from behind by Barbara Bach.

8. **December 13, 1982**
   Headline: "Yoko and Sean"
   Cover text: "Two years later, a poignant look at the lives of Lennon's widow and son."
   Photo: A photo of Sean being embraced from behind by Yoko.

9. **November 14, 1983**
   Headline: "Paul McCartney–Richest Man in Showbiz"
   Cover text: "Here's what he's making, and a look at other money machines, including Sinatra, Parton, Carson, Eastwood, Streisand, and Stallone."
   Photo: A photo of Paul holding up his left index finger, as if to say "Number 1."

10. **February 20, 1984**
    Headline: "John's Last Songs"
    Cover text: "Yoko's bittersweet story of Lennon's final days, and their new hit album."
    Photo: A photo of John and Yoko in the recording studio, both wearing headphones and sunglasses, and sharing one overhead microphone.

11. **March 24, 1986**
    Headline: "Madonna's Beatle Boss"
    Cover text: "George Harrison emerges as a movie mogul to take the Penns in hand."
    Photo: A headshot of George with an inset photo of Madonna.

12. **June 22, 1987**
    Headline: "Celebrating the '60s Summer of Love"
    Cover text: "It's 20 years later. Do you know where your love beads are?"
    Photo: A Peter Max *"Yellow Submarine"*-ish painting with individual *Sgt. Pepper* photos of the Beatles laid in for a two-page foldout collage effect.

13. **February 23, 1987**
    Headline: "The Chilling Story Behind the Murder of John Lennon"

Cover text: None.

Photo: A photo of John in a gray cap and sunglasses with an inset photo of his murderer, Mark David Chapman, holding a battered copy of J. D. Salinger's *Catcher in the Rye.*

14. **August 15, 1988**

    Headline: "A Secret Life"

    Cover text: "The shocking, long-awaited biography by Albert Goldman reveals the JOHN LENNON his fans never knew."

    Photo: A headshot of John in sunglasses and gray cap. (It looks almost identical to the photo used for the February 23, 1987, cover.)

15. **August 22, 1988**

    Headline: "Under Yoko's Spell"

    Cover text: "From the explosive new biography of John Lennon, scenes of despair, drugs and domination by his wife"

    Photo: A late 1980 photo of John and Yoko in New York.

16. **August 28, 1989**

    Headline: "On the Road Again"

    Cover text: "Newly sober Ringo Starr talks about his 20-year bender and joins a retro-rock invasion by The Who, Jefferson Airplane, the Doobie Brothers, and even the Bee Gees. And could this be the new Stone Age?"

    Photo: A photo of an unsmiling Ringo in a blue sport jacket and sunglasses holding his arms up in an open-handed stance like a magician's flourish.

17. **May 4, 1998**

    Headline: "Paul's Tragic Loss—The Love of My Life"

    Cover text: "In 29 years of marriage, Paul and Linda McCartney spent only 11 days apart. Friends talk about her final courage—and their inspiring love story."

    Photo: A photo of Linda being embraced from behind by Paul.

18. **April 3, 2000**

    Headline: "Paul Finds Love Again"

    Photo: A photo of Paul and Heather Mills.

- - - - - - - - - - - - - - -

Except for cash registers ringing, of course

At the 1938 Oscar ceremony, composer Jerome Kern made the
memorable comment, "Of all the noises I think music is the least
annoying."

- - - - - - - - - - - - - - -

The "Movies About Classical Composers" List

Longhair music movies

1936 *Beethoven*
1934 *Blossom Time* (Franz Schubert)
1941 *Rossini*
1943 *Heavenly Music* (Beethoven)
1945 *A Song to Remember* (Chopin)
1947 *Song of Love* (Robert Schumann and Johannes Brahms)
1947 *Song of Scheherazade* (Rimsky-Korsakov)
1948 *The Mozart Story*
1953 *Giuseppe Verdi*
1959 *The Life and Loves of Mozart*
1960 *Song Without End* (Liszt)
1970 *Song of Norway* (Edvard Grieg)
1971 *The Music Lovers* (Tchaikovsky)
1971 *Tchaikovsky*
1974 *Mahler*
1975 *Lisztomania*
1976 *Mozart: A Childhood Chronicle*
1984 *Amadeus*

1985 *Forget Mozart*

1985 *Wagner: The Complete Epic*

1985 *Wagner: The Movie*

1986 *The Mozart Brothers*

1988 *Beethoven's Nephew*

1991 *Impromptu* (Chopin)

1992 *Beethoven Lives Upstairs*

1994 *Immortal Beloved* (Beethoven)

For Your Consideration . . .

THE "L" LIST

Ricki Lake *Hairspray* (1988); *Serial Mom* (1994)

Burt Lancaster *Local Hero* (1983); *Tough Guys* (1986)

Martin Landau *Crimes and Misdemeanors* (1989); *Ed Wood* (1994)

Diane Lane *Lonesome Dove* (1989); *Murder at 1600* (1997)

Nathan Lane *The Birdcage* (1995); *Mouse Hunt* (1997)

Jessica Lange *The Postman Always Rings Twice* (1981); *Tootsie* (1982)

Anthony LaPaglia *Betsy's Wedding* (1990); *One Good Cop* (1991)

Denis Leary *The Ref* (1993); *Wag the Dog* (1997)

Sheryl Lee *Twin Peaks: Fire Walk With Me* (1992); *John Carpenter's Vampires* (1997)

Spike Lee *Do the Right Thing* (1989); *Malcolm X* (1992)

Jennifer Jason Leigh *Single White Female* (1992); *Dolores Claiborne* (1994)

Jack Lemmon *The Odd Couple* (1968); *Glengarry Glen Ross* (1992)

Jerry Lewis *The Nutty Professor* (1963); *King of Comedy* (1982)

Juliette Lewis *Cape Fear* (1991); *Natural Born Killers* (1994)

Laura Linney *Primal Fear* (1996); *The Truman Show* (1998)

Ray Liotta *GoodFellas* (1990); *Article 99* (1992)

John Lithgow *The World According to Garp* (1982); *Terms of Endearment* (1983)

Christopher Lloyd *One Flew Over the Cuckoo's Nest* (1975); the *Back to the Future* series (1985–1990)

Shelley Long *The Money Pit* (1986); *Hello Again* (1987)
Jennifer Lopez *Selena* (1997); *U-Turn* (1997)
Traci Lords *Cry-Baby* (1990); *Stephen King's The Tommyknockers* (1993)
Jon Lovitz *A League of Their Own* (1992); *City Slickers 2: The Legend of Curly's Gold* (1994)
Rob Lowe *St. Elmo's Fire* (1985); *Wayne's World* (1992)

You no like-a the way we talk? C'mere.

At the 1949 Oscar ceremony, presenter James Hilton (*Mrs. Miniver,* 1942; *Foreign Correspondent,* 1940) awarded Roberto Rossellini the Oscar for Best Story and Screenplay for *Paisan* ... but he pronounced Rossellini's name with an exaggerated Italian accent that brought smirks to the faces of many in the crowd.

Reel Holy: Pope John Paul II's Top 10 Movies

Before we go any further, let me assure you that if I come off as a tad critical of my beloved Roman Catholic Church in this chapter, it's because I have a right to: I was born into a Catholic family, I was baptized a Catholic, I made my first Holy Communion and Confirmation, and my Catholic wife and I were married in a Catholic ceremony. I even used to go to Confession and was an altar boy when I was younger.

Also, I probably won't have too much to say about it, but when I'm on my deathbed (which will be at least sixty or more years from now—I'll be 48 when this book comes out ... talk about thinking positively, eh?), my family will probably call in a Catholic priest to give me the last rites.

The Roman Catholic Church has come under quite a bit of fire in the past few decades. The number of young men entering the priest-hood has plummeted; scandals involving priests are common; Catholic grammar schools are closing all over the country; and weekly attendance at Mass has dropped precipitously in the past twenty years or so, result-ing in parishes merging with other parishes in order to share pastors.

Why?

Many blame the church's unwavering, *really* hardline, ultraconserv-ative dogma: No abortion, no birth control (of *any* kind except the rhythm method), no masturbation, no premarital sex, no married priests, no women priests, no divorce, homosexuals should abstain from rela-tionships as a sacrifice to God, and other unwavering precepts that paint a picture of a church completely out of touch with the modern—and real—world.

But I have hope.

Why?

Because of this list of movies Pope John Paul II recently released as approved for the Catholic faithful to watch. (Following this, *Il Papa* released a CD of him saying prayers with a contemporary music sound-track. And believe it or not, the Pontiff had a *Billboard* hit.)

The pope's number-one recommended movie—*Schindler's List*—shows full frontal male and female nudity; explicit sexuality; painful-to-watch, graphic scenes of murder, sadism, and brutal violence; countless scenes of children in constant peril (including scenes of children being killed), and more "fucks" uttered than can be counted.

When I was in St. Rose's Grammar School in the sixties, the Catholic Church routinely issued lists of movies that were "objection-able" for Catholics to watch . . . and graphic nudity was one of the cri-teria that would guarantee a movie an "O" rating (which was the Vatican equivalent of an "X").

That's why there is hope that things are slowly—but perceptibly—changing. The Roman Catholic Church, with 900 million followers worldwide (62 million in the U.S.) is the largest Christian church in the world. It boasts some of the most elaborate codified rituals to be found in organized religion, and serious Catholics find enormous comfort in their faith. But many Catholics are leaving the church because of the previously discussed constraints. These lapsed Catholics are eager to return and most would if the church would lighten up *just a little.* And I'll tell you how they could do it: Allow women priests and married priests. Don't hold your breath waiting for this to happen, though. But if it did? The Catholic Church might just end up taking over the world.

For the pope to recommend *Schindler's List* as his *number-one* pick shows an enlightenment sorely lacking in earlier proclamations from Rome.

The Pope's Picks

1. *Schindler's List* **(1993)** This is Steven Spielberg's *magnum opus* and one of the all-time greatest celluloid renderings of the Holocaust story ever. The pope obviously picked this because of its powerful illustration of the power of the human spirit and how one person's good and moral deed can affect countless others and change history. *(Directed by Steven Spielberg. 195 minutes, rated R. With Liam Neeson, Ben Kingsley, Ralph Fiennes, Embeth Davidtz, Caroline Goodall, Jonathan Sagalle, Mark Ivanir. Written by Steven Zaillian, based on the book by Thomas Kenneally.)*

2. *The Gospel According to St. Matthew* **(1964)** This is the film that many consider to be the definitive cinematic telling of the story of Jesus. Italian director Pier Paolo Pasolini (who was a Marxist when he wrote and directed this film) used a cast of mostly unknown amateur actors (including his mother) and based his script solely on the writings of St. Matthew. The result is a stately and powerful film that leans towards an emphasis on Jesus's radical social agenda over his divinity. This editorial subtext makes this pick by the pope even more intriguing. *(Directed by Pier Paolo Pasolini. 142 minutes. With Enrique Irazoqui, Susanna Pasolini, Margherita Caruso, Marcello Morante, Mario Socrate. Written by Pier Paolo Pasolini, based on the Gospel of St. Matthew.)*

3. *Life Is Beautiful* **(1998)** Another Holocaust movie makes the Pope's list. (Maybe the Pope is expressing some guilt over the Church's alleged inaction during the War? Just wondering.) Italian actor/writer/director Robert Benigni won two Academy Awards (Best Actor and Best Foreign Film) for this poignant story of Guido (played by the star) a part-Jewish Italian who is taken to a German concentration camp with his young son during World War II. To spare the boy the pain and horror of the truth about where

they are, Guido concocts an elaborate game that he steadfastly plays out until its inevitable, tragic end. Again, this is a film that emphasizes the power of the human spirit in the darkest of times and in the most horrible of ordeals. *(Directed by Roberto Benigni. 114 minutes, rated R. With Roberto Benigni, Nicoletta Braschi (Mrs. Benigni), Giustino Durano, Sergio Bustric, Horst Buchholz. Written by Roberto Benigni and Vincenzo Cerami.)*

4. *Modern Times* **(1936)** This classic (partly silent) film about the dehumanization of man and the evils of assembly line work and an automated society is still spot-on in terms of its ultimate message, especially in our increasingly impersonal and computerized age. This movie articulates the church's "dignity of human life" ideology and thus, is a natural to be one of the pope's picks. *(Directed by Charlie Chaplin. 87 minutes. With Charlie Chaplin, Paulette Goddard, Henry Bergman, Stanley Sandford, Gloria De Haven, Chester Conklin. Written by Charlie Chaplin.)*

5. *Jesus of Nazareth* (1977) No big surprise that the pope would include this film in his Top 10, eh? This epic telling of Jesus's story is a magnificent artistic achievement by Italian director Franco Zeffirelli. It originally aired as a three-night TV miniseries starring Robert Powell, who played a blue-eyed Jesus with power and sensitivity. Olivia Hussey played his mother, the Virgin Mary; and Anne Bancroft played Mary Magdalene with a dramatic intensity that is in stark contrast to her occasional comedic roles (*Silent Movie* [1976], *Fatso* [1980], *Home for the Holidays* [1995], etc.). *Jesus of Nazareth* is an unqualified classic and the film that many consider to be the single best cinematic interpretation of the story of Jesus to date. *(Directed by Franco Zeffirelli. 371 minutes. With Robert Powell, Olivia Hussey, Anne Bancroft, James Mason, Laurence Olivier, Rod Steiger, Ernest Borgnine, Claudia Cardinale, Anthony Quinn. Written by Franco Zeffirelli).*

6. *Ben-Hur* **(1959)** Everyone talks about the 8-minute, 40-second chariot race in this epic, but the story of the wealthy Palestinian Jew who angers the Roman emperor Messala—his former childhood friend—and is forced to serve as a galley slave, is high drama that is superb on *all* levels: writing, acting, direction, cinematography, and more. Ben-Hur (Heston) ultimately returns to exact

revenge against his old friend, resulting in the aforementioned chariot race staged by stunt artist Yakima Canutt. This scene is so intense, it even had its own director, Andrew Marton. *(Directed by William Wyler. 212 minutes. With Charlton Heston, Stephen Boyd, Jack Hawkins, Haya Harareet, Hugh Griffith, Martha Scott, Sam Jaffe, Cathy O'Donnell, Finlay Currie. Written by Karl Tunberg, based on the novel by Gen. Lew Wallace.)*

7. *A Man for All Seasons* (1966) King Henry VIII (Shaw) wants to divorce his wife Catherine of Aragon so he can marry his mistress Anne Boleyn, who he believes will give him the son he so passionately desires. Because the Roman Catholic Church will not grant his divorce "variance" request, Henry defies the pope, breaks from the church, and forms the Church of England. Sir Thomas More (Scofield) is the Chancellor of England who refuses to support the king's apostasy and ends up martyred for his integrity and commitment to the Vatican. This is one of those movies where you feel as though you are transported back in time to the era of the film, and the brilliant script (based on Robert Bolt's play of the same name), award-winning performances, and nuanced characterizations all combine to form a truly sublime work of cinematic art. (The fact that More was willing to die for the Catholic Church also makes it a terrific endorsement of Catholicism and probably played a role in the pope picking this as one of his Top 10.) *(Directed by Fred Zinnemann. 120 minutes. With Paul Scofield, Robert Shaw, Orson Welles, Wendy Hiller, Susannah York, Leo McKern, John Hurt, Nigel Davenport, Vanessa Redgrave. Written by Constance Willis and Robert Bolt, based on Bolt's play.)*

8. *2001: A Space Odyssey* (1968) This is an odd choice for the pope, but also another film that bespeaks a new openness at the highest levels of the Roman Catholic Church. The "dangers of technology/sanctity of man" subtext/object lesson of the movie (as played out by the plotline that has HAL the computer taking over) might be why the Vatican recommended this movie for its faithful. But the main premise of the *2001* story is that mankind has been in contact with unknown, unseen aliens for millennia, and that they may have influenced man's evolution—which could be said to contradict biblical creationism and the church's longstanding (but now

modified) antievolution stance. The church now acknowledges that biblical teaching and the scientific fact of evolution can peacefully coexist; and they also agree that the "Big Bang" theory does not, de facto, conflict with biblical creation myths. This is a good sign, since the thinking of many theologists and scientists is beginning to merge at the point of the universe's beginning: The theologians admit that the Big Bang theory is probably scientifically correct; the scientists admit that the cause of the Big Bang itself might very well have been a supernatural (as in "miraculous") event. And now the pope recommends a movie that says we may be descended from aliens. Maybe the twenty-first century really will be an era of enlightenment. *(Directed by Stanley Kubrick. 139 minutes. With Keir Dullea, Gary Lockwood, William Sylvester, Dan Richter, with Douglas Rain as the voice of HAL. Written by Arthur C. Clarke and Stanley Kubrick, based on Clarke's short story, "The Sentinel.")*

9. ***8-1/2* (1963)** This black-and-white classic is one of Italian filmmaker Federico Fellini's greatest films, and it is a sublime work of art that has inspired countless writers and filmmakers since its release in 1963. (See especially Woody Allen's brilliant *Stardust Memories* [1980] which not only is a blatant homage to Fellini and *8-1/2*, but may actually be Woody's own version of the Italian masterpiece.) In *8-1/2*, Fellini is at his most self-analytical. It is about a renowned Italian filmmaker who wants to make an autobiographical movie, and it is told in almost a stream-of-consciousness voice, as the director (and we) wander through his subconscious, his childhood memories, his fears, his insecurities, his reflections about art, and his feelings about the people he considers most important in his life.

Why did Pope John Paul II pick *8-1/2* as one of his Top 10 films? Probably because of its message that personal self-reflection is fulfilling and revelatory. Or maybe he just didn't want to slight the great Fellini, seeing as how he had already picked a Pasolini film? (It later was transformed into the Broadway musical *Nine*.) *(Directed by Federico Fellini. 135 minutes. With Marcello Mastroianni, Claudia Cardinale, Anouk Aimee, Sandra Milo, Barbara Steele, Rosella Falk, Eddra Gale, Mark Herron, Madeleine LeBeau, Caterina Boratto. Written by Tullio Pinelli, Ennio Flaiano, Brunello Rondi, and Federico Fellini.)*

10. *The Leopard* (1963) Another Italian film, this one by Visconti, makes the pope's cut. This powerful drama featured Burt Lancaster as the head of a Sicilian dynasty having difficulty adjusting to the "Risorgimento," the late nineteenth-century unification of Italy. *The Leopard* includes an hour-long banquet scene that some critics consider one of the greatest set pieces in cinematic history. *(Directed by Luchino Visconti. 205 minutes. With Burt Lancaster, Alain Delon, Claudia Cardinale, Rina Morelli, Paolo Stoppa. Written by Suso Cecchi D'Amico, Pasquale Festa Campanile, Massimi Franciosa, Enrico Medioli, and Luchino Visconti.)*

- - - - - - - - - - - - - - - -

Artists—writers, painters, singers, sport figures, musicians—have always been the ones who changed the culture, more than politicians, more than a lot of others.

John Travolta
Playboy, March 1996

- - - - - - - - - - - - - - - -

For Your Consideration . . .

The "M" List

Ralph Macchio *The Karate Kid* (1984); *My Cousin Vinny* (1992)
Andie MacDowell *Groundhog Day* (1993); *Four Weddings and a Funeral* (1994)
Shirley MacLaine *Terms of Endearment* (1983); *Guarding Tess* (1994)
William H. Macy *Fargo* (1996); *Boogie Nights* (1997)
Madonna *Desperately Seeking Susan* (1985); *A League of Their Own* (1992)
John Malkovich *Places in the Heart* (1984); *In the Line of Fire* (1993)
Steve Martin *The Jerk* (1979); *Leap of Faith* (1992)
Mary Stuart Masterson *Fried Green Tomatoes* (1991); *Benny & Joon* (1993)

Mary Elizabeth Mastrantonio *The Color of Money* (1986); *The Abyss* (1989)

Samantha Mathis *Pump Up the Volume* (1990); *The American President* (1995)

Walter Matthau *The Odd Couple* (1968); *JFK* (1991)

Matthew McConaughey *A Time to Kill* (1996); *Contact* (1997)

Kelly McGillis *Witness* (1985); *The Accused* (1988)

Bette Midler *Beaches* (1988); *The First Wives Club* (1996)

Matthew Modine *Short Cuts* (1993); *And the Band Played On* (1993)

Demi Moore *A Few Good Men* (1992); *G. I. Jane* (1997)

Julianne Moore *Short Cuts* (1993); *Boogie Nights* (1997)

Mary Tyler Moore *Ordinary People* (1980); *Flirting With Disaster* (1995)

Rob Morrow *Quiz Show* (1994); *Last Dance* (1996)

Dermot Mulroney *Copycat* (1995); *My Best Friend's Wedding* (1997)

Eddie Murphy *Trading Places* (1983); *Beverly Hills Cop* (1984)

Bill Murray *What About Bob?* (1991); *Groundhog Day* (1993)

Mike Myers *Wayne's World* (1992); *Austin Powers: International Man of Mystery* (1997)

Hey, bridges take a long time to build!

The Best Director Oscar for 1957 went to David Lean for *The Bridge on the River Kwai.* The movie took so long to complete, Lean's wife reportedly divorced him on grounds of desertion.

The American Film Institute's 100 Greatest American Movies

I go to fewer and fewer movies that I give two shits about.
Most are packages of negative spirit, designed to insulate
those who have and pretend to offer something from those
who don't. I'm interested in films only when the filmmaker's
dreams are being shared with me, not when he or she is
saying, "You don't have enough dreams yourself, so I'm
going to make some up for you." When I walk into a
theater, I'm just hoping, "Please, don't lie to me."
　　　　　　　　　—SEAN PENN, *PLAYBOY,* NOVEMBER 1991

I am now going to irritate the American Film Institute by commenting on their "100 Greatest American Movies" list and telling you what I think of the placement of certain films on their list.

But, hey, that's what the movies are all about, right?

I have seen some critics rank a movie "Four Stars" and a "Must See," while other critics rank the *same film* as a Bomb.

Any attempt to rank anything in numerical order will inevitably start arguments. (I know firsthand of what I speak: In my 1998 book, *The Italian 100,* I ranked the one hundred most influential Italians, and to this day I am still asked why I ranked Frank Sinatra below Vivaldi and Enrico Fermi.)

Entertainment Weekly, a magazine notorious for lists of this kind, agrees with the AFI's voters and ranks *Citizen Kane* as the greatest American film of all time. (Although they break their choices up into categories, *Citizen Kane* made the number-one spot on their Drama list.)

The AFI has impressive credentials, but then so do I, and so do you . . . because we all love movies and we watch them whenever we can.

For the following list, I comment where I feel a comment is necessary. If a film is listed in its slot without my two cents, you can assume I generally agree with its ranking by the AFI.

NOTE: The AFI is a private organization funded by membership dues devoted to preserving and restoring "our disappearing film heritage." The AFI recently discovered and preserved *Richard III* (1912), the oldest surviving American movie known to exist. Membership in AFI also helps support scholarships for young filmmakers; assists in making workshops and seminars available to the general public; and supports the AFI Los Angeles International Film Festival. If you're interested in joining, visit their web site at http://www.afionline.com.

1. *Citizen Kane* (1941) Definitely a "Top 10" film, but the greatest American movie ever made? I'm not sure I agree with this choice as the Number 1 film.

2. *Casablanca* (1942) I would not have ranked this film this high. Again, Top 10 for certain, but I'm not convinced it's Number 2.

3. *The Godfather* (1972) Excellent film and ranked appropriately.

4. *Gone With the Wind* (1939) No complaints here.

5. *Lawrence of Arabia* (1962) An epic that might be one of the quintessential examples of the genre, appropriately ranked.

6. *The Wizard of Oz* (1939) Great, although this might have deserved somewhat lower ranking.

7. *The Graduate* (1967) Good movie, but is this really a Top 10 film? And should it be ranked higher than *Schindler's List, Raging Bull, Amadeus,* and others? I think not.

8. *On the Waterfront* (1954) Right where it belongs.

9. *Schindler's List* (1993) This definitely should have been higher, I think; perhaps in the Top 5.

10. *Singin' in the Rain* (1952) Too high, I think.

11. *It's a Wonderful Life* (1946) Definitely belongs on the list but maybe somewhat lower?

12. *Sunset Boulevard* (1950) Too high.

13. *The Bridge on the River Kwai* (1957) Maybe a little too high.

14. *Some Like It Hot* (1959) Too high.

15. *Star Wars* (1977) Lower than *Some Like It Hot?* Hmmmm.

16. *All About Eve* (1950)

17. *The African Queen* (1951)

18. *Psycho* (1960) Should be lower.

19. *Chinatown* (1974) Too high.

20. *One Flew Over the Cuckoo's Nest* (1975) Should be a little higher.

21. *The Grapes of Wrath* (1940)

22. *2001: A Space Odyssey* (1968)

23. *The Maltese Falcon* (1941)

24. *Raging Bull* (1980) Should be higher.

25. *E.T. The Extra-Terrestrial* (1982) Should be higher.

26. *Dr. Strangelove* (1964) Should be higher.

27. *Bonnie and Clyde* (1967) Should be lower.

28. *Apocalypse Now* (1979)

29. *Mr. Smith Goes to Washington* (1939)

30. *The Treasure of the Sierra Madre* (1948)

31. *Annie Hall* (1977) If Woody was only going to get one spot on the list, *Manhattan* might have been a better choice.

32. *The Godfather, Part II* (1974) If *The Godfather* is ranked at Number 3, and the almost unanimous view among film lovers and *Godfather* fans is that 2 is as good as (if not better than) 1, then why is this classic ranked at the ridiculously low Number 32?

33. *High Noon* (1952)

34. *To Kill a Mockingbird* (1962)

35. *It Happened One Night* (1934)

36. *Midnight Cowboy* (1969) Should be lower.

37. *The Best Years of Our Lives* (1946)

38. *Double Indemnity* (1944)

39. *Doctor Zhivago* (1965)

40. *North by Northwest* (1959)

41. *West Side Story* (1961)

42. *Rear Window* (1954)

43. *King Kong* (1933) Above *Amadeus, M*A*S*H, Forrest Gump,* etc.? Seems much too high.

44. *The Birth of a Nation* (1915) Should be lower.

45. *A Streetcar Named Desire* (1951)

46. *A Clockwork Orange* (1971) Probably should be a little higher.

47. *Taxi Driver* (1976) Should be much higher.

48. *Jaws* (1975) Should be higher.

49. *Snow White and the Seven Dwarfs* (1937) Too high.

50. *Butch Cassidy and the Sundance Kid* (1969) Too high.

51. *The Philadelphia Story* (1940)

52. *From Here to Eternity* (1953)

53. *Amadeus* (1984) Should be considerably higher.

54. *All Quiet on the Western Front* (1930) Should be lower.

55. *The Sound of Music* (1965)

56. *M*A*S*H* (1970) Should be higher.

57. *The Third Man* (1949)

58. *Fantasia* (1940)

59. *Rebel Without a Cause* (1955)

60. *Raiders of the Lost Ark* (1981) Maybe too high.

61. *Vertigo* (1958)

62. *Tootsie* (1982) Could be a little higher.

63. *Stagecoach* (1939)

64. *Close Encounters of the Third Kind* (1977)

65. *The Silence of the Lambs* (1991) Should be much higher.

66. *Network* (1976) Maybe a little too low.

67. *The Manchurian Candidate* (1962)

68. *An American in Paris* (1951) Maybe a little too high.

69. *Shane* (1953)

70. *The French Connection* (1971)

71. *Forrest Gump* (1994) Should be higher.

72. *Ben-Hur* (1959)

73. *Wuthering Heights* (1939) Too high.

74. *The Gold Rush* (1925)

75. *Dances With Wolves* (1990) Too low.

76. *City Lights* (1931)

77. *American Graffiti* (1973) Seems too high.

78. *Rocky* (1976) Maybe too high.

79. *The Deer Hunter* (1978) Should be higher.

80. *The Wild Bunch* (1969)

81. *Modern Times* (1936)

82. *Giant* (1956)

83. *Platoon* (1986) Should be higher.

84. *Fargo* (1996) Should be much higher.

85. *Duck Soup* (1933)

86. *Mutiny on the Bounty* (1935)

87. *Frankenstein* (1931) Too high.

88. *Easy Rider* (1969) There's no way this should have been ranked higher than *GoodFellas*, *Pulp Fiction*, or *Unforgiven*. Sorry, it's a terrific film, but those three are cinematic classics.

89. *Patton* (1970)

90. *The Jazz Singer* (1927)

91. *My Fair Lady* (1964)

92. *A Place in the Sun* (1951)

93. *The Apartment* (1960) A little too low.

94. *GoodFellas* (1990) Should have been much higher.

95. *Pulp Fiction* (1994) Should have been much higher.

96. *The Searchers* (1956)

97. *Bringing Up Baby* (1938)

98. *Unforgiven* (1992) Should have been higher.

99. *Guess Who's Coming to Dinner* (1967)

100. *Yankee Doodle Dandy* (1942) Not sure this would even make my Top 100.

- - - - - - - - - - - - - - - -

Sound familiar?

At the 1979 ceremony, Dustin Hoffman won a Best Actor Oscar for his performance in *Kramer vs. Kramer.* During his acceptance speech, he said, "There are sixty thousand actors in the Screen Actors Guild who don't work. You have to practice accents while you're driving a taxicab 'cause when you're a broke actor, you can't write and you can't paint. Most actors don't work and a few of us are so lucky to have a chance." Three years later, Hoffman would give a similar speech, but this time in character as Michael Dorsey, the out of work acting teacher who dons a dress and becomes a national hit on a soap opera as "Dorothy Michaels" in the enormously popular *Tootsie.*

- - - - - - - - - - - - - - - -

People Magazine's 86 "Movie" Covers

For a magazine that's supposed to be about people, *People* sure does do a lot of cover stories about movies!

To be fair, the overwhelming majority of *People*'s cover stories have been about, well, people. But eighty-six times during the past twenty-five years or so (through the fall of 1999), the mag devoted a cover to a current movie.

Reading through this list is a revelation. Movies that were apparently huge news at the time (*The Fan, High Road to China, Tarzan, Sahara, Bolero, Rhinestone, Bad Influence*) now aren't even a blip on the pop culture landscape; while movies that are now carved-in-stone classics (*Star Wars, Airplane!, Raiders of the Lost Ark, E.T. The Extra-Terrestrial, Broadcast News*) were covered as brand-new releases, with an offhandedness often seen in contemporary entertainment coverage. NOTE: Each "movie" cover is listed by date, followed by the film that scored the cover story, followed by a description of the photo (or photos) on the mag's cover.

1. July 18, 1977; *Star Wars;* C-3PO.

2. May 29, 1978; *Pretty Baby;* Brooke Shields.

3. August 14, 1978; *Star Wars;* Carrie Fisher and Darth Vader.

4. January 8, 1979; *Superman;* Christopher Reeve as Superman.

5. April 16, 1979; *The China Syndrome;* Michael Douglas being embraced from behind by Jane Fonda.

6. July 23, 1979; *Rocky II;* Sylvester Stallone in yellow robe and red boxing gloves embracing Talia Shire.

7. August 13, 1979; *Moonraker;* Richard Kiel as "Jaws," Lois Chiles, and Roger Moore.

8. September 17, 1979; *The Amityville Horror;* Margot Kidder.

9. April 7, 1980; *American Gigolo;* a bare-chested Richard Gere.

10. July 28, 1980; *The Shining;* Jack Nicholson in a tux and an inset photo of the "Here's Johnny!" scene from the movie.

11. August 4, 1980; *The Blue Brothers;* Dan Aykroyd and John Belushi in costume (black suit, white shirt, black tie, sunglasses) as the Blue Brothers.

12. August 11, 1980; *The Blue Lagoon;* Brooke Shields and Christopher Atkins embracing as their characters from the movie. They're both in costume, which essentially consists of nothing but tiny loincloths . . . oh, and they're both topless, too; Brooke's hair strategically covers her breasts. (This was the tenth best-selling issue in *People* magazine's history. Must have been 'cause the movie was so good.)

13. September 8, 1980; *Airplane!;* Lloyd Bridges, Robert Hays, Julie Hagerty, Kareem Abdul-Jabbar, Peter Graves, and the "blowup" copilot from the movie.

14. September 15, 1980; *Dressed to Kill;* Angie Dickinson, and an inset photo from the movie.

15. September 22, 1980; *Shogun;* Richard Chamberlain, in costume from the movie.

16. January 19, 1981; *9 to 5;* Dolly Parton, Jane Fonda, and Lily Tomlin.

17. June 8, 1981; *The Fan;* Lauren Bacall.

18. July 6, 1981; *Superman 2;* Christopher Reeve. (Interestingly, the cover copy reads, "He beds Lois in his Man of Steel sequel, but in film—and fact—he shuns marriage like Kryptonite. This was obviously before Reeve met the love of his life, wife Dana, a singer and actress who has taken care of him since his accident.)

19. July 20, 1981; *Raiders of the Lost Ark;* Harrison Ford and Karen Allen in costume from the movie, posing for the camera with their arms around each other.

20. July 27, 1981; *Tarzan;* Bo Derek, with an inset photo from the movie.

21. August 10, 1981; *Endless Love;* Brooke Shields.

22. August 17, 1981; *Blow Out;* John Travolta and Nancy Allen.

23. August 31, 1981; *Star Wars;* Mark Hamill and Yoda.

24. September 14, 1981; *Arthur;* Dudley Moore and Susan Anton.

25. October 5, 1981; *Mommie Dearest;* Faye Dunaway.

26. February 8, 1982; *Taps;* Timothy Hutton.

27. April 12, 1982; *On Golden Pond;* Henry Fonda with an inset photo of daughter Jane Fonda holding an Oscar.

28. May 3, 1982; *High Road to China;* Tom Selleck and Bess Armstrong in costume from the movie.

29. June 21, 1982; The *Rocky* saga; Sylvester Stallone in costume as Rocky, holding his infant son, Seargeoh.

30. June 28, 1982; *E.T. The Extra-Terrestrial;* Henry Thomas and E.T.

31. July 12, 1982; *Annie;* Aileen Quinn and the dog.

32. August 23, 1982; *E.T. The Extra-Terrestrial;* E.T. holding a Princess phone.

33. January 17, 1983; *Tootsie;* Dustin Hoffman in costume as Dorothy Michaels and also as himself.

34. February 28, 1983; *Sahara;* Brooke Shields and a camel.

35. March 7, 1983; *Staying Alive;* Director Sylvester Stallone, with John Travolta in costume as his character Tony from the movie.

36. April 4, 1983; *E.T. The Extra-Terrestrial;* An Oscar and an inset photo of E.T.

37. June 6, 1983; *Return of the Jedi;* Carrie Fisher as Princess Leia (in the famous yellow bikini) and Jabba the Hut in a scene from the movie.

38. June 13, 1983; *Psycho II;* Tony Perkins standing in front of the *Psycho* house.

39. July 18, 1983; The James Bond saga; Roger Moore and six Bond babes.

40. July 25, 1983; *Staying Alive;* John Travolta, Cynthia Rhodes, and Finola Hughes, all in costume from the movie.

41. September 12, 1983; *National Lampoon's Vacation;* Chevy Chase holding his infant son, Cydney.

42. December 19, 1983; *Two of a Kind;* John Travolta and Olivia Newton-John.

43. January 23, 1984; *Silkwood;* Cher.

44. February 6, 1984; *Terms of Endearment;* Shirley Maclaine and Debra Winger in the "lying on the bed talking" scene from the movie.

45. February 27, 1984; *Bolero;* Bo Derek.

46. March 19, 1984; *Harry & Son;* Paul Newman.

47. April 2, 1984; *Footloose;* Kevin Bacon.

48. April 9, 1984; *Splash;* Daryl Hannah in costume as Madison the mermaid from the movie.

49. May 28, 1984; *The Natural;* Robert Redford in a baseball uniform from the movie.

50. July 2, 1984; *Indiana Jones and the Temple of Doom;* Harrison Ford and Kate Capshaw in costume from the movie.

51. July 9, 1984; *Rhinestone;* Sylvester Stallone and Dolly Parton in costume from the movie.

52. March 18, 1985; *Mask;* Cher and Rocky Dennis, the real-life boy whose life story was the basis for her and Eric Stoltz's powerful movie.

53. July 1, 1985; *Goonies;* Cyndi Lauper.

54. July 8, 1985; *Prizzi's Honor;* Jack Nicholson and Anjelica Huston.

55. July 28, 1986; *Back to School* and *Ruthless People; Back to School*'s Rodney Dangerfield and *Ruthless People*'s Danny DeVito.

56. August 18, 1986; *Heartburn;* Meryl Streep and Jack Nicholson in three photos from the movie.

57. November 3, 1986; *Peggy Sue Got Married;* Kathleen Turner and three inset photos from *Body Heat, Prizzi's Honor,* and *Romancing the Stone.*

58. March 9, 1987; *Platoon;* Charlie Sheen and an inset photo of him from the movie.

59. April 20, 1987; *The Secret of My Success;* Michael J. Fox.

60. October 26, 1987; *Fatal Attraction;* Michael Douglas and Glenn Close.

61. January 25, 1988; *Moonstruck;* Cher.

62. February 1, 1988; *Broadcast News;* Albert Brooks, Holly Hunter, and William Hurt.

63. June 20, 1988; *Big Business;* Bette Midler and Lily Tomlin.

64. March 19, 1990; *Bad Influence;* Rob Lowe.

65. June 11, 1990; *Bird on a Wire;* Mel Gibson and Goldie Hawn.

66. July 2, 1990; *Dick Tracy;* Madonna and Warren Beatty.

67. November 19, 1990; *Dances With Wolves;* Kevin Costner.

68. January 21, 1991; *Mermaids;* Cher.

69. June 24, 1991; *Thelma & Louise;* Geena Davis and an inset photo of her and Susan Sarandon from the movie.

70. July 8, 1991; *Soapdish;* Sally Field.

71. December 23, 1991; *Hook;* Dustin Hoffman in costume as Hook from the movie, and an inset photo of Julia Roberts as Tinkerbelle.

72. July 13, 1992; *Batman Returns;* Michelle Pfeiffer and an inset photo of Michelle in costume as Catwoman from the movie.

73. June 10, 1996; *Mission: Impossible;* Tom Cruise.

74. June 24, 1996; *Striptease;* Demi Moore.

75. July 22, 1996; *Independence Day;* Will Smith.

76. October 14, 1996; *The First Wives Club;* Goldie Hawn, Diane Keaton, and Bette Midler.

77. November 11, 1996; *Ransom;* Mel Gibson.

78. August 4, 1997; *Air Force One;* Harrison Ford.

79. January 26, 1998; *Titanic;* Leonardo DiCaprio and an inset photo of him and Kate Winslet from the movie.

80. March 16, 1998; *Titanic;* Leonardo DiCaprio and Kate Winslet from the movie (the same photo as on the January 26, 1998 cover).

81. June 8, 1998; *The Horse Whisperer;* Robert Redford.

82. July 27, 1998; *Lethal Weapon 4;* Mel Gibson.

83. August 3, 1998; *Saving Private Ryan;* Tom Hanks.

84. August 17, 1998; *There's Something About Mary;* Cameron Diaz and an inset photo of her and Matt Dillon from the movie.

85. August 30, 1999; *Runaway Bride;* an article about "real-life" runaway brides, a tie-in to the hit Julia Roberts movie.

86. October 15, 1999; *The Sixth Sense;* an article titled "Is There a Sixth Sense?," a tie-in to the hit Bruce Willis movie.

18 Movies About the Holocaust

Often painful to watch, these films are important contributions to the history of the nightmare known as the Holocaust.

1. *The Diary of Anne Frank* (1959)

2. *The Pawnbroker* (1965)

3. *The Garden of the Finzi-Continis* (1971)

4. *Holocaust* (1978)

5. *The Last Metro* (1980)

6. *Playing for Time* (1980)

7. *Sophie's Choice* (1982)

8. *The Holcroft Covenant* (1985)

9. *Shoah* (1985)

10. *Au Revoir Les Enfants* (1987)

11. *Hanna's War* (1988)

12. *Enemies, a Love Story* (1989)

13. *Europa, Europa* (1991)

14. *The Last Butterfly* (1992)

15. *Schindler's List* (1993)

16. *Les Misérables* (1995)

17. *Life Is Beautiful* (1998)

18. *The Devil's Arithmetic* (1999)

For Your Consideration . . .

THE "N" LIST

Kathy Najimy *Soapdish* (1991); *Sister Act* (1992)
Liam Neeson *Schindler's List* (1993); *Michael Collins* (1996)
Sam Neill *The Piano* (1993); *Jurassic Park* (1993)
Judd Nelson *St. Elmo's Fire* (1985); *The Breakfast Club* (1985)
Bob Newhart *Cold Turkey* (1971); *In and Out* (1997)
Paul Newman *The Sting* (1973); *The Verdict* (1982)
Jack Nicholson *One Flew Over the Cuckoo's Nest* (1975); *As Good As It Gets* (1997)
Nick Nolte *Down and Out in Beverly Hills* (1986); *Cape Fear* (1991)
Edward Norton *American History X* (1998); *Fight Club* (1999)

- - - - - - - - - - - - - - - - - -

**It's really called the
Academy of Motion Picture Arts and Sciences and Gymnastics**

At the 1957 ceremony, Kirk Douglas did a handstand over the head of Burt Lancaster and then Lancaster held Douglas above his head and carried him off stage. At the 1958 ceremony, Douglas stood on Lancaster's shoulders and then they both did somersaults. At the 1991 ceremony, Jack Palance dropped to the floor and did four one-armed push-ups.

- - - - - - - - - - - - - - - - - -

34 Actors and 1 Actress Who Have Played the President of the United States

American presidents have always been rich fodder for Hollywood. The movies have given us portrayals of real presidents (John Quincy Adams, Harry Truman, Thomas Jefferson, Richard Nixon, Abraham Lincoln, Franklin D. Roosevelt, John F. Kennedy); fake presidents; black presidents; and even a woman president.

For those of you interested in how (a drum roll and tons of reverb, please) the *Most Powerful Man in the World* has been portrayed on the silver screen and on TV over the past sixty years, these thirty-five flicks will allow you to cinematically OD on the Oval Office.

Just don't watch too many of these around election time: Some of them may make you not want to vote anymore.

1. Morgan Freeman as President Beck in *Deep Impact* (1998)

2. John Travolta as President Jack Stanton in *Primary Colors* (1998)

3. Roy Scheider as President Carlson in *Executive Target* (1997)

4. Ronny Cox as President Jack Neil in *Murder at 1600* (1997)

5. Phil Hartman as the president in *The Second Civil War* (1997)

6. Harrison Ford as President James Marshall in *Air Force One* (1997)

7. Gene Hackman as President Alan Richmond in *Absolute Power* (1997)

8. Anthony Hopkins as President John Quincy Adams in *Amistad* (1997)

9. Sam Waterston as the president in *The Shadow Conspiracy* (1997)

10. Paul Winfield as the president in *The Assassination File* (1996)

11. Jack Nicholson as President Dale in *Mars Attacks!* (1996)

12. Dan Aykroyd as President William Haney; Jack Lemmon as President Russell P. Kramer; and James Garner as President Matt Douglas in *My Fellow Americans* (1996)

13. Bill Pullman as President Thomas J. Whitmore in *Independence Day* (1996)

14. Michael Douglas as President Andrew Shepard in *The American President* (1995)

15. Gary Sinise as President Harry Truman in *Truman* (1995)

16. Anthony Hopkins as President Richard Nixon in *Nixon* (1995)

17. Sam Waterston as President William Foster in *The Enemy Within* (1994)

18. Nick Nolte as President Thomas Jefferson in *Jefferson in Paris* (1994)

19. Hugh Wilson as the voice of the president in *Guarding Tess* (1994)

20. Kevin Kline as President Bill Mitchell in *Dave* (1993)

21. Jim Curley as the president in *In the Line of Fire* (1993)

22. Lane Smith as President Richard Nixon in *The Final Days* (1989, TV)

23. Sam Waterston as President Abraham Lincoln in *Gore Vidal's Lincoln* (1988, TV)

24. Charles Howerton as President Calvin Craig in *Assassination* (1987)

25. Donald Pleasance as the president in *Escape From New York* (1981)

26. Bob Newhart as President Manfred Link in *First Family* (1980)

27. Henry Fonda as the president in *Meteor* (1979)

28. Edward Hermann as President Franklin D. Roosevelt in *Eleanor & Franklin* (1976, TV)

29. Zero Mostel as the president in *Fore Play* (1975)

30. William Devane as President John F. Kennedy in *Missiles of October* (1974, TV)

31. Tod Andrews as President Jeremy Haines in *The President's Plane Is Missing* (1971, TV)

32. Polly Bergen as President Leslie McCloud in *Kisses for My President* (1964)

33. Franchot Tone as the president in *Advise and Consent* (1962)

34. Henry Fonda as President Abraham Lincoln in *Young Mr. Lincoln* (1939)

35. Walter Huston as President Judson Hammon in *Gabriel Over the White House* (1933)

36. And finally ... a great TV series about the presidency: Martin Sheen as President Josiah Bartlett in *The West Wing* (1999–).

44 Models Who Act

Being a model (if you're successful at it, of course) is often a great job: You get paid thousands of dollars a day for looking beautiful and wearing cool clothes. But being a movie star is an even *better* job and that's why so many models try to make the switch from modeling to acting.

This plan is fine ... if you, the model, happen to possess a modicum (and hopefully much more) of acting ability and can amplify your tried-and-true *photographic* presence into a much more demanding *screen* presence.

There are a few legendary breakouts in this tradition, most notably Kim Basinger, Courteney Cox, Cindy Crawford, and Liv Tyler, as well as Cameron Diaz, Geena Davis, Andie MacDowell, René Russo, and Susan Sarandon, all of whom are former models who, thankfully, are also extremely talented actors.

Others have not been so lucky.

Standouts

Kim Basinger After a couple of forgettable roles, Basinger got her big break in 1983 with a photo spread in *Playboy*. That same year she became a "Bond girl" in *Never Say Never Again*, which she followed a couple of years later with an incredibly erotic (and frequently naked) performance as Mickey Rourke's lover in *9-1/2 Weeks* (1986). Basinger won a Best Supporting Actress Academy Award for her performance in *L.A. Confidential* (1997).

Courteney Cox Courteney Cox has been successful in both movies and on TV and currently stars in the most popular comedy on the tube, *Friends*. She has appeared in several successful films (even though she has appeared in a few forgettable flicks (*Down Twisted* [1987]; *Battling For Baby* [1992]), and it's clear that she has both the looks and the talent to continue with a thriving acting career. She may still do commercials from time to time, but we can be pretty sure that her résumé now reads "Actress," not "Model Who Acts."

Cindy Crawford This is the woman who defines the word "super-model." Breathtakingly gorgeous, Cindy also has a charming, nondiva personality that has served her well on talk shows. Guys love Cindy and girls want to be like her. (Kathy Ireland has a similar type of following.) She has done runway modeling, print ads, TV commercials, hosting (she had her own show, *House of Style*, on MTV), books, and in 1995 she made the leap to the big screen with *Fair Game*, the second adaptation of Paula Gosling's novel of the same name. (The first was 1986's execrable *Cobra*.) She costarred with William Baldwin and even though she was awarded the Golden Raspberry Award that year for Worst New Star, I thought she did just fine in her screen debut — and looked fetching in the tank top she wore during much of the movie.

Cameron Diaz This beautiful and bubbly blonde got her start as a model but successfully made the transition (in a big way) to acting when she starred in the Jim Carrey megahit, *The Mask* (1994). Diaz projects an irresistible charm in front of the camera and after her *Mask* feature film debut, she made five films in quick succession (*The Last Supper* (1995); *She's the One, Feeling Minnesota, Head Above Water* [all 1996]; and *Keys to Tulsa* [1997]) but none of these really did much to boost her career. But then this Pretty Girl starred in the 1997 hit *My Best Friend's Wedding* (with Julia Roberts) and almost stole the movie away from the Pretty Woman. (Diaz's pitiable—but ultimately enchanting) karaoke performance in *Wedding* is legendary and may actually persuade you to never cross the threshold of a karaoke bar ever again.) The following year she crossed over into the realm of superstar with her, ahem, seminal performance in the enormous comedy hit, *There's Something About Mary.* Cameron Diaz starred (with Drew Barrymore and Lucy Lui) in the feature film remake of *Charlie's Angels* (2000).

Susan Sarandon This intense brown-haired beauty got her start in commercials and print ads and made the transition to acting in the edgy drama *Joe* (1970). Since that auspicious start, Sarandon has made over fifty movies, including some undeniable classics such as *Pretty Baby* (1978—a hooker with a heart—and an underaged virginal daughter for sale); *Atlantic City* (1980—watch for the lemon scene); *The Hunger* (1983—lesbian vampires . . . how's that for high concept?); *Bull Durham* (1988—too sexy for words); *The Player* (1992, as herself!); *Little Women* (1994—in what might be the all-time greatest portrayal of Alcott's character Marmee March to date); *Dead Man Walking* (1995—her best performance so far); and, of course, *The Rocky Horror Picture Show* (1975—she never suspected what this movie would become) and *Thelma & Louise* (1991—or for that matter, this one either). Sarandon and her life partner Tim Robbins (he directed her in *Dead Man Walking*) are outspoken and politically active, but this has not prevented them from both doing superb work both in front of and behind the cameras.

Liv Tyler Daughter of Aerosmith's lead singer Steven Tyler and *Playboy* Playmate Bebe Buell, Liv has been in front of the camera since her teenage debut in her father's "Crazy" video in 1994. She is gorgeous, talented, has a show business pedigree, and will probably be one of the stars of the next decade. (She also has a cool synergy going with her dad: Aerosmith did a song for *Armageddon,* which was nominated for an Oscar. Liv introduced her dad's band's performance of the song at the Academy Awards ceremony in 1999. Wouldn't you love to hear what *this* family talks about around their dinner table?)

Other Models Who Now Act

Maude Adams

Tyra Banks

Marisa Berenson

Candice Bergen

Halle Berry

Josie Bissett

Susan Blakely

Naomi Campbell

Joanna Cassidy

Geena Davis

Angie Everhart

Melanie Griffith

Patti Hansen

Mariel Hemingway

Natasha Henstridge

Whitney Houston

Elizabeth Hurley

Lauren Hutton

Iman

Kathy Ireland

Beverly Johnson

Jessica Lange

Kelly Lynch

Andie MacDowell

Ali McGraw

Elle Macpherson

Demi Moore

Michelle Pfeiffer

Paulina Porizkova

Priscilla Presley

René Russo

Cybill Shepherd

Brooke Shields

Anna Nicole Smith

Sharon Stone

Uma Thurman

Twiggy

Sela Ward

For Your Consideration . . .

THE "O" LIST

Chris O'Donnell *Scent of a Woman* (1992); *The Chamber* (1996)

Rosie O'Donnell *A League of Their Own* (1992); *The Flintstones* (1994)

Gary Oldman *True Romance* (1993); *Air Force One* (1997)

Annette O'Toole *Cat People* (1982); *Cross My Heart* (1988)

Peter O'Toole *Becket* (1964); *My Favorite Year* (1982)

- - - - - - - - - - - - - - - - -

"Southern sensibilities"—Can you say oxymoron?

In the early sixties, racism was rampant in the United States and truth be told, we *have* come a long way, baby. At the 1963 Oscar ceremony, Sidney Poitier won a Best Actor Oscar for his performance in *Lilies of the Field*. He received his statuette from Anne Bancroft and gave her a brief hug in appreciation. *Time* magazine's TV reviewer later wrote, "In fictional television such a touchingly sincere and realistic scene would have been written out lest Southern sensibilities be disturbed."

- - - - - - - - - - - - - - - - -

Singles: 30 Actors Who Directed One Film

[Directors are] there to answer any of the questions that come up from any department, and if you're not prepared to give guidance to those who request it (and they request it several times a minute, it seems), you'll have a tough time not being run over by the steam-powered train that is production.

—DIRECTOR MICK GARRIS

All of the stars in this chapter really want to . . . *act*!?

Wait a minute. Isn't it usually the other way around? Actors are always whining about *really* wanting to direct, aren't they?

This list looks at thirty actors and actresses who, as of 2000, have directed *one* theatrical feature but who are still far better known for their acting than for their directing. (Some of these "one-timers" may have also directed a TV episode or some other short feature, but for the purposes of this chapter, we are only considering their theatrical releases.)

What is interesting is that it seems that if actors are serious about moving into directing (if not full-time then at least on a fairly regular basis), they direct *more than one film,* often in quick succession.

One wonders if the "one-timers" listed here, instead, got a taste of what directing is all about—the endless pressure, countless decisions, ultimate responsibility, and the need (and ability) to micromanage—and determined (perhaps correctly, considering the number of crap movies released each year) that all of those factors were a burden that could impede the crafting of their *own* cinematic art, which previously had been expressed through acting. Perhaps they then decided that having a trailer to rest in between takes and only having to learn *their own* lines was more to their liking.

Of course, when it comes to some of the younger artists on this list (Matthew Broderick, Steve Buscemi, Kevin Bacon, etc.) the fact that they've only directed one film might just be due to their busy acting career that has prevented them from finding the time to both act and direct.

But in the case of some of the old-timer one-timers (Alan Arkin, Marlon Brando, Richard Burton, etc.) the fact that they directed one film in the sixties or seventies and then went back to acting could lead us to believe that being the captain of the ship was not to their liking, eh?

Alan Arkin

Best known for: Superb naturalistic performances in such films as *The Russians Are Coming, The Russians Are Coming* (1966), *The In-Laws* (1979), *Glengarry Glen Ross* (1992), and *Grosse Pointe Blanke* (1997). Father of actor Adam Arkin.

Directorial debut: *Little Murders* (1971), a black comedy scripted by Jules Feiffer that is generally thought to be as good today as it was three decades ago.

Dan Aykroyd

Best known for: His starring role as a Not-Ready-for-Prime-Time Player in the early years of TV's *Saturday Night Live,* plus a series of roles in often great comedies such as *The Blues Brothers* (1980), *Trading Places* (1983), and *Ghostbusters* (1984), with an occasional terrific dramatic performance thrown in, in films like *Driving Miss Daisy* (1989), and *Sneakers* (1992).

Directorial debut: *Nothing but Trouble* (1991), a horror comedy that is nothing but forgettable.

KEVIN BACON

Best known for: A long string of terrific performances from a young actor/musician who is unquestionably one of the ten best American actors working today, ranging from the comedic—*National Lampoon's Animal House* (1978), *Diner* (1982), *Picture Perfect* (1996), to the dramatic—*Criminal Law* (1989), *Flatliners* (1990), *JFK* (1991), *Sleepers* (1996), *Apollo 13* (1995)—to the Academy Award caliber (*A Few Good Men* (1992), *Murder in the First* (1995). Oh, and let's not forget the game *Six Degrees of Kevin Bacon,* the goal of which is to connect Bacon to any other American actor in as few steps ("degrees") as possible. (The game even has its own web site.) Here's an example: Connect Kevin Bacon with Marilyn Monroe. Easy. Marilyn Monroe was in *Some Like It Hot* with Jack Lemmon who was in *JFK* with Kevin Bacon. Trust me: This game quickly becomes addictive and not all are that easy. And if you expand the game to include people other than actors, then I have a Bacon Number of 2: I interviewed Ron Howard for my 1987 book *Mayberry, My Home Town,* Ron Howard directed Kevin Bacon in *Apollo 13.* Fun, no?

Directorial debut: *Losing Chase* (1996), a powerful drama set on Martha's Vineyard about the troubled relationship between a newly hired "mother's helper" (played by Bacon's wife Kyra Sedgwick) and a woman recovering from a nervous breakdown.

MARLON BRANDO

Best known for: A lifetime of incredible performances, including unforgettable early roles in *A Streetcar Named Desire* (1951) and *On the Waterfront* (1954), and peaking with, of course, *The Godfather* (1972), *Last Tango in Paris* (1973), and *Apocalypse Now* (1979).

Directorial debut: *One-Eyed Jacks* (1961), a psychological Western with stunning visuals and a great performance by Brando both in front of and behind the camera. (Brando took over from Stanley Kubrick about halfway through the shooting.)

MATTHEW BRODERICK

Best known for: A string of charismatic performances in such entertaining films as *WarGames* (1983), *Family Business* (1989), *The Freshman* (1990), *The Road to Wellville* (1994), *The Cable Guy* (1996), and especially *Ferris Bueller's Day Off* (1986).

Directorial debut: *Infinity* (1996), a biopic of the life of Nobel Prize-winning physicist Richard Feynman. The screenplay was written by Broderick's mother Patricia and, in addition to directing, Broderick played Feynman. The film costarred Patricia Arquette.

RICHARD BURTON

Best known for: A lifetime of great performances (although he'd never won a Best Actor Academy Award), including roles in *The Robe* (1953), *The Longest Day* (1962), *The Sandpiper* (1965), *Who's Afraid of Virginia Woolf?* (1966), and *Wagner,* the 1985 epic biography of Richard Wagner.

Directorial debut. *Doctor Faustus* (1968), an unsuccessful adaptation of Christopher Marlowe's retelling of the Faust tale. Burton plays the hapless fellow who sells his soul to the devil and Elizabeth Taylor plays Helen of Troy. This is only worth watching if you are a passionate Burton/Taylor fan; if not, it's an ordeal to sit through.

STEVE BUSCEMI

Best known for: His extremely unusual looks and his very intense acting style. Buscemi's most memorable performances have been in dark, often ultraviolent thrillers like *Barton Fink* (1991), *Reservoir Dogs* (1992), *Pulp Fiction* (1994), and *Fargo* (1996), although he was also very funny as the drunk wedding guest (and later lead singer) in the 1997 Adam Sandler hit comedy, *The Wedding Singer.*

Directorial debut: *Trees Lounge* (1996), a dark comedy about a loser (Buscemi) who loses his job, ends up hanging around a bar all day, and finally takes a job driving an ice cream truck. Universally praised as being well written, acted, and directed, *Trees Lounge* was an impressive directorial debut for Buscemi and showed that he was obviously so good at it, he will likely direct again (his appearance in this chapter notwithstanding!).

JOHN CANDY

Best known for: A long list of roles as the funny fat guy in such comedies as *Stripes* (1981), *Splash* (1984), *Volunteers* (1985), *Summer Rental* (1985), *Planes, Trains, and Automobiles* (1987), and *Home Alone* (1990), although he also excelled in a straight dramatic role in *JFK* (1991). Candy's final film (before his untimely death while shooting 1994's *Wagons East*) was the 1995 satire *Canadian Bacon* (which was the directorial debut of *Roger and Me*'s Michael Moore).

Directorial debut: *Hostage for a Day* (1994), a made-for-TV comedy in which George Wendt plays a stressed-out guy going through a midlife crisis who decides to fake his own kidnapping. Candy also had a cameo.

DYAN CANNON

Best known for: An interesting blend of comedic and dramatic performances, beginning with the wild satire *Bob & Carol & Ted & Alice* (1969) and including roles in *The Anderson Tapes* (1971), *Revenge of the Pink Panther* (1978), *Honeysuckle Rose* (1980), *Deathtrap* (1982), and *Out to Sea* (1997).

Directorial debut: *The End of Innocence* (1990), the story of a woman who has a nervous breakdown and tries to put her life back together. Cannon also wrote and starred in this film that is uncertain whether it's a comedy or a drama. Some critics (most notably Leonard Maltin) wondered aloud if Cannon had gotten in over her head by trying to handle directing, acting, and writing chores. Evidence he may be right could be the fact that the movie took so long to put together that it costars Rebecca Schaeffer as a young Cannon, and the film appeared two years *after* Schaeffer was murdered by an obsessed fan.

CHER

Best known for: A short list of memorable (and in the case of *Moonstruck*, Oscar-winning) performances, including roles in *Come Back to the Five and Dime, Jimmy Dean, Jimmy Dean* (1982), *Silkwood* (1983), *Mask* (1985), *The Witches of Eastwick* (1987), and *Mermaids* (1990). Oh, yeah . . . and she's also known for a bunch of best-selling albums and for being one-half of Sonny & Cher.

Directorial debut: *If These Walls Could Talk* (1996), a made-for-HBO movie that covers the abortion issue and how it affects four different women over a span of four decades, from the fifties through the nineties. Cher shared directing chores with Nancy Savoca (*Household Saints,* 1993), and it's obvious that her personal involvement was able to snare such big name stars as Demi Moore, Anne Heche, Sissy Spacek, and Jada Pinkett Smith. (Cher also appeared in the film.)

TOM CRUISE

Best known for: Being one of the all-time biggest box-office draws and for starring in a string of incredibly successful hits, including *Risky Business* (1983), *Top Gun* (1986), *Rain Man* (1988), *A Few Good Men* (1993), *The Firm* (1993), *Interview With the Vampire* (1994), *Mission: Impossible* (1996), and *Jerry Maguire* (1996). Cruise's steamy 1999 blockbuster *Eyes Wide Shut* (which was Stanley Kubrick's final film and which costarred Cruise's then wife Nicole Kidman) just added to his bankability and incomparable star status.

Directorial debut: *The Frightening Frammis* (1993), one segment of an anthology of three individual films released as *Fallen Angels 1.* Cruise's contribution (*Frammis*) was an adaptation of a Jim Thompson story about a grifter and a mysterious woman and starred Peter Gallagher and Isabella Rossellini. Cruise did not even have a cameo in the film.

GERARD DEPARDIEU

Best known for: A string of widely varying roles and brilliant performances in over fifty films, ranging from serious historical dramas such as *The Return of Martin Guerre* (1983) and *Cyrano de Bergerac* (1990) to broad comedies like *Green Card* (1990) and *Bogus* (1996). A native of France, Depardieu is one of the few European actors to garner a successful American following.

Directorial debut: *Tartuffe* (1984), a French language adaptation of the play of the same name by Molière. Depardieu also starred in the well-received film (which was released in the U.S. with English subtitles).

ROBERT ENGLUND

Best known for: Playing the notoriously evil, undead child murderer Freddy Kreuger (complete with gruesome burn scars, battered fedora, and a glove that had knives for fingers) in the above-average *Nightmare on Elm Street* horror series.

Directorial debut: *976-EVIL* (1988), a horror movie (big surprise there, eh?) about a teenager who can dial Hell direct. A decent sequel (*976-EVIL 2: The Astral Factor*, directed by Jim Wynorski) followed in 1991.

MARTY FELDMAN

Best known for: A series of extremely funny comedic performances, perhaps best epitomized by his role as the bug-eyed Hunchback with the shifting hump in Mel Brooks's hilarious 1974 classic *Young Frankenstein.* (That's Frahnk-en-steen, by the way.)

Directorial debut: *The Last Remake of Beau Geste* (1977), a funny Foreign Legion spoof that Feldman also cowrote and starred in.

MORGAN FREEMAN

Best known for: As he is one of the top actors on the contemporary screen, Freeman's presence in a film elevates it to something better than it would have been without him. Some of his most memorable films include *Brubaker* (1980), *Harry & Son* (1984), *Clean and Sober* (1988), *Glory* (1989), *Robin Hood: Prince of Thieves* (1991), *Unforgiven* (1992), *Seven* (1995), *Kiss the Girls* (1997), *Amistad* (1997), and his two greatest roles (both of which garnered Freeman Best Actor Oscar nominations), Hoke in *Driving Miss Daisy* (1989) and Red in *The Shawshank Redemption* (1994).

Directorial debut: *Bopha!* (1993), an earnest drama about a South African police officer (Danny Glover) and his activist son during the final days of apartheid. Adapted from the play by Percy Mtwa, the film also starred Malcolm McDowell and Alfre Woodard and was shot on location in Zimbabwe.

BOBCAT GOLDTHWAIT

Best known for: His trademark "screaming nervous guy" persona, created for his stand-up comedy performances, and which he also began using in films.

Directorial debut: *Shakes the Clown* (1992), a very strange, oddly compelling, but ultimately disastrous movie that takes place in Palookaville, a bizarre all-clown town where Shakes and his colleagues practice their craft at birthday parties and then drink themselves into oblivion at the town's all-clown bar. The idea of an all-clown town is a funny idea and it could have worked, but Goldthwait's script is lame and much of it is not funny.

LARRY HAGMAN

Best known for: His role as J. R. Ewing on the popular 1978–1991 TV drama, *Dallas,* and his role as Major Nelson on the popular sixties sitcom *I Dream of Jeannie.* Even though Hagman has also had a successful film career, ranging from memorable performances in *Fail-Safe* (1964), *Ensign Pulver* (1964), *S.O.B.* (1981), and *Primary Colors* (1998), he seems to be best remembered for his two classic TV characters.

Directorial debut: *Son of Blob* (1972), a stupid sequel to the 1950s camp sci-fi classic, *The Blob.* After Hagman's *Dallas* success, *Son of Blob* was rereleased in 1982 with the tag line, "The Film That J.R. Shot!" It didn't help.

RICHARD HARRIS

Best known for: A lifetime of stunning and classic performances, including roles in *Mutiny on the Bounty* (1962), *Camelot* (1967), *Unforgiven* (1992), *Wrestling Ernest Hemingway* (1993), and *Smilla's Sense of Snow* (1996), a private life of which gossip columns are made, and his unforgettable 1968 recording of "MacArthur Park" (still don't know what leaving the cake out in the rain is all about. Good song though).

Directorial debut: *The Hero* (1971), a drama shot partly in Israel about a young boy and the soccer star he idolizes. Harris also starred in the film.

GOLDIE HAWN

Best known for: A career of comedic roles in which she often plays the adorable daffy blonde, epitomized by such films as *Shampoo* (1975), *Foul Play* (1978), *Private Benjamin* (1980), *Protocol* (1984), *Overboard* (1987), *Housesitter* (1992), and *The First Wives Club* (1996).

Directorial debut: *Hope* (1997), an above average, made-for-cable drama about a young girl growing up in the segregated South during the Cuban Missile Crisis. It starred Jena Malone (*Bastard out of Car-*

olina, 1996; *Contact,* 1997) as the young girl, and costarred Christine Lahti, Catherine O'Hara, and the late J. T. Walsh.

ANTHONY HOPKINS

Best known for: British actor Anthony Hopkins had appeared in more than thirty films by the time he starred in, and won, a Best Actor Oscar for his performance as the cannibalistic serial killer Hannibal Lecter in *The Silence of the Lambs* (1991), and yet that role is what most people today remember him for. And well we should. Lecter may have been the greatest performance of Hopkins's career, which includes memorable roles in such classics as *The Lion in Winter* (1968), *A Bridge Too Far* (1977), *Magic* (1978), and *The Elephant Man* (1980). Hopkins's "post–*Lambs*" career is no less impressive, including fabulous performances in such films as *Howards End* (1992), *Chaplin* (1992), *Shadowlands* (1993), *The Remains of the Day* (1993), *Legends of the Fall* (1994), *Nixon* (1995), and *Amistad* (1997). (Hopkins may be the only British actor to have played two American presidents—Richard Nixon and John Quincy Adams—during his career.)

Directorial debut: *August* (1995), an okay adaptation of Anton Chekhov's play "Uncle Vanya," transplanted to 1890s Wales. The film starred Hopkins, Kate Burton, Leslie Phillips, Gawn Grainger, and Rhian Morgan. Hopkins not only starred in and directed *August,* he also composed the music for the film.

ERIQ LASALLE

Best known for: His ongoing role as the intense, arrogant, and brilliant surgical resident Peter Benton on the number one show in America, the Michael Crichton–created *ER.*

Directorial debut: *Rebound: The Legend of Earl "The Goat" Manigault* (1996), a faithful telling of the life story of a neighborhood basketball player who had a shot at the NBA but turned to drugs instead, ended up in prison, but then made a final "rebound" and turned his life around. The best thing in this made-for-cable flick directed by "Dr. Benton," is the performance of Don Cheadle (*Things To Do In Denver When You're Dead,* 1995; *Boogie Nights,* 1997) as Earl "The Goat" Manigault.

DENIS LEARY

Best known for: His inspired stand-up comedy concerts, his appearances on MTV in commercials about Cindy Crawford, and some very sharp performances in films ranging from *The Ref* (1993) and *Natural Born Killers* (1994), to *Wag the Dog* (1997), *Suicide Kings* (1997), and *The Real Blonde* (1998).

Directorial debut: *National Lampoon's Favorite Deadly Sins* (1995), an anthology of three sketches about greed, anger, and lust, codirected by Leary with David Jablin. Leary starred in the "Lust" segment as a security guard who spies on his neighbor. The film also starred Joe Mantegna, Annabelle Sciorra, Andrew Dice Clay, Brian Keith, and Farrah Forke.

JOHN COUGAR MELLENCAMP

Best known for: Ironically, Mellencamp is not really well known for doing anything in the movie business. John Cougar Mellencamp is a rock singer/songwriter best known for such huge hits as "Little Pink Houses" and "Jack and Diane." Mellencamp had never acted (unless you want to count appearing in music videos) or directed prior to *Falling From Grace*.

Directorial debut: *Falling From Grace* (1992), an adaptation of a Larry McMurtry story about a country singer (Mellencamp) who returns to his small Indiana hometown to celebrate his grandfather's eightieth birthday. Amazingly, reviews of this film have ranged from four stars to BOMB. (And critics want to know why people refuse to take them seriously.) It costarred Mariel Hemingway as Mellencamp's wife and Kay Lenz as the former girlfriend he invites back into his life.

VIC MORROW

Best known for: Morrow appeared in close to two dozen movies before his bizarre death in 1982 during the shooting of *Twilight Zone: The Movie*. Some of his films included *God's Little Acre* (1958) and *Dirty Mary Crazy Larry* (1978), but he is probably best remembered for his starring role as Sgt. Chip Saunders in the popular war series *Combat* (1962–1967).

Directorial debut: *A Man Called Sledge* (1970, Italian), a standard Western about a gunslinger who leads his gang on a quest to find a hidden cache of gold. When they find it, they end up fighting over it. This movie is notable for casting the affable (and usually "good guy") James Garner as a villain. It costarred Dennis Weaver, Claude Akins, and Laura Antonelli.

AL PACINO

Best known for: Being an actor's actor in a range of powerful roles and incredible performances that define a standard of excellence, including the *Godfather* series (1972–1990), *And Justice for All . . .* (1979), *Scarface* (1983), *Scent of a Woman* (1992), *Glengarry Glen Ross* (1992), *Heat* (1995), and *Donnie Brasco* (1996).

Directorial debut: *Looking for Richard* (1996), an odd pseudo-documentary of sorts (no, not a "mockumentary") about Pacino's many stagings of Shakespeare's *Richard III* over a four-year period. A wide range of world-class actors (both acting and commenting on Shakespeare) contribute to the film. Participants include Alec Baldwin, Kevin Spacey, Aidan Quinn, F. Murray Abraham, Kenneth Branagh, John Gielgud, James Earl Jones, Kevin Kline, Estelle Parsons, Vanessa Redgrave, Winona Ryder, Harris Yulin, Penelope Allen, Kevin Conway, Pacino himself, and others. *Looking for Richard* also explores Pacino's unending quest to understand the play and he even takes to the streets of New York to ask passersby what, if any, significance Shakespeare has in their lives. These scenes are the most fascinating as we get to see the legendary Pacino strolling about New York like a Woody Allen character, as home on the streets of Manhattan as on any vaulted stage. Pacino is obviously first and foremost an actor, and, thus, it is sublimely appropriate that his first directorial effort is a film about finding the right way to interpret a play and all its roles. *Looking for Richard* is, in the end, a film about the art and craft of *acting*.

CHRISTOPHER REEVE

Best known for: Playing Superman in the movies, and, sadly, for ending up completely paralyzed from an unfortunate horse riding accident in the early 1990s.

Directorial debut: *In the Gloaming* (1997), a sensitive, tragic, and poignantly rendered telling of the story of a young man with AIDS (Robert Sean Leonard) who returns home to die. Reeve directed *In the Gloaming* from a wheelchair and yet, he did as good (and perhaps even better) a job than some directors who do not have to deal with such a devastating and prohibitive disability. The performances are uniformly superb and the narrative accurately portrays the emotional (and logistical—insurance problems, equipment and nursing needs, etc.) nightmare parents must go through as they watch one of their children get sicker and sicker and ultimately die. Glenn Close is incredible as the boy's mother. Bridget Fonda costars as the angry and bitter sister, David Straithairn is the closed-off father, and Whoopi Goldberg excels as the hospice nurse who helps Leonard (and the rest of the family) through his final days. Based on a short story by Alice Elliott Dark.

Martin Sheen

Best known for: A long career of wonderfully crafted and nuanced performances, both as a leading man and in supporting roles. Memorable Martin Sheen films include *Apocalypse Now* (1979), *The Dead Zone* (1983), *Wall Street* (1987), *The American President* (1995), and his directorial debut, *Cadence* (1989). (Not to mention his terrific work as President Josiah Bartlet on TV's *The West Wing*.) It should also be noted that another of Sheen's claims to fame is fathering two of our most popular younger actors, Charlie Sheen (who worked with his father in *Wall Street* and *Cadence*) and Emilio Estevez, plus daughter Renée, who also has a recurring role in *The West Wing*.

Directorial debut: *Cadence* (1989), the powerful story of an insubordinate soldier in the 1960s sentenced to serve time in an all-black stockade as his punishment. Martin Sheen plays the hard-assed sergeant whose job it is to whip the prisoner into submission; his son Charlie Sheen plays the soldier. Martin's son (and Charlie's brother) Ramon Estevez plays one of the prisoners. Laurence Fishburne is another of them.

Frank Sinatra

Best known for: A recording career that defines American popular music and an acting career that includes an Oscar. Sinatra was a seminal influence on an entire generation of singers, musicians, songwriters, and entertainers.

Directorial debut: *None but the Brave* (1965), a war drama about U.S. and Japanese soldiers who bond after they're both stranded on an island during World War II. Sinatra played a doctor in this decent, but unremarkable effort.

RINGO STARR

Best known for: Being a Beatle. Anything else Ringo has done during his career has not even come close to what he accomplished as one of the Fab Four.

Directorial debut: *Born to Boogie* (1972), a documentary about Marc Bolan and his band T Rex. Read what you will into the fact that this film was never released in the United States.

RIP TORN

Best known for: Lately? Playing Larry Sanders's seasoned producer Artie on the brilliant HBO series *The Larry Sanders Show* (now in reruns following a successful multiyear run on cable). Rip Torn is a Hollywood veteran, though, and is also known for memorable roles in such films as *The King of Kings* (1961), *The Man Who Fell to Earth* (1976), *A Shining Season* (1979), *Defending Your Life* (1991), and the enormously popular 1997 hit, *Men in Black*.

Directorial debut: *The Telephone* (1987), a woeful effort in which Whoopi Goldberg plays an unemployed actress with mental problems. Whoopi sued to prevent the film's release, but was unsuccessful. *The Telephone* was scripted by Harry Nilsson and Terry Southern and also starred Amy Wright, Elliot Gould, and John Heard.

- - - - - - - - - - - - - - - - - -

Bernardo Bertolucci asked me to do *The Sheltering Sky,* but I was pregnant with Dakota—I wasn't going to have an abortion to do a movie.

Melanie Griffith
Movieline, April 1999

- - - - - - - - - - - - - - - - - -

47 Terrific Christmas Movies

VCRs spin . . . are you listening?

1942 *Holiday Inn* Rival song-and-dance men work to turn a Connecticut farm into a holiday season inn. This is the movie that gave the world Irving Berlin's "White Christmas." (Bing Crosby, Fred Astaire.)

1945 *Christmas in Connecticut* Barbara Stanwyck stars as a magazine writer assigned to entertain a war veteran and her boss over the Christmas holidays. (Barbara Stanwyck, Dennis Morgan, Sydney Greenstreet, Reginald Gardiner, S. Z. Sakall.) (Arnold Schwarzenegger directed the TV remake.)

1946 *It's a Wonderful Life* Is this the ultimate Christmas movie? It just may be. It is shown countless times throughout the holiday season and is one of the most heartwarming and morally uplifting movies ever made. It isn't Christmas without at least one watching of this classic. (And stay away from the colorized version. With the magnificent black-and-white edition available, watching the colorized version is like drinking decaffeinated coffee: Why bother?) (James Stewart, Donna Reed, Lionel Barrymore, Thomas Mitchell, Ward Bond, Sheldon Leonard, Ellen Corby.)

1947 *Miracle on 34th Street* Is Kris Kringle really Santa Claus? This classic movie asks that question and leaves the answer up to you. (But we all know he is, don't we?) (Maureen O'Hara, John Payne, Edmund Gwenn, Gene Lockhart, Natalie Wood, Porter Hall, William Frawley.) (Forget the TV remake and the one in 1994 with Richard Attenborough.)

1951 *A Christmas Carol* This is the film that many consider the best adaptation of Dickens's classic tale. Leonard Maltin believes that this "[s]uperb film is too good to be shown only at Christmastime." (He's right.) (Alastair Sim, Jack Warner, Kathleen Harrison, Mervyn Jones, Hermione Baddeley.)

1954 *White Christmas* In this Irving Berlin songfest, two army buddies play at a Vermont inn to raise money for charity. (Bing Crosby, Danny Kaye, Rosemary Clooney.)

1961 *Babes in Toyland* A glorious Disney adaptation of Victor Herbert's timeless operetta. (Annette Funicello, Ray Bolger, Ed Wynn.)

1962 *Mr. Magoo's Christmas Carol* This five-star animated film features Mr. Magoo as Ebenezer Scrooge and includes songs by Jule Styne and Bob Merrill. Many consider this the best *animated* version of Dickens's classic to date. (Animated.)

1964 *Rudolph the Red-Nosed Reindeer* The wonderful Rankin/Bass stop-motion animation version of the classic Christmas story (that also boats a cameo from the Abominable Snowman!). (Animated.)

1965 *A Charlie Brown Christmas* The heartwarming story of Charlie Brown's attempt to save a forlorn little Christmas tree in the film in which the "Peanuts" crew made their animated debut. (Animated.)

1965 *How the Grinch Stole Christmas* The classic Christmas special based on the beloved Dr. Seuss book, narrated by Boris Karloff. (Animated.)

1969 *The Christmas Tree* During the holidays, a young boy's relationship with his wealthy father (William Holden) changes on discovering that the boy is terminally ill. (William Holden, Virna Lisi, Bourvil, Brook Fuller, Madeleine Damien.)

1970 *Scrooge* A charming musical adaptation of Dickens's *A Christmas Carol* with Albert Finney starring as old Ebenezer. (Albert Finney, Alec Guinness, Edith Evans, Kenneth More, Lawrence Naismith.)

1973 *A Dream for Christmas* A black minister moves his family from Arkansas to Los Angeles to work with an inner-city congregation in a church fated for destruction. (Hari Rhodes, Beah Richards, Lynn Hamilton, George Spell, Juanita Moore.)

1977 *A Flintstones Christmas* Fred, Wilma, Barney, Thelma, and the other denizens of Bedrock have an exciting and unpredictable holiday when Fred and Barney take over for an absent Santa. (Animated.)

1978 *A Christmas to Remember* An elderly farm couple take in their city-raised grandson for the holidays during the Depression. (Jason Robards, Eva Marie Saint, Joanne Woodward, George Perry, Bryan Englund.)

1979 *Christmas Lilies of the Field* In this heartwarming Christmas followup to the Oscar–nominated 1963 film, *Lilies of the Field*, Homer Smith returns to the chapel he built in the Arizona desert and is "persuaded" by Mother Maria to build a much-needed orphanage. (Billy Dee Williams, Maria Schell, Fay Hauser, Judith Piquet, Hanna Hertelendy.)

1980 *A Christmas Without Snow* A recently-divorced woman gets involved in a church choir at Christmas . . . and also ends up getting involved in the choir members's lives. (Michael Learned, John Houseman, Ramon Bieri, James Cromwell, Valerie Curtin.)

1980 *Yogi's First Christmas* Yogi and Boo-Boo come out of hibernation for their first Christmas ever to help save Jellystone Park from destruction for a new highway. (Animated.)

1983 *A Christmas Story* This is humorist Jean Shepherd's charming memoir of growing up in the 1940s and wanting a Red Ryder BB gun for Christmas. (Peter Billingsley, Darren McGavin, Melinda Dillon, Ian Petrella, Scott Schwartz.)

1983 *Trading Places* Eddie Murphy gets into the holiday spirit by pretending he's a legless war veteran. And that's just the *beginning* of this hilarious holiday movie. (Eddie Murphy, Dan Aykroyd, Ralph Bellamy, Don Ameche, Jamie Lee Curtis, Denholm Elliott.)

1984 *Gremlins* A wonderful black comedy set at Christmas and concerning a rather unusual (and excitable) Yuletide present. (Zach Galligan, Phoebe Cates, Hoyt Axton, Frances Lee McCain, Keye Luke, Judge Reinhold.)

1984 *The Night They Saved Christmas* Three kids try to save Santa's toy factory from destruction by an evil oil company in this wonderful film that features Art Carney as St. Nick. (Jaclyn Smith, Art Carney, Paul LeMat, Mason Adams, June Lockhart, Paul Williams.)

1985 *A Jetson Christmas Carol* Mr. Spaceley makes George Jetson work on Christmas Eve and the family wonders if their holiday plans are doomed. (Animated.)

1985 *One Magic Christmas* Santa Claus and a guardian angel (played by Harry Dean Stanton!) conspire to help a mom going through hard times regain the holiday spirit. (Mary Steenburgen, Gary Basaraba, Harry Dean Stanton, Arthur Hill.)

1985 *Santa Claus: The Movie* Dudley Moore plays an innocent elf named Patch who ends up involved with an evil toymaker. (Dudley Moore, John Lithgow, David Huddleston, Burgess Meredith, Judy Cornwell.)

1986 *Casper's First Christmas* Casper celebrates his first Christmas with his pals Yogi Bear, Quick Draw McGraw, and Huckleberry Hound. (Animated.)

1986 *The Family Circus Christmas* An animated film based on the doings of the beloved syndicated cartoon strip family and set during the Christmas season. (Animated.)

1987 *Miracle Down Under* This heartwarming Christmas tale about a small boy who helps a mean old skinflint regain his Christmas spirit is set in the Australian outback. (This film is also known as *Bushfire Mountain and the Christmas Visitor.*) (Dee Wallace, John Waters, Charles Tingwell, Bill Kerr, Andrew Ferguson.)

1987 *Planes, Trains, and Automobiles* Steve Martin wants nothing more than to get home for the holidays, and the irrepressible John Candy seems to be doing everything in his power to stop him! (Steve Martin, John Candy.)

1988 *Ernest Saves Christmas* Ernest tries to help Santa on Christmas Eve. Know wuddamean? (Jim Varney, Douglas Seale, Oliver Clark, Noelle Parker, Robert Lesser.)

1988 *Funny Farm* Chevy Chase moves to the rural, impossibly quaint, small town of Redbud to write his novel, but finds the bucolic life is not what he thought it would be. He and his wife try to use an "old-fashioned Christmas" as a ruse to sell their place and get back to the city. (Chevy Chase, Madolyn Smith.)

1988 *Roots: The Gift* It's Christmas 1770 and Kunta Kinte and Fiddler try to escape from slavery via the Underground Railroad. (Lou Gossett Jr., LeVar Burton.)

1988 *Scrooged* Bill Murray stars as the unlikeliest Scrooge ever in this contemporary all-star reworking of the Dickens story. (Bill

Murray, Karen Allen, John Forsythe, John Glover, Bobcat Goldthwait, David Johansen, Carol Kane, Robert Mitchum, Michael J. Pollard, Alfre Woodard, Jamie Farr, Robert Goulet, Buddy Hackett, John Houseman, Lee Majors, Pat McCormick, Brian Doyle-Murray, Mary Lou Retton.)

1988 *The Christmas Wife* In this excellent drama, a lonely widower "hires" a woman to be his companion over the Christmas holidays in a mountain cabin. (Jason Robards, Julie Harris, Don Francks, James Eckhouse, Patricia Hamilton, Deborah Grover.)

1989 *National Lampoon's Christmas Vacation* This hilarious movie pits the fervently-in-the-spirit Clark Griswold against the multifaceted problems and perils of the holiday season. (Chevy Chase, Beverly D'Angelo, Juliette Lewis, Johnny Galecki, Randy Quaid, Julia Louis-Dreyfus, Miriam Flynn, William Hickey, Mae Questel, E. G. Marshall, Doris Roberts, John Randolph, Diane Ladd.)

1989 *Prancer* A troubled girl finds an injured reindeer just before Christmas and helps the animal regain its health. (Sam Elliott, Rebecca Harrell, Cloris Leachman, Rutanya Alda, Abe Vigoda, Michael Constantine.)

1989 *When Harry Met Sally . . .* Harry and Sally love and fight through several years—and a couple of Christmases and New Years—together. (Meg Ryan, Billy Crystal, Carrie Fisher, Bruno Kirby, Steven Ford.)

1990 *Home Alone* Eight-year-old Kevin is inadvertently left "home alone" for Christmas and has to contend with two bungling burglars. (Macauley Culkin, Catherine O'Hara, Joe Pesci, Daniel Stern, John Heard, John Candy.)

1992 *Home Alone 2: Lost in New York* This time, Kevin spends Christmas in Manhattan—and so do the burglars! (Macauley Culkin, Catherine O'Hara, Joe Pesci, Daniel Stern, John Heard, John Candy.)

1992 *The Muppet Christmas Carol* Kermit and Miss Piggy do Dickens! (Michael Caine, The Muppets.)

1993 *Sleepless in Seattle* Tom Hanks and Meg Ryan are perfect together in this romantic comedy about a widower and the woman who hears him talk about his deceased wife on a radio program. (Tom Hanks, Meg Ryan, Bill Pullman, Ross Malinger, Rosie O'Donnell, Gaby Hoffmann, Rita Wilson, Rob Reiner.)

1994 *Little Women* An absolutely magnificent version of the Louisa May Alcott classic that takes the "little women" through a momentous Christmas season. (There were three earlier adaptations of the book—1933, 1949, 1978—to compare with and yet this one shines above them all.) (Winona Ryder, Susan Sarandon, Gabriel Byrne, Trini Alvarado, Samantha Mathis, Claire Danes, Kirsten Dunst, Christian Bale, Eric Stoltz, John Neville, Mary Wickes.)

1994 *The Santa Clause* Tim Allen plays a divorced dad who inadvertently causes Santa Claus's death when he frightens the old fellow and Santa falls off Allen's roof. Dad puts on the jolly guy's suit and begins to transform into Santa, first physically, and then, ultimately, spiritually and emotionally. A sentimental winner that became an instant annual Christmas classic. (Tim Allen, Judge Reinhold, Wendy Crewson, Eric Lloyd, Peter Boyle, Mary Gross.)

1995 *While You Were Sleeping* Sandra Bullock is at her most adorable as the (phony) fiancée who ends up becoming part of the family of her comatose heartthrob in this delightful romantic comedy that takes place during the Christmas season. (Sandra Bullock, Bill Pullman, Peter Gallagher, Jack Warden, Peter Boyle.)

1996 *Jingle All the Way* Ahnuld tries to do comedy. In this innocuous Yuletide comedy, Arnold Schwarzenegger plays a harried dad on a Christmas Eve mission to find his son the only toy he really wants for Christmas: A Turbo Man. Dubious hilarity ensues. (Arnold Schwarzenegger, Sinbad, Phil Hartman, Rita Wilson, Robert Conrad, Martin Mull, James Belushi, Harvey Korman.)

2000 *How the Grinch Stole Christmas* This Ron Howard–directed comedy was an enormous hit at the box office and boasted another astonishing performance by the versatile Jim Carrey. Based on the book by Dr. Seuss, the movie tells of the evil Grinch's attempt to steal Christmas from the lovable Who people, small folk who live in Whoville (which, as we all know from our childhoods) is inside a snowflake. (Jim Carrey, Jeffrey Tambor,

Taylor Momsen, Christine Baranski, Bill Irwin, Anthony Hopkins, Josh Ryan Evans, Molly Shannon.)

For Your Consideration . . .

THE "P" LIST

Al Pacino *Scarface* (1983); *Glengarry Glen Ross* (1992)

Chazz Palminteri *A Bronx Tale* (1993); *The Usual Suspects* (1995)

Gwyneth Paltrow *Seven* (1995); *Shakespeare in Love* (1998)

Anna Paquin *The Piano* (1993); *Amistad* (1997)

Mary-Louise Parker *Fried Green Tomatoes* (1991); *Boys on the Side* (1994)

Sarah Jessica Parker *Honeymoon in Vegas* (1992); *The First Wives Club* (1996)

Dolly Parton *9 to 5* (1980); *Steel Magnolias* (1989)

Mandy Patinkin *Yentl* (1983); *The Doctor* (1991)

Bill Paxton *Aliens* (1986); *Twister* (1996)

Christopher Penn *Reservoir Dogs* (1992); *True Romance* (1993)

Sean Penn *Dead Man Walking* (1995); *The Game* (1997)

Rosie Perez *Do the Right Thing* (1989); *It Could Happen to You* (1994)

Elizabeth Perkins *Big* (1988); *Avalon* (1990)

Joe Pesci *Raging Bull* (1980); *GoodFellas* (1990)

Lori Petty *Cadillac Man* (1990); *A League of Their Own* (1992)

Michelle Pfeiffer *Scarface* (1983); *The Witches of Eastwick* (1987)

Lou Diamond Phillips *La Bamba* (1987); *Courage Under Fire* (1996)

River Phoenix *Running on Empty* (1988); *Sneakers* (1992)

Bronson Pinchot *Risky Business* (1983); *True Romance* (1993)

Brad Pitt *Legends of the Fall* (1994); *Seven* (1995)

Oliver Platt *A Time to Kill* (1996); *Bulworth* (1998)

Kelly Preston *Twins* (1988); *Jerry Maguire* (1996)

Bill Pullman *While You Were Sleeping* (1995); *Independence Day* (1996)

- - - - - - - - - - - - - - - - -

True colors

No doubt about it: Joan Crawford was a genuine, unadulterated diva in her time, and modern poseurs could take a lesson from this tempestuous celluloid queen. For the 1964 ceremony, Crawford had the identical gown made for her in both black and white fabrics. Why? Because she had heard that Deborah Kerr, who was to present immediately before her, had looked at fabrics in both colors but no one knew which she had chosen to wear the night of the event. To make sure she would not follow Kerr in the same color dress, Crawford stood by backstage until she saw what Kerr was wearing and then she immediately dressed in the opposite color. And, for the record, Kerr wore white; Crawford (hurriedly) wore black.

- - - - - - - - - - - - - - - - -

Whacked! 7 Mob Movies and 1 Mob TV Series

There are a lot of movies out there about organized crime, wise guys, the Mafia, the Mob, drug cartels, and other bad boys who are extremely orderly. This is a look at eight of the all-time best.

1–3. *The Godfather series* (1972–1990) This series is the definitive cinematic statement on the Mafia, both as it exists here in the U.S and its roots in Italy. The first film, *The Godfather*, is an undeniable classic (it is ranked *number 3* on the AFI's list of the 100 greatest American movies of all time) and some of its greatest lines—"I'll make him an offer he can't refuse"; "Luca Brazzi sleeps with the fishes"; "Never go against the family"—have become part of our pop culture. Part II is equally brilliant and is one of those rare sequels (*Terminator 2* is another) that is as good as the original. Part III is less successful but still a worthwhile viewing experience.

4. *GoodFellas* (1990) Nobody does wiseguy movies like director and writer Martin Scorsese, and *GoodFellas* is unquestionably his Mob

magnum opus. Henry Hill (Ray Liotta) tells us at the beginning of *Goodfellas* that "As far back as I can remember I always wanted to be a gangster." And become a gangster he does as the movie takes us through his beginnings running errands for the wiseguys, master-minding truck heists, getting addicted to cocaine, and ending up turning State's evidence, ratting out his wiseguy cohorts, and ending up in the government's Witness Protection Program. Each scene in *GoodFellas* is like an exquisitely constructed minimovie, some of the most memorable being Tommy's (Joe Pesci) "I amuse you?" scene; Henry's pistol-whipping defense of his girlfriend Karen (Lorraine Bracco); the Billy Batts scenes ("Now go home and get your fucking shine box"); the late night dinner with Tommy's mother (played by Scorsese's real mother); the incredible tracking shot that takes Henry and Karen from the street outside the Copacabana, through the kitchen, to a front row table, without a cut; and Jimmy's (Robert De Niro) shakedown of Morrie for the week's vig (interest). (Not to mention the fabulous names of some of the wiseguys, like Pete the Killer, Fat Andy, Frankie the Wop, Freddie No Nose, Sally Balls, Nicky Eyes, Jimmy Two Times ["I'm gonna get the papers, get the papers."], and, of course, Johnny Roastbeef.) Alternately shockingly violent and hilariously funny, *GoodFellas* was based on a true story by Nicholas Pileggi and finds Scorsese and his cast at their best.

5. *Casino* (1995) This could be subtitled, "How the Mob Built Las Vegas 101." Scorsese, De Niro, and Pesci revisit an area they know very well, and this time they bring along Sharon Stone, in what might be the best performance of her career.

6. *A Bronx Tale* (1993) Robert De Niro made his directorial debut with this powerful Mob drama written by star Chazz Palminteri (and based on his play of the same name). A nine-year-old Italian-American boy named Calogero witnesses a Mob hit and doesn't rat. Mob boss Sonny (Palminteri) takes the kid under his wing (he's already connected at the age of nine!) and it isn't long before he is seduced by the power and glamour of Sonny and his crew. The kid's father (played by De Niro), a low-key, hard-working bus driver, is totally against his son's involvement with Sonny, but as the boy grows up, he finds he has less and less influence on the way his son thinks. Ultimately, hard choices—by all involved—must be made. Palminteri is superb; De Niro's direction, confident and engaging.

7. ***Donnie Brasco* (1996)** Johnny Depp plays an FBI agent working undercover in the Mob as Donnie "The Jeweler" Brasco. He hooks up with Lefty (Al Pacino) and immediately reports to his superiors that he's got "his hooks" in him. Lefty takes Donnie under his wing and Donnie instantly becomes "connected." Lefty explains to him that introducing Donnie as "a friend of mine" means he's connected; if he had introduced him as "a friend of ours," it would mean he was a "made guy." Even though this flick runs hot and cold in terms of pacing, it is based on a true story (as were *Good-Fellas* and *Casino*) and Depp and Pacino's performances keep interest at a peak. Is *Donnie Brasco* worth seeing? Fuhgeddaboudit!

Must-Whack TV

8. ***The Sopranos* (1999–, HBO)** Mob boss Tony Soprano (James Gandolfini in a star-making performance) starts having anxiety attacks and when his MRI is negative, he starts seeing psychiatrist Dr. Melfi (Lorraine Bracco) for help in dealing with whatever anxieties and stresses are causing him to pass out. This brilliant original HBO series has the same premise as the 1999 Billy Crystal/Robert De Niro comedy *Analyze This*, but like *GoodFellas*, even though there may be laughs in *The Sopranos*, this series sure as hell couldn't be described in *TV Guide* with the word "comedy."

The Sopranos are family people: They attend their kids' soccer games and musical recitals, and Tony's wife Carmella (HBO's *Oz's* Edie Falco) is involved with the community and their church. But Tony also whacks guys who deserve it and has to vie with a power-hungry uncle for control of the New Jersey "business." And then there's Tony's mother, a manipulative shrew who is not averse to putting out a contract on her own son's life. Like I said, there may be funny moments in *The Sopranos*, but this ain't no sitcom. *The Sopranos* received rave reviews and excellent ratings in its first season and it was wisely renewed for three more seasons. If the quality of *The Sopranos* remains consistent (and there's no reason why it shouldn't considering the talent both in front of and behind the camera) then the real crime would be if *this show* got whacked. If you don't have HBO you're missing a great series.

"Directed by Alan Smithee"
A List of 45 Hollywood Embarrassments

The question "Who ought to be boss?" is like asking "Who ought to be the tenor in the quartet?" Obviously, the man who can sing tenor.

—HENRY FORD

Who is Alan Smithee?

Alan Smithee is a prolific director with dozens of films and TV shows to his credit. He has been working in Hollywood since the mid-1950s and continues to churn out both feature films and TV productions to this day.

Smithee is a recluse, however: He has never granted an interview nor does a photograph of the busy auteur exist. Alan Smithee makes J. D. Salinger and Thomas Pynchon look as outgoing as Charles Nelson Reilly during the years when Johnny Carson hosted *The Tonight Show.*

Smithee never has been to a Hollywood premiere and yet his movies play all over the world.

Who is Alan Smithee?

Alan Smithee is nobody, because Alan Smithee does not exist.

"Alan Smithee" is a pseudonym the Directors Guild of America allows its members to use when they ultimately decide they do not want their name to appear on a film which they directed.

There are many reasons why a director would choose not to be associated with a film; the main one being that he is mortally embarrassed by the finished product. (Interestingly, it seems there has yet to be a female director who opted for the "Smithee" credit.) Perhaps the performances were so atrocious, he couldn't salvage the film. Perhaps the script went through so many changes, he couldn't salvage the film. Perhaps the studio intrusively (and detrimentally) stuck their nose into the production of the film, and he couldn't salvage the film.

Or maybe *all* of that happened and the end result was that the movie just plain *sucked.*

Whatever the reason, a director has the option of donning the "Cloak of Smithee" when he sees fit, and this feature looks at some of those who chose to do just that, and the works from which they so desperately wanted to disassociate themselves.

This chapter also looks at directors who released a film under their own name and then chose to "go Smithee" when a butchered version of the film appeared on TV or on airplanes. I have tried to provide the real name of the director when I could; for some films, though, this info simply does not exist in any of the standard industry references.

20 Feature Films

1. *Fade-In* (1968) (really Jud Taylor) A film editor (Barbara Loden) has an affair with a man she meets (Burt Reynolds) while working on location. After a brief theatrical release; it ultimately came out on video as *Iron Cowboy.* (Reynolds had not yet made *Deliverance* when he did *Fade-In.*)

2. *Death of a Gunfighter* (1969) (really Robert Totten and Don Siegel) A town tries to do away with its no-good sheriff (Richard Widmark) who refuses to be fired. Lena Horne is the love interest.

3. *The Barking Dog* (1978) None of the standard film references provide any info whatsoever about this one. Must have been a real "dog," eh? (Sorry.)

4. *Stitches* (1985) (really Rod Holcomb) Medical students play practical jokes with corpses and body parts. This loser starred Eddie Albert and Parker Stevenson, who was hot at the time from his recurring role on the TV series *Falcon Crest.*

5. *Appointment With Fear* (1985) (really Razmi Thomas) An insane asylum inmate (who conveniently happens to be in a coma) is the chief suspect in a murder case.

6. *Morgan Stewart's Coming Home* (1987) (really Paul Aaron and Terry Windsor) A politician brings his son (Jon Cryer) home from boarding school to present a wholesome family image for an upcoming race . . . but sonny boy refuses to play along. Wacky mayhem ensues.

7. *Let's Get Harry* (1987) (really Stuart Rosenberg) A soldier of fortune (Robert Duvall) leads a bunch of Americans on a mission to South America to rescue their kidnapped friend (Mark Harmon). Also starred Gary Busey. Decent cast, but excessively lame script. If you blinked, you missed the theatrical release of this stinker.

8. *Ghost Fever* (1987) (really Lee Madden) In this *Ghostbusters*-rip-off, two idiot cops (Sherman Hemsley and Luis Avalos) try to evict a bunch of ghosts from a haunted mansion. Where's Weezy when you need her?

9. *I Love N.Y.* (1988) (really Gianni Bozzacchi) Scott Baio plays a young photographer in love with a renowned actor's daughter in this disaster of a romantic comedy.

10. *The Shrimp on the Barbie* (1990) (really Michael Gottlieb) Cheech Marin plays a guy from L.A. who relocates to Australia where he is hired to impersonate the fiancé of a wealthy heiress . . . just to piss off her father. One can't help but see this as a (failed) attempt to cash in on the (ultimately short-lived) "Down Under" craze started in 1986 with *Crocodile Dundee* and its 1988 sequel.

11. *Solar Crisis* (1990) (really Richard Sarafian) In the year 2050, the sun starts sending out solar flares that threaten to incinerate the earth. A stalwart team of scientists must save the planet.

12. *Bloodsucking Pharaohs of Pittsburgh* (1990) (really Dean Tschetter) How great a title is this, eh? Cannibals terrorize Pittsburgh. Sounds good to me! But director Tschetter apparently did not want to be associated with this camp spin on *Night of the Living Dead*.

13. *Gypsy Angels* (1994) This movie starred *Wheel of Fortune*'s letter-turner Vanna White and is remembered today for the fetching Vanna's very, very, *very* brief topless scene. (You saw more in her *Playboy* lingerie photo spread.) Vanna plays a stripper who tries to help an injured stunt pilot recover. Rent this if you like planes.

14. *Raging Angels* (1995) A rock band is a front for a satanic cult in this stinker that culminates in a good vs. evil battle over downtown Los Angeles.

15. *Hellraiser: Bloodline* (1996) (really Kevin Yagher) This could also be called *Pinhead: A Biography*. But even die-hard Clive Barker/

Hellraiser fans weren't thrilled with this final installment in the popular horror series.

16. *Firehouse* (1997)

17. *Sub Down* (1997) (really Gregg Champion)

18. *Illusion Infinity* (1998)

19. *To Light the Darkness* (1999) (really Vance Kotrla)

20. *Starforce* (2000)

6 Edited Versions

It's a real pity that the acclaimed directors of these six wonderful films had to resort to the Smithee pseudonym because of the unconscionable butchering of their movies for venues other than the theater. Let's face it: Certain films contain absolutely necessary violence, profanity, or nudity. These elements are integral to an honest rendering of the writer's and director's vision. Many films are extremely intense and often brilliant in their final form, and yet some schlub editor can take his or her scissors to the final, meticulously crafted product and arbitrarily slash and burn at will, eliminating anything that might offend the oh-so-delicate sensibilities of the network TV audience or the passengers of an airplane.

Well, the hell with that, I say. Don't give these movies to these butchers if they won't run them the way they were originally made. Let the network TV watchers *do without.* If they want to see *Heat,* let them rent it. It is an *artistic crime* to do to some of these films what the networks censors do to them. And what's most aggravating is the hypocrisy of the Big Three networks. When Steven Spielberg sold TV rights of *Schindler's List* to NBC, he sold it *as is:* no cuts, and limited interruptions. (And this was non-negotiable.) Now, remember that *Schindler's List* is a movie that has full frontal male and female nudity, incredibly graphic scenes of murder and brutal violence, countless scenes of children in constant peril, and more "fucks" uttered than can be counted. And guess what? The network said, fine, okay, no problem, and they aired the acclaimed movie—*twice*—the way it was made—in its theatrical, R-rated version. And no one squawked.

The republic did not collapse, and the streets were not flooded with rioting citizens stirred into a frenzy by what they had seen on their TV.

Imagine that. Perhaps it's time that the networks start giving the American viewing public a little credit?

1. *Backtrack* (1989) (really Dennis Hopper—European release only) For some reason, this film was cut up against Hopper's wishes and released in Europe as *Catchfire*. That version was (wisely) credited to Smithee.

2. *The Guardian* (1990) (really William Friedkin—butchered TV version only) This is a perfect example of the kind of film the networks should not buy for broadcast. This movie is about a couple who unwittingly hires a baby-sitter who happens to be a fanatical Druid intent on feeding her infant charge to a tree. Human sacrifice and infanticide on network TV? What were they thinking?

3. *Scent of a Woman* (1992) (really Martin Brest—drastically cut airplane version only) A wonderful film that won a slew of awards gets massacred into a G-rated abomination so it can be played on an airplane. Sheesh. No wonder Brest opted for Smithee for this version.

4. *Thunderheart* (1992) (really Michael Apted—TV version only) This brilliant film about a murder on a Sioux reservation contained violence and language that were edited out for network broadcast. This film was coproduced by Robert De Niro and was praised for its realistic attention to detail regarding Sioux customs and culture. It was based in part on an acclaimed documentary about Indian activist Leonard Peltier called *Incident at Oglala*. Critics were almost unanimous in their praise of the film . . . until the network "editors" got their hands on it.

5. *Rudy* (1993) (really David Anspaugh—butchered TV version only) This warm and funny football movie was originally rated PG. What in the world could the network censors have found so offensive that they had to butcher it to the point where director Anspaugh went the Smithee route?

6. *Heat* (1995) (really Michael Mann—butchered TV version only) This film is a perfect example of the kind of movie that simply does not belong on mainstream, network TV . . . if they are going to cut it to ribbons and make it unrecognizable when compared to its stunning, original version. What's next? The story of Jesus with the crucifixion eliminated because it's too violent?

18 Made-for-TV Movies and TV Episodes

All of these TV movies or episodes of TV series were directed by Alan Smithee for one reason of another. Why? There are probably many reasons, some of which could include displeasure with the final script/performances/editing/whatever; an unwillingness to be associated with the subject (the O.J. movie might fall into this category); or just a desire to disassociate from TV work completely for whatever reason.

Some of these productions (especially the later TV movies) are probably relatively easy to catch some night on a cable station or perhaps even on video. The early stuff (*Mrs. Jarvis, Fade-In,* etc.) might be more difficult to find, but all are worth watching if only to try and guess what it was that brought Alan Smithee out of his celluloid closet for these works.

1. *The Indiscreet Mrs. Jarvis* (1955)
2. *Fade-In* (1968) (really Jud Taylor)
3. *The Challenge* (1970)
4. *City in Fear* (1980) (really Jud Taylor)
5. *Fun and Games* (1980) (really Paul Bogart)
6. *Moonlight* (1982) (really Jackie Cooper and Rod Holcomb)
7. The *Twilight Zone* TV series episode "Paladin of the Lost Hour" (1985)
8. The *MacGyver* TV series episode "MacGyver" (1985)
9. The *MacGyver* TV series episode "The Heist" (1985)
10. *Dalton: Code of Vengeance II* (1986)
11. *Riviera* (1987) (really John Frankenheimer)
12. *The Owl* (1991)
13. *Bay City Story* (1992)
14. *Call of the Wild* (1993) (really Michael Uno)
18. *Fatal Charm* (1992) (Fritz Kiersch)
15. *Birds II: The Land's End* (1994) (really Rick Rosenthal)
16. *While Justice Sleeps* (1994)

17. *The O.J. Simpson Story* (1994) (Jerrold Freedman)
18. *The Disciples* (1999) (Kirk Wong)

In a League of Its Own

An Alan Smithee Film: Burn, Hollywood, Burn (1997) (really Arthur Hiller) This movie made several "Worst of" year-end lists and probably for good reason. Successful Hollywood screenwriter Joe Eszterhas (*Basic Instinct, Sliver, Showgirls, Jade*) scripted this attack on the mindlessness of Tinseltown, shooting for irony and satire, but achieving neither.

A British director played by Eric Idle resorts to stealing the negative of his latest film because he is extremely displeased with the results after a meddling producer (Ryan O'Neal) gets his hands on it and butchers it in editing. Why does he have to steal the negative? Because this director's real name is "Alan Smithee" and since this is the name the Directors Guild of America uses for disputed films (which Idle's film in the movie *is* . . . stay with me, now), the movie will be released with his name on it—even though it's *not* his name, if you follow this logic.

In a bizarre twist of real-world events, director Arthur Hiller actually removed his name from the film after producer Eszterhas edited the movie in a way with which Hiller was not pleased. Was this a publicity stunt to promote the "art imitates life imitates art" subtext of the film? Perhaps.

Whatever the truth though, the film (which also starred Coolio, Sandra Bernhard, and Richard Jeni) is told in mock documentary form and is almost unwatchable, except for the parade of Hollywood big shot cameos, including movie stars Sylvester Stallone, Whoopi Goldberg, Jackie Chan, and Billy Bob Thornton; celeb interviewer Larry King; writer Dominick Dunne, producer Robert Evans, and screenwriter Shane Black (*Lethal Weapon* and *The Last Action Hero*).

So let's sum up: *An Alan Smithee Film* is a movie about a director named Alan Smithee who wants to pull his name off a fictitious movie. The *real* movie is ultimately credited to the pseudonymous director "Alan Smithee," because the *real* director pulled his name off the project. Only in Hollywood, eh?

- - - - - - - - - - - - - - -

The weird thing in Hollywood is they'll still smile at you, but the bottom line is they're thinking: You prick, you scumbag, I hope you choke on your own shit! Why don't you gag on your own genitals?

Robin Williams
Playboy, January 1992

- - - - - - - - - - - - - - -

46 Blaxploitation Movies (and 2 Honorable Mentions)

Fur hats, high heels (for men), Day-Glo jackets, Cadillacs, and "Mr. T"–inspired jewelry.

Let us all offer thanks that this trend in movies is now over.

1970

Cotton Comes to Harlem

1971

Shaft
*Sweet Sweetback's Baadasssss
   Song*

1972

Across 110th Street
Blacula
Shaft's Big Score
Slaughter
Superfly
Top of the Heap

1973

Black Caesar
Black Vampire
Blackenstein
Cleopatra Jones
Coffy
Detroit 9000
Hell up in Harlem
The Mack
Savage!
Scream Blacula Scream
Shaft in Africa
Slaughter's Big Ripoff
Superfly T.N.T.

1974

Black Belt Jones
Black Godfather
Foxy Brown
No Way Back
Three the Hard Way
Truck Turner

1975

Black Gestapo
Bucktown
Cleopatra Jones and the Casino of Gold
Dolemite
Friday Foster
Let's Do It Again
Mean Johnny Barrows
Sheba, Baby
Soul Vengeance

1976

Avenging Disco Godfather
Dolomite 2: Human Tornado
Dr. Black, Mr. Hyde
Hot Potato
J.D.'s Revenge

1977

The Guy From Harlem
Monkey Hustle

1982

One Down, Two to Go!

1983

Big Score

HONORABLE MENTION TO . . .

Doctor Detroit (1983)
Jackie Brown (1998)

For Your Consideration . . .

THE "Q" LIST

Dennis Quaid *Enemy Mine* (1985); *Flesh + Bone* (1993)
Randy Quaid The *National Lampoon Vacation* series (1983–1996); *LBJ: The Early Years* (1988)

- - - - - - - - - - - - - - - - -

Unless, of course, she was forced to attend the ceremony, too.

All her protests that she had been coerced and threatened into making the movie notwithstanding, *Deep Throat* star Linda Lovelace must have been at least a little bit favorably disposed toward the movie and her participation in it: She attended the 1973 Oscars ceremony decked out in a white lace dress and wide-brimmed hat, arriving in a coach drawn by two white horses.

- - - - - - - - - - - - - - - - -

Oscar Upsets?
15 Best Picture Academy Awards
That Might Raise Eyebrows Today

One has to wonder what some Academy voters are thinking when they make their picks. *In the Heat of the Night* is a great picture, but did it deserve to beat *The Graduate,* a film the American Film Institute ranked as Number 7 on their list of the 100 Greatest American Films? (*In the Heat of the Night* did not even make the Top 100.) Should *Patton* have beaten *M*A*S*H?* Should *Ordinary People* have beaten *Raging Bull?* And most glaringly, should *Rocky* have beaten *All the President's Men, Network,* and *Taxi Driver?*

Here is a look at fifteen Academy Award Best Picture Oscars that, when viewed with 20/20 hindsight, give pause, to say the least.

1. In 1941, *How Green Was My Valley* beat *Citizen Kane.*

2. In 1956, *Around the World in 80 Days* beat *Giant* and *The Ten Commandments.*

3. In 1961, *West Side Story* beat *The Hustler* and *Judgment at Nuremburg.*

4. In 1964, *My Fair Lady* beat *Dr. Strangelove* and *Zorba the Greek.*

5. In 1967, *In the Heat of the Night* beat *The Graduate* and *Guess Who's Coming to Dinner.*

6. In 1970, *Patton* beat *M*A*S*H* and *Five Easy Pieces.*

7. In 1971, *The French Connection* beat *A Clockwork Orange* and *The Last Picture Show.*

8. In 1973, *The Sting* beat *The Exorcist.*

9. In 1976, *Rocky* beat *All the President's Men, Network,* and *Taxi Driver.*

10. In 1979, *Kramer vs. Kramer* beat *All That Jazz, Apocalypse Now, Breaking Away,* and *Norma Rae.*

11. In 1980, *Ordinary People* beat *Raging Bull* and *The Elephant Man.*

12. In 1981, *Chariots of Fire* beat *Reds.*

13. In 1990, *Dances With Wolves* beat *GoodFellas.*

14. In 1992, *Unforgiven* beat *A Few Good Men* and *Scent of a Woman.*

15. In 1996, *The English Patient* beat *Fargo, Jerry Maguire,* and *Shine.*

---

5. Lighten up. Stars should stop taking themselves so seriously. Pretend it's the Golden Globes, and relax.... 7. Enough of the Academy. We never again want to hear from the Academy president—whoever he is—or industry lobbyist Jack Valenti, either.

TV critic **Matt Roush**
(from "10 Ways to Fix the Oscars")
TV Guide, April 10, 1999

The Feature Film Debuts of 23 Best Actress Academy Award Winners

1. **Julie Andrews** (*Mary Poppins,* 1964)

   Debut *Mary Poppins* (1964), directed by Robert Stevenson; with Dick Van Dyke, Ed Wynn, Hermione Baddeley, David Tomlinson, Glynis Johns.

   Julie Andrews certainly got her movie career off to an auspicious start. She won an Academy Award for her film *debut*, playing the magical nanny Mary Poppins who changes the lives of everyone she meets in this Disney classic. How does one follow such an opening act? A year later (after her equally winning *The Americanization of Emily*) Andrews scored again—big time—with her performance as Maria Von Trapp in *The Sound of Music* for which she won a Golden Globe Award and received a Best Actress Oscar nomination.

2. **Anne Bancroft** (*The Miracle Worker,* 1962)

   Debut *Don't Bother to Knock* (1952), directed by Roy Ward; with Richard Widmark, Marilyn Monroe, Elisha Cook Jr., Jim Backus, Lurene Tuttle, Jeanne Cagney, Donna Corcoran.

   Anne Bancroft made her film debut as Richard Widmark's girlfriend in this Marilyn Monroe drama. Monroe plays an unstable baby-sitter who has a liaison with Widmark. They are interrupted by his daughter (Bancroft) and Monroe decides to kill the girl.

3. **Ingrid Bergman** (*Gaslight,* 1944, and *Anastasia,* 1956)

   Debut *The Count of the Old Town* (1934), directed by Edvin Adolphson and Sigurd Wallen; with Edvin Adolphson, Sigurd Wallen, Valdemar Dahlquist.

   This adaptation of a Swedish play by Arthur and Siegfried Fischer featured Bergman as a young virgin seduced by a mysterious stranger.

4. **Cher** (*Moonstruck,* 1987)

   Debut *Wild on the Beach* (1965), directed by Maury Dexter; with Sonny Bono.

Cher played herself—i.e., one half of the then-hot Sonny and Cher singing duo—in this lame beach movie. She followed this with the equally forgettable *Good Times* in 1967. Cher would eschew the movies until 1982 when she returned to the silver screen with a wonderful performance in *Come Back to the Five and Dime, Jimmy Dean, Jimmy Dean.*

5. **Olivia De Havilland** (*To Each His Own*, 1946, and *The Heiress*, 1949)

    Debut *A Midsummer Night's Dream* (1935), directed by Max Reinhardt; with James Cagney, Dick Powell, Joe E. Brown, Hugh Herbert, Ian Hunter, Mickey Rooney, Victor Jory, Arthur Treacher, Billy Barty.

    Shakespeare, of course. James Cagney and Mickey Rooney costarred. Seriously.

6. **Sally Field** (*Norma Rae*, 1979 and *Places in the Heart*, 1984)

    Debut *The Way West* (1967), directed by Andrew V. McLaglen; with Kirk Douglas, Robert Mitchum, Richard Widmark, Lola Albright, Michael Witney, Stubby Kaye, Jack Elam.

    Field made her debut in this awful adaptation of the Pulitzer Prize–winning novel by A. B. Guthrie Jr. The talented actress would have to wait until 1976 and her performance in *Sybil* to garner the fame she deserved.

7. **Jane Fonda** (*Klute*, 1971, and *Coming Home*, 1978)

    Debut *Tall Story* (1960), directed by Joshua Logan; with Anthony Perkins, Ray Walston, Marc Connelly, Anne Jackson, Tom Laughlin.

    Fonda plays a cheerleader enamored of Anthony Perkins. *Psycho* appeared the same year. Guess she hadn't seen it, eh?

8. **Jodie Foster** (*The Silence of the Lambs*, 1991, and *The Accused*, 1988)

    Debut *Napoleon and Samantha* (1972), directed by Bernard McEveety; with Johnny Whitaker, Michael Douglas, Will Geer, Henry Jones.

    A Disney adventure about an orphan, a college student, a pet lion, and Samantha (Foster), all of whom run away from home.

9. **Audrey Hepburn** (*Roman Holiday*, 1953)

   Debut *Roman Holiday* (1953), directed by William Wyler; with Gregory Peck, Eddie Albert, Tullio Carminati.

   Hepburn plays a princess who pretends to be a commoner and has a romance with reporter Gregory Peck. For forty years this Best Screenplay Oscar winner was credited to Ian McLellan Hunter, who acted as the "front" for the blacklisted real writer, Dalton Trumbo. AMPAS awarded Trumbo a posthumous Oscar in 1993. (Even though *Roman Holiday* is considered Hepburn's film debut, she had a brief cameo as a cigarette girl in *The Lavender Hill Mob* [1951] when she was a mere lass of twenty-two, as well as a few other forgettable roles.)

10. **Katharine Hepburn** (*On Golden Pond*, 1981; *The Lion in Winter*, 1968; *Guess Who's Coming to Dinner*, 1967; and *Morning Glory*, 1933)

    Debut *A Bill of Divorcement* (1932), directed by George Cukor; with John Barrymore, Billie Burke, Henry Stephenson, David Manners, Paul Cavanagh, Elizabeth Patterson.

    Hepburn played Barrymore's daughter in this drama about a World War I vet who returns home after a stint in a mental hospital. When Hepburn's mother divorces her husband, she ends up taking care of her father and finally getting to know him.

11. **Helen Hunt** (*As Good As It Gets*, 1997)

    Debut *Rollercoaster* (1977), directed by James Goldstone; with George Segal, Richard Widmark, Timothy Bottoms, Henry Fonda, Susan Strasberg, Harry Guardino.

    Hunt's first theatrical film was this melodramatic disaster film about, duh, a sabotaged rollercoaster.

12. **Holly Hunter** (*The Piano*, 1994)

    Debut *The Burning* (1981), directed by Tony Maylam; with Brian Matthews, Leah Ayres, Brian Backer, Larry Joshua, Jason Alexander, Ned Eisenberg, Garrick Glenn, Carolyn Houlihan, Fisher Stevens, Lou David.

    Friday the 13th spurred many imitators, some good, some not so, as evidenced by this lame slasher flick set—where else?—at a summer camp. Mayhem ensues. (Good Tom Savini gore effects though.)

13. **Diane Keaton** (*Annie Hall,* 1977)

    Debut *Lovers and Other Strangers* (1970), directed by Cy Howard; with Gig Young, Bea Arthur, Bonnie Bedelia, Anne Jackson, Harry Guardino, Michael Brandon, Richard Castellano, Cloris Leachman, Anne Meara.

    A young couple decides to get married—after the two have already lived together for over a year. There are some very funny moments in this film based on a play by Renée Taylor and Joseph Bologna. Its song "For All We Know" won an Oscar.

14. **Grace Kelly** (*The Country Girl,* 1954)

    Debut *Fourteen Hours* (1951), directed by Henry Hathaway; with Paul Douglas, Richard Basehart, Barbara Bel Geddes, Debra Paget, Agnes Moorehead, Howard da Silva.

    A guy threatens to jump off a building ledge. A genuinely suspenseful thriller presented almost as a pseudodocumentary.

15. **Jessica Lange** (*Blue Sky,* 1994)

    Debut *King Kong* (1976), directed by John Guillermin; with Jeff Bridges, Charles Grodin, Rene Auberjonois, John Randolph, Ed Lauter, John Agar.

    This tepid Dino DeLaurentiis remake of the 1933 Fay Wray classic marks the film debut of Lange, who plays the bimbette "Dwan" (you know, like Dawn but with two letters reversed?), who at one point asks hero Jeff Bridges, "Did you ever meet anyone before whose life was saved by *Deep Throat?*" It seems that Dwan refused to watch a below-decks screening of the porno film on the doomed yacht where the action takes place and thus, she was on deck when the ship went down. Jessica Lange was flagrantly wasted in *King Kong.* Her talent was hard to miss, though, and she later went on to such classic films (and performances) as *All That Jazz, The Postman Always Rings Twice, Frances, Tootsie, The Music Box,* and *Cape Fear.*

16. **Shirley MacLaine** (*Terms of Endearment,* 1983)

    Debut *The Trouble With Harry* (1955), directed by Alfred Hitchcock; with John Forsythe, Edmund Gwenn, Mildred Natwick, Mildred Dunnock, Royal Dano.

    A young boy finds a dead body in a small town and no one knows who killed him or what to do with the corpse. This dark comedy is one of Hitchcock's funniest (yes, funniest) films, and MacLaine shines in her feature debut.

17. **Frances McDormand** (*Fargo*, 1996)
     Debut *Blood Simple* (1985), directed by Joel Coen; with John Getz, M. Emmet Walsh, Dan Hedaya, Samm-Art Williams.

     McDormand debuted in this noir thriller about a cuckolded hubby who hires a scumbag private detective to kill his wife and her lover. The *Fargo* actress (married to director Joel Coen) excelled, and then went on to another offbeat winner, *Raising Arizona* (1987), but she was at her absolute best in *Fargo*—one of the all-time great American films—as the pregnant police chief Marge Gunderson. You betcha.

18. **Susan Sarandon** (*Dead Man Walking*, 1995)
     Debut *Joe* (1970), directed by John G. Avildsen; with Peter Boyle, Dennis Patrick, Audrey Caire, Patrick McDermott.

     Sarandon played a hippie whose father murders her druggie boyfriend. Peter Boyle plays a hardhat bigot who discovers the murder and then blackmails the dad. This was an impressive debut for a gifted actress who gave an Oscar-winning performance in *Dead Man Walking* (1995).

19. **Sissy Spacek** (*Coal Miner's Daughter*, 1995)
     Debut *Prime Cut* (1972), directed by Michael Ritchie; with Lee Marvin, Gene Hackman, Angel Thompson, Gregory Walcott.

     The future "Carrie" made her debut in this trashy crime melodrama that one film critic described as an "orgy of drug trafficking, prostitution, extortion, loan-sharking, fisticuffs and gangsters." He was right.

20. **Meryl Streep** (*Sophie's Choice*, 1982)
     Debut *Julia* (1977), directed by Fred Zinnemann; with Jane Fonda, Jason Robards, Vanessa Redgrave, Maximilian Schell, Hal Holbrook, Rosemary Murphy, Lisa Pelikan.

     Streep's debut feature film performance was as Anne Marie in this gripping adaptation of Lillian Hellman's fictional memoir *Pentimento*. Fonda was amazing as Hellmann; Redgrave played her childhood friend Julia. The story revolves around Hellman's attempt to smuggle money into Germany during World War II to help her friend. Redgrave won an Oscar; Streep's next movie was the magnificent *The Deer Hunter.*

21. **Barbra Streisand** (*Funny Girl,* 1968)

Debut *Funny Girl* (1968), directed by William Wyler; with Omar Sharif, Walter Pidgeon, Kay Medford, Anne Francis.

Like Julie Andrews and Audrey Hepburn before her, Barbra Streisand won an Academy Award for her debut feature film performance in *Funny Girl,* the story of comedian Fanny Brice and her success with the Ziegfeld Follies. Streisand previously had played Brice in the Broadway musical of it. (Streisand also would play her in the 1975 sequel, *Funny Lady.* Omar Sharif returned briefly for the sequel as well as gambler Nick Arnstein. Great songs in both.)

22. **Elizabeth Taylor** (*Who's Afraid of Virginia Woolf?*, 1966, and *Butterfield 8,* 1960)

Debut *There's One Born Every Minute* (1942), directed by Harold Young; with Hugh Herbert, Tom Brown, Peggy Moran, Guy Kibbee, Gus Schilling, Edgar Kennedy, Carl "Alfalfa" Switzer.

Liz played the ten-year-old daughter of a wacky dad in this lame family comedy about the father's "adventures" running a pudding company. Eighteen years after this inauspicious debut, she would win the Oscar for *Butterfield 8.*

23. **Joanne Woodward** (*The Three Faces of Eve,* 1957)

Debut *Count Three and Pray* (1955), directed by George Sherman; with Van Heflin, Raymond Burr, Nancy Kulp.

Woodward played an orphan in this post–Civil War drama about a fiery pastor whose influence on his new flock is not always good.

■ ■ ■ ■ ■ ■ ■ ■ ■ ■ ■ ■ ■ ■ ■

Hollywood is interested in twenty-seven, not forty. It's something I never wanted to believe was true. And I don't understand why that should be. As you get older, you get better as an actress. I have.

Melanie Griffith
Movieline, April 1999

■ ■ ■ ■ ■ ■ ■ ■ ■ ■ ■ ■ ■ ■ ■

For Your Consideration . . .

THE "R" LIST

Robert Redford *All the President's Men* (1976); *Sneakers* (1992)

Christopher Reeve The *Superman* series (1978–1987); *Above Suspicion* (1995)

Keanu Reeves *Speed* (1994); *The Matrix* (1999)

Rob Reiner *This Is Spinal Tap* (1984); *Primary Colors* (1998)

Judge Reinhold *Fast Times at Ridgemont High* (1982); The *Beverly Hills Cop* series (1984–1994)

Paul Reiser *Diner* (1982); *Aliens* (1986)

Burt Reynolds *Semi-Tough* (1977); *Boogie Nights* (1997)

Ving Rhames *Pulp Fiction* (1994); *Don King: Only in America* (1997)

Christina Ricci *The Addams Family* (1991); *The Opposite of Sex* (1998)

Peter Riegert *Local Hero* (1983); *Barbarians at the Gate* (1993)

Molly Ringwald *Sixteen Candles* (1984); *Betsy's Wedding* (1990)

Tim Robbins *The Player* (1992); *The Shawshank Redemption* (1994)

Eric Roberts *The Pope of Greenwich Village* (1984); *Runaway Train* (1985)

Julia Roberts *Pretty Woman* (1990); *My Best Friend's Wedding* (1997)

Mimi Rogers *The Rapture* (1991); *Full Body Massage* (1995)

Mickey Rourke *The Pope of Greenwich Village* (1984); *Barfly* (1987)

Kurt Russell *The Mean Season* (1985); *Captain Ron* (1992)

René Russo *Tin Cup* (1996); *Ransom* (1996)

Meg Ryan *When Harry Met Sally . . .* (1989); *Courage Under Fire* (1996)

Winona Ryder *Heathers* (1989); *Little Women* (1994)

■ ■ ■ ■ ■ ■ ■ ■ ■ ■ ■ ■ ■ ■ ■ ■ ■

Naked ambition, Part 2

The 1973 ceremony is most remembered for being the one at which a naked man streaked across the stage, prompting David Niven's clever ad-lib, "Ladies and gentlemen, that was bound to happen. Just think, the only laugh that man will probably ever get is for stripping and showing off his shortcomings." The streaker was Robert Opal, the 33-year-old owner of a San Francisco sex shop. (Five years later Opal was found murdered in his shop.) *Daily Variety* accused the Academy of being a party to the stunt, calling it "a most unfortunate lapse of judgment." Academy bigwig Jack Haley Jr. denied having anything to do with it and told reporters that if he had wanted to have someone streak naked across the stage of the Dorothy Chandler Pavilion on live TV, he "would have used a pretty girl instead."

■ ■ ■ ■ ■ ■ ■ ■ ■ ■ ■ ■ ■ ■ ■ ■ ■

People Magazine's 14 Sexiest Men Alive (and 1 Sexiest Couple) Alive

J.F.K. Jr. was mortified when he was picked for this "honor" in 1988. Other winners may not have been.

1985   Mel Gibson (February 4)

1986   Mark Harmon (January 27)

1987   Harry Hamlin (March 30)—This was the worst-selling "Sexiest Men" issue in *People*'s history. (The November 30 issue this year featured Jay Leno on the cover with, yes, "The Sexiest Man Alive" next to his smiling face. Beneath this though, was, "Just kidding—he paid us to say that.")

1988   John F. Kennedy Jr. (September 12)—This was the best-selling "Sexiest Men" issue in *People*'s history.

1989   Sean Connery (December 18)

1990   Tom Cruise (July 23)

1991   Patrick Swayze (August 26)

1992   Nick Nolte (March 16)

1993   Richard Gere and Cindy Crawford ("Sexiest *Couple* Alive";
October 18)

1994   No winner. (This was the year that Nancy Kerrigan was
assaulted during the Olympics, Michael Jackson was charged
with child abuse and then married Elvis's daughter, John Candy
died, Kurt Cobain killed himself, Paula Jones accused Bill
Clinton of sexual harassment, Jackie Kennedy died, O. J.
Simpson stood trial for double murder, and serial killer Jeffrey
Dahmer was murdered in prison. Guess it was too busy a news
year for a "Sexiest Man" cover, eh?)

1995   Brad Pitt (January 30)

1996   Denzel Washington (July 29)

1997   George Clooney (November 17)

1998   Harrison Ford (November 16)

1999   Richard Gere (November 15)

2000   Brad Pitt (November 13)

- - - - - - - - - - - - - - - - -

Fame is like being a pretty girl: People turn and look at you. But
that's about all I've gotten out of it. I have found that it doesn't get
you laid, and you don't get as much free stuff as you think.

Anthony Edwards
Playboy, July 1997

- - - - - - - - - - - - - - - - -

The "Movies With Memorable (for a Multitude of Reasons!) Bathroom Scenes" List

We're sure the makers of these films are flushed with pride!

Psycho (1960)

High Anxiety (1977)

Midnight Express (1978)

American Gigolo (1979)

Dressed To Kill (1980)

He Knows You're Alone (1980)

9 to 5 (1980)

The Shining (1980)

An American Werewolf in London (1981)

Stripes (1981)

An Officer and a Gentleman (1982)

Poltergeist (1982)

Porky's (1982)

Breathless (1983)

National Lampoon's Vacation (1983)

Scarface (1983)

Silkwood (1983)

St. Elmo's Fire (1985)

About Last Night . . . (1986)

Fatal Attraction (1987)

Full Metal Jacket (1987)

Bull Durham (1988)

Married to the Mob (1988)

Working Girl (1988)

Tie Me Up! Tie Me Down! (1990)

Jurassic Park (1993)

Color of Night (1994)

Dumb & Dumber (1994)

Forrest Gump (1994)

Natural Born Killers (1994)

Pulp Fiction (1994)

Copycat (1995)

Jerry Maguire (1996)

Liar Liar (1996)

Austin Powers: International Man of Mystery (1997)

American History X (1998)

Wild Things (1998)

There's Something About Mary (1998)

For Your Consideration . . .

THE "S" LIST

Laura San Giacamo *Pretty Woman* (1990); *Nina Takes a Lover* (1994)

Adam Sandler *Happy Gilmore* (1996); *The Wedding Singer* (1997)

Mia Sara *Ferris Bueller's Day Off* (1986); *Timecop* (1994)

Susan Sarandon *Thelma & Louise* (1991); *Dead Man Walking* (1995)

Greta Scacchi *The Coca-Cola* (1984); *The Player* (1992)

Rick Schroder *The Champ* (1979); *Lonesome Dove* (1989)

Arnold Schwarzenegger The *Terminator* series (1984–1991); *True Lies* (1994)

David Schwimmer *Breast Men* (1997); *Apt Pupil* (1998)

Annabella Sciorra *Cadillac Man* (1990); *What Dreams May Come* (1998)

Kyra Sedgwick *Singles* (1992); *Phenomenon* (1996)

Tom Selleck *Three Men and a Baby* (1987); *In and Out* (1997)

Jane Seymour *Somewhere in Time* (1980); the *War and Remembrance* series (1988–1989)

Ally Sheedy *WarGames* (1982); *The Breakfast Club* (1985)

Charlie Sheen *Platoon* (1986); *Wall Street* (1987)

Martin Sheen *Apocalypse Now* (1979); *The American President* (1995)

Talia Shire The *Godfather* series (1972–1990); the *Rocky* series (1976–1990)

Pauly Shore *Encino Man* (1992); *Son-in-Law* (1993)

Martin Short The *Father of the Bride* series (1991–1995); *Merlin* (1998)

Elisabeth Shue *Soapdish* (1991); *Leaving Las Vegas* (1995)

O. J. Simpson *Roots* (1977); the *Naked Gun* series (1988–1994)

Lori Singer *Footloose* (1984); *Short Cuts* (1993)

Gary Sinise *Forrest Gump* (1994); *Ransom* (1996)

Ione Skye *Say Anything* (1989); *Gas Food Lodging* (1992)

Christian Slater *Heathers* (1989); *True Romance* (1993)

Will Smith *Independence Day* (1996); *Men in Black* (1997)

Jimmy Smits *Old Gringo* (1989); *Switch* (1991)

Wesley Snipes *Passenger 57* (1992); *Murder at 1600* (1997)

Mira Sorvino *Mighty Aphrodite* (1995); *Romy and Michele's High School Reunion* (1997)

Sissy Spacek *Coal Miner's Daughter* (1980); *'Night, Mother* (1986)

Kevin Spacey *Glengarry Glen Ross* (1992); *American Beauty* (1999)

James Spader *sex, lies and videotape* (1989); *Crash* (1995)

Sylvester Stallone The *Rocky* series (1976–1990); *Cliffhanger* (1993)

Mary Steenburgen *Melvin and Howard* (1980); *Cross Creek* (1983)

Daniel Stern The *Home Alone* series (1990–1992); the *City Slickers* series (1991–1994)

Frances Sternhagen *Misery* (1990); *Doc Hollywood* (1991)

Ben Stiller *Flirting With Disaster* (1995); *There's Something About Mary* (1998)

Eric Stoltz *The Waterdance* (1991); *Pulp Fiction* (1994)

Sharon Stone *Casino* (1995); *Last Dance* (1996)

Madeleine Stowe *Short Cuts* (1993); *Bad Girls* (1994)

David Straithairn *Sneakers* (1992); *In the Gloaming* (1997)

Meryl Streep *Sophie's Choice* (1982); *Postcards From the Edge* (1990)

Barbra Streisand *The Owl and the Pussycat* (1970); *Nuts* (1987)

Donald Sutherland *M*A*S*H* (1970); *Citizen X* (1995)

Kiefer Sutherland *A Few Good Men* (1992); *A Time to Kill* (1996)

Kristy Swanson *Flowers in the Attic* (1987); *Buffy the Vampire Slayer* (1992)

Patrick Swayze *Dirty Dancing* (1987); *Ghost* (1990)

21 Robin Williams Movies

Behold the work of a cinematic genius!

Serious Robin Williams Movies

1. *The World According to Garp* (1982)
2. *Moscow on the Hudson* (1984)
3. *Seize the Day* (1986)
4. *Dead Poets Society* (1989)
5. *Awakenings* (1990)
6. *The Fisher King* (1991)
7. *Being Human* (1994)
8. *Good Will Hunting* (1997)
9. *What Dreams May Come* (1998)
10. *Jakob the Liar* (1999)
11. *Bicentennial Man* (1999)
12. *A.I.: Artificial Intelligence* (2001)

Funny Robin Williams Movies

1. *Survivors* (1983)
2. *Good Morning, Vietnam* (1987)
3. *Mrs. Doubtfire* (1993)
4. *The Birdcage* (1995)
5. *Jack* (1996)
6. *Father's Day* (1996)
7. *Flubber* (1997)
8. *Deconstructing Harry* (1997)
9. *Patch Adams* (1998)

For Your Consideration . . .

THE "T" LIST

Quentin Tarantino *Reservoir Dogs* (1992); *Pulp Fiction* (1994)

Lea Thompson The *Back to the Future* series (1985–1990); *Some Kind of Wonderful* (1987)

Billy Bob Thornton *Sling Blade* (1996); *Primary Colors* (1998)

Uma Thurman *Pulp Fiction* (1994); *The Truth About Cats and Dogs* (1996)

Jennifer Tilly *Liar Liar* (1996); *Bound* (1996)

Meg Tilly *The Big Chill* (1983); *Agnes of God* (1985)

Marisa Tomei *My Cousin Vinny* (1992); *The Paper* (1994)

Lily Tomlin *9 to 5* (1980); *Flirting With Disaster* (1995)

John Travolta *Saturday Night Fever* (1977); *Pulp Fiction* (1994)

Jeanne Tripplehorn *Basic Instinct* (1992); *The Firm* (1993)

Chris Tucker *Jackie Brown* (1997); *Rush Hour* (1998)

Janine Turner *Steel Magnolias* (1989); *Cliffhanger* (1993)

Kathleen Turner *The War of the Roses* (1989); *Serial Mom* (1994)

Liv Tyler *That Thing You Do!* (1996); *Stealing Beauty* (1996)

47 Things You May Not Know About Some of the Biggest Movies of All Time

1. In some video versions of *Airplane!* (1980), the scene in which the little girl's IV line is ripped out of her arm is missing. Also, British television on occasion has edited out the scenes of Captain Over's "gladiator movie" advances to the young boy.

2. In *Annie Hall* (1977), the guy Alvy (Woody Allen), described to Annie (Diane Keaton) as the "winner of the Truman Capote look-alike contest," was played by Truman Capote.

3. When Robert Duvall's character Kilgore in *Apocalypse Now* (1979) angrily throws down his megaphone, it was because director Francis Ford Coppola frequently did the exact same thing on the set, and Duvall "borrowed" the gesture from him.

4. In *Batman* (1989), the name of the Flugelheim Museum is spelled with an extra "e" on a sign. Also in *Batman*, the guy leading the

procession in the "Who can you trust?" sequence is Prince *before* he became "The Artist Formerly Known as . . ."

5. The "herpes simplex ten" scene in *Beverly Hills Cop* (1984) was completely improvised by Eddie Murphy and committed to film in a mere fifteen minutes of shooting.

6. The scene in *Bonnie and Clyde* (1967) when part of Warren Beatty's head blows off was a deliberate reference to the Zapruder film that showed President Kennedy's head being blown off in the same manner.

7. In *Casablanca* (1942), Humphrey Bogart's cigarette magically changes length from long to short and back to long again in several shots.

8. Even though the Academy Award-winning movie *Chariots of Fire* is based on a true story, researchers have chronicled at least fifty errors of fact in the script, ranging from details about the main character Eric Liddell to stats about the 1924 Paris Olympics.

9. There were actually *three* "Rosebud" sleds made for *Citizen Kane* (1941). Two were burned during production of the film; the third and final Rosebud was bought by director Steven Spielberg in the late eighties for $60,000.

10. In 1985, New York location shooting for *Crocodile Dundee* (1986) was delayed for an entire day because Hurricane Gloria was bearing down on Manhattan.

11. In *Dirty Harry* (1972), a movie theater marquee is seen showing *Play Misty for Me*, star Clint Eastwood's previous (at the time) movie.

12. In the opening reception scene in *Duck Soup* (1933), Groucho's coat changes from a gray one with braids to a formal tuxedo coat with tails and back to the braided coat, all in the same scene.

13. In *Easy Rider* (1969), the guy buying the cocaine in the airport scene at the beginning of the movie was legendary record producer Phil Spector.

14. The teacher in the classroom scene in *E.T. The Extra-Terrestrial* (1982) was played by superstar Harrison Ford, the husband of cowriter and producer Kathleen Kennedy (and Spielberg friend), but you never see Ford's face.

15. In *The Big Chill* (1983), the corpse of Alex was played by Kevin Costner. His scenes were cut from the released version of the film. (Costner's face is never shown but that *is* his body being dressed for burial in the opening scenes of the movie.) Director Lawrence Kasdan refused to restore the scenes for the film's anniversary re-release.

16. The green puke Regan sprays all over Father Merrin in *The Exorcist* (1973) was made of oatmeal and pea soup.

17. At the 1940 Academy Awards ceremony, when Walt Disney was awarded the Thalberg Award, David O. Selznick specifically praised him for employing a wide range of classical music (including Bach, Tchaikovsky, and Beethoven) in the animated feature *Fantasia,* now considered a classic of the genre. At the time, however, *Fantasia* was a box-office disaster and Disney actually began crying and, during his Thalberg acceptance speech, apologized for making it. "We all make mistakes," he sobbed. "*Fantasia* was one but it was an honest one." *Fantasia* ultimately became one of Disney's most popular animated features and has become a cult favorite for several generations of moviegoers.

18. According to the wall clock in the kitchen sink sex scene in *Fatal Attraction* (1987), Michael Douglas and Glenn Close's bonk lasted an astonishing one hour and fifty minutes. In one scene, the clock is shown to read 4:45; in a later scene, it reads 6:35. Now that's stamina.

19. The village seen in James Whale's 1931 classic *Frankenstein* had actually been constructed for the previous year's *All Quiet on the Western Front* (which also had been produced by *Frankenstein*'s producer Carl Laemmle Jr.). Waste not, want not, eh?

20. When James Caan was riddled with bullets at the toll plaza in one of the most powerful scenes in *The Godfather* (1972), his face shows the agony of being shot to death. But Caan wasn't acting. By necessity, there had to be a great deal of explosive rigging on Caan's body in order to effectively simulate all the bullets Sonny was supposed to be taking. When they were triggered, it hurt like hell.

21. In *Goldfinger* (1964), James Bond kills the thug who has come to assassinate him by hurling an electric heater into the tub where the killer had fallen. Why did the girl Bond had been necking with have an electric *heater—turned on*—in a sweltering *tropical* paradise?

(Also, did you know that Bond creator Ian Fleming got the super-spy's name from a book called *Birds of the West Indies?* The author of the book was, of course, James Bond.)

22. In *Gone With the Wind* (1939), we never see the O'Hara mansion from the front. Why? Because it was only a fake studio front piece and the door was off-center. (Most of the trees and bushes were fakes, too.) Also, an electric light bulb is seen in a lamppost outside the makeshift hospital in 1864 . . . fifteen years before Edison invented the lightbulb in 1879.

23. An unknown Dustin Hoffman received only $17,000 for his role in *The Graduate* (1967), and he had to apply for unemployment insurance after shooting wrapped.

24. In *Grease* (1978), John Travolta's car has "John" written on it in grease in a scene at the drive-in. The only problem is that Travolta's character was named Danny.

25. At the beginning of *A Hard Day's Night* (1964), the Beatles are seen running onto a train. They are each wearing the clothes they arrived in on the set that day, and in the next scene (which chronologically follows the "running" scene), they are all dressed differently.

26. The famous "night in the haystack" scene in *It Happened One Night* (1934) was filmed during the day in a circus tent. The cricket sounds were dubbed in later, the first time ambient sounds were added to a scene after it was shot.

27. All the perspiration we see in *Lawrence of Arabia* (1962) is fake sweat. Actual sweat evaporates in seconds in the real 130°F. Desert heat in which the movie was shot.

28. Even though M*A*S*H stands for Mobile Army Surgical Hospital, the acronym is never explained in the 1970 movie, *M*A*S*H.*

29. In *One Flew Over the Cuckoo's Nest* (1975), the supporting actors (mostly unknown at the time, including Danny DeVito, Christopher Lloyd, Brad Dourif, and Vincent Schiavelli) were so good at playing Jack Nicholson's fellow inmates, moviegoers debated at the time of the film's release whether the actors were actually mental patients.

30. The submarine seen in *Raiders of the Lost Ark* (1981) was the same sub that was used in the German U-boat movie *Das Boot* (also 1981).

31. In *Rambo: First Blood Part II* (1985), there is a killing every 2.1 minutes, for a total of 44, including 5 knife deaths, 2 strangulations, 14 bow and arrow deaths, 15 gunshot deaths, 3 explosion deaths, and 2 from being attacked by a helicopter. Sylvester Stallone later compared his performance in *Rambo* to that of James Dean's in *East of Eden* (1955).

32. The house in which Plato (Sal Mineo) lived in *Rebel Without a Cause* (1955) also appeared in Billy Wilder's *Sunset Boulevard* (1950).

33. In the scarf sequence of *Singin' in the Rain* (1952) (about an hour and twenty minutes into the movie), it is rumored that if you look close enough, you can see Cyd Charisse's pubic hair through her diaphanous costume. Apparently she wasn't wearing underwear during the scene and there *is* a hint of a shadow, but it could be anything. Whether or not anything can be seen in the final version of the film, though, it *is* true that Charisse did initially pose a problem for costume designer Walter Plunkett during shooting of the scene. Legend has it that after trying a few different costume modifications to conceal her as much as possible, Plunkett, finally satisfied, proclaimed, "Don't worry, fellas. We've got Cyd Charisse's crotch licked!"

34. In *Snow White and the Seven Dwarfs* (1937), the dwarfs' names are Doc, Grumpy, Happy, Sleepy, Bashful, Sneezy, and Dopey. The names originally proposed for the dwarfs, however, were Awful, Biggo-Ego, Biggy, Biggy-Wiggy, Blabby, Daffy, Dirty, Doleful, Gabby, Gaspy, Gloomy, Hoppy, Hotsy, Hungry, Jaunty, Neurtsy, Nifty, Shifty, Snoopy, Soulful, Thrifty, Weepy, and Woeful.

35. In *Some Like It Hot* (1959), George Raft sees a young hood flipping a coin and asks the kid, "Where did you pick up that cheap trick?" The coin flip is a bit Raft himself made famous almost thirty years earlier in *Scarface* (1932). (The hood, by the way, was played by Edward G. Robinson Jr.)

36. In publicity photos for *The Sound of Music* (1965), a case of oranges from Israel is seen, although the crates didn't make it into the final film. The problem? The movie took place ten years before the state of Israel came into existence.

37. *Star Wars* (1977), directed by George Lucas, has a character named Luke Skywalker. Try saying the character's first name and last initial—"Luke S"—a few times. How's *that* for an obscure director's cameo?

38. The computer in *2001: A Space Odyssey* (1968) is named HAL. Try substituting each of the three letters of HAL with the next letter in the alphabet; i.e., I-B-M. Was this some hidden slap at the computer giant? Writer Arthur C. Clarke said no, it was a coincidence, since HAL was supposed to stand for *H*euristically-programmed *Al*gorithmic computer.

39. Jerry Garcia of the Grateful Dead can be seen in the crowd scene in India in *Close Encounters of the Third Kind* (1977).

40. The horse that Thomas Mitchell (playing Scarlett's father Gerald O'Hara) rode in *Gone With the Wind* (1939) later became the Lone Ranger's horse Silver in the movie version of the adventures of the popular TV hero.

41. Frank Zappa's bizarre, almost indescribable film *200 Motels* (1971) was shot in the same studio in which Stanley Kubrick had filmed *2001: A Space Odyssey* (1968) three years earlier. The black monolith from Kubrick's classic can actually be seen in one scene of Zappa's movie.

42. In *Beetlejuice* (1988), when Geena Davis (Barbara) and Alec Baldwin (Adam) are waiting for their interview with their afterlife caseworker, at one point Dan Aykroyd and John Belushi, in character as Jake and Elwood Blues of *The Blue Brothers* (1980), briefly can be seen through the venetian blinds in the office.

43. Quentin Tarantino always inserts references to Big Kahuna Burgers and Red Apple cigarettes in his scripts. They appear in *True Romance* (1993), *Pulp Fiction* (1994), *From Dusk Till Dawn* (1996), and *Four Rooms* (1995). These burgers and butts also appear, however, in a *non*-Tarantino movie, *Romy and Michele's High School Reunion* (1997). Why? Because Tarantino and *Romy* star Mira Sorvino were a couple when the movie was made. (They since have split.)

44. *Sesame Street*'s lovable Bert and Ernie characters were named after the two characters with those names in *It's a Wonderful Life* (1946).

45. In Disney's animated *Hunchback of Notre Dame* (1996), a satellite dish can be seen on the roof of one of the buildings in the "Out There" scene.

46. Bugs Bunny's, ahem, "bunny" can be seen in one frame of *The Wabbit Who Came to Dinner* (1948), when Bugs steps out of the shower and wraps a towel around his waist.

47. Demonic maniac Michael Myers's mask in the original *Halloween* (1978) was actually a store-bought *William Shatner* mask that the makeup people painted white. (They had no budget for big-time makeup effects.)

■ — ■ — ■ — ■ — ■ — ■ — ■ — ■ — ■ — ■ — ■ — ■ — ■ — ■ — ■ — ■

The best lesson I learned . . . was from William Shatner, when he hosted *Saturday Night Live.* Every week I'd be all anxiety-ridden and tense . . . but when Shatner hosted the show, he seemed so relaxed, I said, "How do you do it?" He said, "I just do it." I knew how to walk. I knew how to speak. So I just did it, and I found it worked. Instead of worrying about being funny, I was fine—perhaps not more funny, but not less funny than when I was all tied up inside.

Jon Lovitz
Playboy, July 1997

■ — ■ — ■ — ■ — ■ — ■ — ■ — ■ — ■ — ■ — ■ — ■ — ■ — ■ — ■ — ■

How Hollywood Can Change $20 Million Into $4 Million in 17 Easy Steps

Superfluous wealth can buy superfluities only.
—HENRY DAVID THOREAU

It ain't easy being a movie star, even if you're making $20 million a movie.

The old adage about it taking money to make money is nowhere more evident than in the list of expenses a wealthy movie star must cover as part of his high-profile career, ranging from a huge federal tax bite to pedicures.

The following profit and loss schedule looks at the life of a hypothetical movie star who gets $20 million a movie. (I'm sure you can think of a few of this ilk.) For the sake of this overview, we are assuming the star does one movie a year, for which he or she earns $20 million.

This list consists of the out-of-pocket expenses the star must take care of him- or herself, even though some of these costs are often picked up by the studio as part of a star's perk package when making a movie.

The chart, based on figures from *USA Today,* is calculated weekly because that's how most non-movie stars (mortals) figure their living costs. We also assumed that the federal tax and state tax would be withheld from the star's weekly paycheck (a convenience for the purposes of this feature; many stars are paid in installments throughout the production of the movie) and made the presumptuous leap that the star might live in California.

Weekly Gross Income:	**$ 384,615.38**
Deductions:	
Federal taxes (39.6%):	$ 152,307.69
California state tax (9.3%):	$ 35,769.23
Total Deductions:	**$ 188,076.92**
Weekly Net Pay:	**$ 196,538.46**

Weekly Personal Living Expenses:

Agent (10%):	$ 38,461.54
Manager (10%):	$ 38,461.54
Business manager (5%):	$ 19,230.77
Security:	$ 5,000.00
Private jet air transportation:	$ 4,807.69
Home mortgage:	$ 1,615.38
Personal assistant:	$ 1,250.00
Nanny:	$ 1,000.00
Publicist:	$ 576.92
Personal trainer:	$ 480.77
Personal stylist:	$ 192.31
Manicures and pedicures:	$ 67.31
Screen Actors Guild dues:	$ 43.46
Haircuts:	$ 34.62
Hair coloring:	$ 30.77
Total personal living expenses:	**$111,253.08**
Net Weekly Profit:	**$ 85,285.38**

From this weekly profit figure, the star must pay for groceries, home utilities, clothing, restaurants, personal purchases, etc. But just for fun, let's assume that this profit is the star's to invest; that all of his or her other expenses do not have to come out of this figure.

This means the star's net profit for the year for this hypothetical movie is **$4,434,839.79.**

Even at the conservative rate of 4% annually, the star would earn **$177,393.58** a year on this money. This gives the celeb another **$3,411.42** a week in interest earnings . . . but if this is all taxable, then out of this figure has to come the federal tax, the state tax . . . sheesh.

No wonder so many celebrities are in therapy.

- - - - - - - - - - - - - - - - - -

In my business, the only way you get as much money as I have is if you don't care about money and you care about comedy; then somehow you end up with money.

Jerry Seinfeld
Us, March 1998

- - - - - - - - - - - - - - - - - -

35 Really, Really, *Really* Long Movies

And you thought *Titanic* was long!

This list consists of movies that require catering.

I used 5 hours as the minimum length required for inclusion on the list, and this still left out almost three dozen films listed in my sources that were released with running times of 4 hours to 4 hours, 58 minutes.

The list begins with the "shortest" films (relatively speaking, that is) and concludes with the longest films known.

1. **5 hours, 2 minutes** *Winifred Wagner und die Geschichte des Hauses Wahnfried* (1975)

2. **5 hours, 5 minutes** *Les Misérables* (1927)

3. **5 hours, 6 minutes** *Petersburgskije Truscoby* (1915)

4. **5 hours, 14 minutes** *Potopi/The Deluge* (1974)

5. **5 hours, 16 minutes** *1900* (1978)

6. **5 hours, 20 minutes** *Vindicta* (1923)

7. **5 hours, 32 minutes** *Les Misérables* (1933)

8. **5 hours, 50 minutes** *Fanny and Alexander* (1983)

9. **5 hours, 54 minutes** *Soldati Svobodi* (1977)

10. **5 hours, 57 minutes** *Little Dorrit* (1988)

11. **6 hours** *Idade de Terra* (1979)

12. **6 hours** *Khan Asparouch* (1982)

13. **6 hours, 10 minutes** *Die Nibelungen* (1924)

14. **6 hours, 24 minutes** *Foolish Wives* (1922)

15. **6 hours, 30 minutes** *Sleep* (1963)

16. **6 hours, 40 minutes** *Hitler: A Film From Germany* (1977)

17. **7 hours** *Der Hund von Baskerville* (1914–1920)

18. **7 hours, 45 minutes** *Français si vous savez* (1973)

19. **7 hours, 58 minutes** *Iskry Plamja* (1925)

20. **8 hours** *Empire* (1964)

21. **8 hours, 27 minutes** *War and Peace* (1963–1967)

22. **8 hours, 32 minutes** *La Roue* (1921)

23. **9 hours** *Wagner* (1983)

24. **9 hours** *Napoleon* (1927)

25. **9 hours, 21 minutes** *Shoah* (1985)

26. **9 hours, 29 minutes** *The Human Condition* (1958–1960)

27. **12 hours, 40 minutes** *Out 1: Noli me tangere* (1971)

28. **12 hours, 43 minutes** *Comment Yukong déplace les montagnes* (1976)

29. **13 hours** *The Old Testament* (1922)

30. **15 hours, 21 minutes** *Berlin Alexanderplatz* (1980)

31. **15 hours, 40 minutes** *Heimat* (1984)

32. **24 hours** **** (1967)

33. **27 hours** *The Burning of the Red Lotus Temple* (1928–1931)

34. **48 hours** *The Longest Most Meaningless Movie in the World* (1970)

35. **85 hours** *The Cure for Insomnia* (1987)

For Your Consideration . . .

THE "U" LIST

Liv Ullmann *Cries and Whispers* (1972); *Scenes From a Marriage* (1974)

Skeet Ulrich *Scream* (1996); *The Newton Boys* (1997)

- - - - - - - - - - - - - - - - - - - -

A classic phony Hollywood moment if there ever was one

At the 1977 ceremony, Debbie Boone sang the nominated song, "You Light Up My Life," which by then had sold about a gazillion copies. Before she started singing, though, she introduced "eleven young ladies affiliated with the John Tracy Clinic for the Deaf." During the song, the audience was told, these young girls would "sing along" with Debbie in sign language for the benefit of the hearing impaired both there in the Dorothy Chandler Pavilion, and in the worldwide TV audience who were not able to hear the brilliant lyrics of the song as Debbie sang them. Well, it turned out that the eleven girls were *not* from the John Tracy Clinic for the Deaf (they were just students randomly picked from a school in Torrance, California); that none of them was actually deaf; and that their "signing" was just convoluted hand gestures made to look like sign language.

- - - - - - - - - - - - - - - - - - - -

The "Movies About Mummies" List

And no, *Mummy Dearest* is not included here.

The Mummy (1932)
The Mummy's Hand (1940)
The Mummy's Tomb (1942)
The Mummy's Curse (1944)
The Mummy's Ghost (1944)
Abbott and Costello Meet the Mummy (1955)
The Curse of the Aztec Mummy (1959)
The Mummy (1959)

The Robot vs. the Aztec Mummy (1959)
Wrestling Women vs. the Aztec Mummy (1959)
Attack of the Mayan Mummy (1963)
Castle of the Living Dead (1964)
Mad Monster Party (1968)
The Mummy's Revenge (1973)
The Awakening (1980)

Sphinx (1981)
Dawn of the Mummy (1982)
The Monster Squad (1987)
Bram Stoker's The Mummy
   (1997)

The Creeps (1997)
The Mummy (1999)
The Mummy Returns (2001)

67 Admitted TV and Movie Star Alcoholics

These celebs have all admitted publicly that they were alcoholics, or the
media has (often gleefully) covered their rehab (or falls from grace).

1. Ann-Margret
2. Tom Arnold
3. Tammy Faye Bakker
4. Diana Barrymore
5. Drew Barrymore
6. Robert Blake
7. Humphrey Bogart
8. Gary Busey
9. Brett Butler
10. Sid Caesar
11. Michael Caine
12. David Caruso
13. Chevy Chase
14. Jeff Conaway
15. Joan Crawford
16. Tony Curtis
17. John Cusack
18. Tyne Daly
19. Shannen Doherty
20. Amanda Donohoe
21. Michael Douglas
22. Robert Downey Jr.
23. Richard Dreyfuss
24. Chad Everett
25. Carrie Fisher
26. Mel Gibson
27. Louis Gossett Jr.
28. Kelsey Grammer
29. Melanie Griffith
30. David Hasselhoff
31. Margaux Hemingway
32. Anthony Hopkins
33. Dennis Hopper
34. John Hurt

35. William Hurt
36. Samuel L. Jackson
37. Elton John
38. Don Johnson
39. Stephen King
40. Kris Kristofferson
41. Nathan Lane
42. John Larroquette
43. Liza Minnelli
44. Mary Tyler Moore
45. Nick Nolte
46. Gary Oldman
47. Al Pacino
48. Sean Penn
49. Chynna Phillips
50. Mackenzie Phillips
51. Richard Pryor

52. Dennis Quaid
53. Robert Redford
54. Charlie Sheen
55. Anna Nicole Smith
56. David Soul
57. Ringo Starr
58. Patrick Swayze
59. Liz Taylor
60. Spencer Tracy
61. Daniel J. Travanti
62. Dick Van Dyke
63. Jan-Michael Vincent
64. John Wayne
65. Robin Williams
66. Bruce Willis
67. Robert Young

I never thought I was an alcoholic; I just drank all my life. But I was a blackout drinker. I would wake up in places and not know how I got there. . . . I was always in excess. When I bought a six-pack of beer, I drank six beers. I didn't save one for the next day. Once I figured this out about myself, it was easy to say, "Okay, I've tried this for twenty-three or whatever years. Let's give this other way a shot and see what happens."

Samuel L. Jackson
Playboy, June 1999

For Your Consideration . . .

THE "V" LIST

Jean-Claude Van Damme *Universal Soldier* (1992); *The Quest* (1996)

Dick Van Dyke *Mary Poppins* (1964); *Cold Turkey* (1971)

Mario Van Peebles *Posse* (1993); *Solo* (1996)

Gore Vidal *Bob Roberts* (1992); *Gattaca* (1997)

Jon Voight *Midnight Cowboy* (1969); *John Grisham's The Rainmaker* (1997)

Toga!

Dan Aykroyd and John Belushi were scheduled to present the Visual Effects Oscar at the 1981 ceremony, but Belushi died of a drug overdose a few weeks before the big night. Producer Howard Koch made Aykroyd promise that he would not mention Belushi during the telecast. (Koch wanted the Academy to play absolutely no part in a tribute to Belushi.) Aykroyd agreed but couldn't get through his presentation without at least acknowledging his best friend's passing. "My partner would have loved presenting this Award with me," Aykroyd said, breaking his promise to Koch. "He was something of a special effect himself."

85 Actresses and Their Most Memorable Nude Scenes

. . . there's more enterprise
In walking naked.
— WILLIAM BUTLER YEATS, "A COAT"
(FROM *RESPONSIBILITIES*, 1914)

This list provides a quick rundown of some of the most memorable nude scenes of a few of our most popular actresses. For each actress, we provide some interesting and entertaining background trivia or info about the movie, the star, and/or the scene.

Interestingly, even though more and more actresses are willing to do nudity these days, no actress or celeb is safe from the hands of the "Fakirs," wizards with Photoshop software and other graphics programs who can seamlessly splice a celebrity's head onto a photo of their choosing. There are Internet newsgroups bursting at the scenes with these fakes and there, the fan can find photos of their faves doing the *nastiest* things!

Several actresses and celebrities (Alyssa Milano and Nancy Kerrigan to name two) sued the owners of Web sites that posted X-rated fakes of them and some won; but now a great many of these incredible composite photos are posted anonymously on the aforementioned newsgroups.

One of the most popular of these Internet newsgroups is **alt.bina ries.pictures.nude.celebrities.fake**.

Recently, hard-core fakes posted there have included pix of Julia Roberts, Gwyneth Paltrow, Shania Twain, Bridget Fonda, Sandra Bullock, Katie Couric, Nicole Kidman, Jewel, Teri Hatcher, and Helen Hunt, just to name a few. (Occasionally, fakirs will do a "For Ladies Only" post which will include X-rated nudes of male heartthrobs like David Duchovny, Bruce Willis, Val Kilmer, Jeff Goldblum and others. And since the "body shots" the fakirs use for the composites are usually pictures of porn stars, these movie stars are always depicted as incredibly endowed! This happens sometimes with the women, too. Now and then a less-than-buxom star such as Gwyneth Paltrow or Liv Tyler will be faked with D cup breasts or bigger!)

For those interested in the real thing, however, the following list will steer you to a glimpse of the stripped, sought-after star.

[Special thanks to Craig Hosoda and his *Bare Facts Video Guide* for doing the primary research that allowed this list to take shape. Craig watches movies and keeps track of the nude scenes. That's right. That's his *job*. Hey, somebody's got to do it, right?!]

Joey Lauren Adams This tiny blond firecracker made an indelible impression in director Kevin Smith's groundbreaking comedy *Chasing Amy* (1997) as a fiercely independent, singing lesbian with a somewhat salacious past. Adams also appeared in Smith's second film, the less successful *Mallrats* and did a brief topless scene.

★ *Mallrats* (1995)

Karen Allen An awful lot of us fell in love with Karen Allen from her performance in *Raiders of the Lost Ark* (1981). As you can imagine, her nude scenes in the 1984 romantic comedy *Until September* drew a lot of *Raiders* fans who might not have wanted to see a chick flick.

★ *Until September* (1984)

Nancy Allen This pretty blonde is seen naked in a locker room scene at the beginning of this Stephen King horror movie about a telekinetic teenage girl who goes on a rampage when she is humiliated at her high school prom. (Carrie's classmates drop a bucket of pig's blood all over her as she stands onstage after being crowned Queen of the Prom.)

★ *Carrie* (1976)

Julie Andrews Mary Poppins *topless*? Yup. When Julie "The hills are alive" Andrews decided to do the first nude scene of her career in *S.O.B.*, it almost didn't matter what the movie was about. The publicity about the nude scene overshadowed the fact that the movie was written and directed by her real-life husband Blake Edwards and that it was essentially a bitter *roman à clef* tirade against the movie business.

★ *S.O.B.* (1981)

Ann-Margret Her nude scene with Jack Nicholson in *Carnal Knowledge* is legendary. She's also seen topless in *Magic*.

★ *Carnal Knowledge* (1971); *Magic* (1978)

Anne Archer She's not really naked in this movie, but her bra and panties scenes are definitely worth checking out.

★ *Fatal Attraction* (1987)

Patricia Arquette One of the two amazing Arquette sisters, both of whom are talented and gorgeous. As the reformed hooker Alabama in *True Romance*, Patricia meets, seduces, and marries Christian Slater in about three minutes, and then gets involved in a cocaine sale that ends up in a bloody shoot-out.

★ *True Romance* (1993)

Rosanna Arquette Rosanna walks around naked in this adaptation of Norman Mailer's book about serial killer Gary Gilmore.

★ *The Executioner's Song* (1982)

Adrienne Barbeau At least Maude's not there for Barbeau's brief topless scene!

★ *Open House* (1987)

Paula Barbieri Even though O.J.'s ex-girlfriend posed naked for *Playboy*, her movies are included in case you wanted to see if she can act while naked.

★ *Red Shoe Diaries: Double or Nothing* (1993); *Night Eyes 4 . . . Fatal Passion* (1995)

Ellen Barkin This movie contains the hottest nude scenes Barkin has done to date.

★ *Siesta* (1987)

Toni Basil Remember the video hit "Mickey"? ("Oh, Mickey, you're so fine, you're so fine, you blow my mind, hey, Mickey"?) That's choreographer/actress Toni Basil who had a brief nude scene in the sixties classic *Easy Rider.*

★ *Easy Rider* (1969)

Kim Basinger This sexy superstar (and soon-to-be-ex-wife of Alec Baldwin) made her (naked) debut in the February 1983 issue of *Playboy* magazine. Even though she had done a couple of movies prior to this appearance, the magazine spread got her a role in the James Bond film

Never Say Never Again (1983) and kicked her film career into over-drive. In 1997, she won a Best Supporting Actress Oscar for her performance in *L.A. Confidential.* These two movies contain the steamiest (and nakedest) scenes Basinger has done to date.

★ *9-1/2 Weeks* (1986); *The Getaway* (1993)

Kathy Bates If there's one thing you can say about Kathy Bates it is that she's gutsy. Not usually considered a sex symbol, Bates actually cavorted naked in this film (although she was covered with mud and leaves) Still, naked is naked, right?

★ *At Play in the Fields of the Lord* (1991)

Jennifer Beals A lot of guys fell in love with Beals because of one scene in her 1983 hit *Flashdance.* You know the one I'm talking about: the scene where she takes her bra off without removing her sweatshirt and pulls it out through her sleeve-hole as a wide-eyed Michael Nouri sits there and watches. Yikes. Jennifer has a couple of brief nude scenes in this 1990 sci-fi thriller.

★ *Club Extinction* (1990)

Annette Bening Mrs. Warren Beatty has never done nudity during her film career . . . except for a not-a-stitch-on nude scene in this nineties noir thriller that also starred Anjelica Huston and John Cusack.

★ *The Grifters* (1990)

Candice Bergen TV's *Murphy Brown* showed her assets in this Italian romance about an American feminist who is pursued by an Italian communist (played by Giancarlo Giannini).

★ *A Night Full of Rain* (1978, Italian)

Elizabeth Berkley Even though she had played a relatively innocent schoolgirl in TV's *Saved by the Bell,* Elizabeth Berkley made headlines with her less-than-innocent feature film debut in *Showgirls.* Berkley is naked in *Showgirls* a lot and even though the Joe Eszterhas script was rather lame, if you're a Berkley fan, then a rental of *Showgirls* is a must. (Tip: Try to find the NC-17 version. It's even steamier than the R version.)

★ *Showgirls* (1995)

Sandra Bernhard The comedienne and actress strips completely naked in front of the camera and then climbs into bed—alone—at the conclusion of this entertaining documentary/concert film.

★ *Sandra After Dark* (1992, HBO)

Jacqueline Bisset People (okay . . . guys) went to see this movie just for the scenes of Bisset swimming around in a white T-shirt that essentially became see-through when she was underwater.

★ *The Deep* (1977)

Lisa Bonet The former *Cosby* child star shocked many of her fans with the steamy nude scenes in this movie about voodoo and Satan.

★ *Angel Heart* (1987, British)

Danielle Brisbois Brisbois played Archie Bunker's niece in *Archie's Place,* the sequel to *All in the Family,* and then took her clothes off in this sequel to the 1974 Angie Dickinson scorcher, *Big Bad Mama.* Wonder what Archie had to say, eh?

★ *Big Bad Mama II* (1987)

Kate Capshaw Mrs. Steven Spielberg had a brief nude scene in *A Little Sex* (her debut) about a cuckolded wife. Married to Mr. Hollywood for years, Capshaw is quite selective about her film choices, which lately have included roles in *The Locusts* (1997), *How To Make an American Quilt* (1995), and *Just Cause* (1994). She recently did a nude lesbian love scene with model Elle Macpherson in Showtime's *A Girl Thing.*

★ *A Little Sex* (1982); *A Girl Thing* (2000)

Lynda Carter Wonder Woman topless. Need we say more?

★ *Bobbi Jo and the Outlaw* (1976)

Phoebe Cates Cates's topless scene by the pool (a fantasy Judge Reinhold uses as he pleasures himself inside the house in the bathroom) is legendary and may have even inspired the bathroom scene in the Farrelly Brothers' 1998 smash, *There's Something About Mary.*

★ *Fast Times at Ridgemont High* (1982)

Glenn Close This respected and talented actress sat naked and weeping in a shower in *The Big Chill* and then a few years later took on the role of Michael Douglas's psychotic mistress in *Fatal Attraction,* in which she not only appeared naked, but had some especially steamy sex scenes (including memorable trysts on a kitchen sink and in an elevator).

★ *The Big Chill* (1983); *Fatal Attraction* (1987)

Jennifer Connelly This gorgeous young goddess surprised everyone with her nude scene in *The Hot Spot.* (She had not done screen nudity prior to this movie.) One critic described Connelly's nude beach scene in this movie with one word: "Wow!"

★ *The Hot Spot* (1990)

Jane Curtin The former *Saturday Night Live* cast member and star of the eighties sitcom *Kate & Allie* is seen topless in this comedy, although since her face is not shown, it is believed to have been a body double.

★ *How to Beat the High Cost of Living* (1980)

Jamie Lee Curtis Watch for the scene in the bedroom when Curtis undresses as Dan Aykroyd watches. As he stares, Jamie covers her bountiful breasts with her hands and then spits at him her line about not only rent and food costing money around here. Classic.

★ *Trading Places* (1983)

Geena Davis Geena is only seen in a bikini in this comedy, but she's seen *a lot* in a bikini, so if you're a Geena Davis fan, this is a must-see.

★ *Earth Girls Are Easy* (1989)

Rebecca DeMornay DeMornay's subway sex scene with Tom Cruise in *Risky Business* is what she's remembered for, but she does more nudity in the 1988 remake of the Bardot classic, *And God Created Woman.*

★ *And God Created Woman* (1988); *The Hand That Rocks the Cradle* (1992)

Dana Delany In *Light Sleeper,* this former *China Beach* star had a very brief nude scene, which whetted her fans' appetite and set them up for her amazing full frontal nude scenes (and S&M scenes) in the otherwise disastrous adaptation of the Anne Rice novel *Exit to Eden.*

★ *Light Sleeper* (1992); *Exit to Eden* (1994)

Laura Dern "Put away your titty," Robert Duvall tells Laura Dern in *Rambling Rose,* after she tries to seduce him. When she reluctantly complies, a collective sigh can be heard throughout Moviedom.

★ *Wild at Heart* (1990); *Rambling Rose* (1991)

Susan Dey This movie is notable for Dey's topless scene with William Katt and has long been a nostalgic cult favorite for *Partridge Family* fans who always wanted to see Laurie Partridge naked.

★ *First Love* (1977)

Fran Drescher One of Fran's bare breasts is seen as she romps around under the covers with Robin Williams in this terrific, albeit underrated comedy/drama.

★ *Cadillac Man* (1990)

Bridget Fonda This wonderful actress from a Hollywood show business family is one of the most "faked" stars; you can see the real thing in two terrific movies. *Single White Female* contains Fonda's most explicit nude scenes, although Quentin Tarantino's *Jackie Brown* is notable for her athletic, standing-up tryst with Robert De Niro.

★ *Single White Female* (1992); *Jackie Brown* (1997)

Jodie Foster This multitalented actress and director won an Academy Award for her role in *The Accused* as a gang-rape victim who fights back. She has not done much nudity in her films, but these three provide the clearest views of the Oscar winner.

★ *The Accused* (1988); *Backtrack* (1989); *Nell* (1994)

Gina Gershon When the stunning Gershon's nude scenes in *Showgirls* are added to Elizabeth Berkely's, a terrible movie becomes a sought-after and greatly cherished collectible, wouldn't you say so?

★ *Showgirls* (1995)

Daryl Hannah Four classics for the serious Daryl Hannah fan. *At Play* and *Splash* offer the best, ahem, views of the blond goddess.

★ *Summer Lovers* (1982); *Reckless* (1984); *Splash* (1984); *At Play in the Fields of the Lord* (1991)

Mariska Hargitay Jayne Mansfield's gorgeous daughter has been spending time of late on the small screen, playing Anthony Edwards's love interest on *ER,* and as costar of *Law and Order SVU.* In 1986, though, she showed off her impressive heritage (and equally impressive derrière) in this lame coming-of-age comedy, which also starred Courtney Thorne-Smith (who would go on to starring roles in *Melrose Place* and *Ally McBeal*).

★ *Welcome to 18* (1986)

Deborah Harry The lead singer of Blondie has a topless scene in this sci-fi thriller by David Cronenberg. Harry appeared in several movies following *Videodrome,* including *Hairspray* (1988), *New York Stories* (1989), *Tales From the Darkside: The Movie* (1990), and *Heavy* (1994), but in 1999 she announced that Blondie was getting back together and was planning a new CD and a tour.

★ *Videodrome* (1983, Canadian)

Teri Hatcher Lois Lane naked. Super, man.

★ *The Cool Surface* (1992); *Heaven's Prisoners* (1995)

Anne Heche The former Mrs. Ellen DeGeneres does not let her private life interfere with her choice of roles, some of which have been steamy, naked, and decidedly heterosexual (with the occasional detour into bisexuality, as in *Wild Side*). These two movies show off Heche at her best.

★ *Rebel Highway: Girls in Prison* (1994, Showtime); *Wild Side* (1995)

Mariel Hemingway These two films provide two different versions of this talented thespian granddaughter of Ernest Hemingway. *Personal Best* is Mariel pre-implants; *Star 80,* Mariel after her enhancement.

★ *Personal Best* (1982); *Star 80* (1983)

Helen Hunt Even though Helen Hunt's nude scene with Greg Kinnear in *As Good As It Gets* was talked about, in actuality it was really more teasing and coy than blatantly naked. In 1991, though, Helen delivered the full monty in *The Waterdance,* which costarred Eric Stoltz as a writer (paralyzed in a hiking accident) with whom she was having an affair prior to his injury. *The Waterdance* is legendary among Helen Hunt fans. (Stoltz later made several appearances as Jamie's [Hunt] old boyfriend on the Paul Reiser/Helen Hunt sitcom *Mad About You.*)

★ *The Waterdance* (1991)

Holly Hunter No one in a million years expected the talented star of such films as *Raising Arizona* (1987), *Broadcast News* (1987), *Roe vs. Wade* (1989), and *The Positively True Adventures of the Alleged Texas Cheerleader-Murdering Mom* (1993)—none of which contained even a hint of Hunter nudity—to strip completely naked for some very explicit nude scenes in this Jane Campion award winner. Hunter won a Best Actress Oscar for her performance.

★ *The Piano* (1993)

Angelina Jolie Jon Voight's stunning daughter is phenomenal in this movie about the heroin-addicted, bisexual supermodel Gia Carangi who died of AIDS at the age of twenty-six. Angelina is also absolutely, completely nude in several scenes and her shamelessness and brazen exhibitionism quite effectively captures the recklessness with which Carangi lived her life.

★ *Gia* (1998, HBO)

Ashley Judd This gorgeous actress is part of the talented Judd clan (her mom Naomi and sister Winonna are hugely popular country music stars) and her film career has included some memorable performances since her impressive debut in *Ruby in Paradise* in 1993. She is extremely naked in both of these films (especially *Norma Jean & Marilyn*), although for many fans, she never looked more appealing than in *A Time to Kill* (1996), in which she played Matthew McConaughey's wife.

★ *Normal Life* (1996); *Norma Jean & Marilyn* (1996, HBO)

Diane Keaton Annie Hall does several nude scenes in this seventies thriller that costarred Richard Gere and which was released the same year she won the Oscar for her performance in Woody Allen's classic comedy *Annie Hall.*

★ *Looking for Mr. Goodbar* (1977)

Nicole Kidman Mrs. Tom Cruise has had a wide-ranging and varied career and has not been averse to nudity. *Eyes Wide Shut* and *Billy Bathgate* contain her most explicit scenes. (Worth noting: Kidman's performance in *To Die For* is one of the best performances by an actress in the nineties.)

★ *Windrider* (1986, Australian); *Dead Calm* (1989); *Billy Bathgate* (1991); *Malice* (1993); *To Die For* (1995); *Eyes Wide Shut* (1999)

Nastassja Kinski This movie is worth a rental just for the scenes in which Kinski walks around the woods naked . . . because she's really a panther, you see.

★ *Cat People* (1982)

Marta Kristen Personally, I craved Angela Cartwright, but there are plenty of you rabid *Lost in Space* fans out there who absolutely worshiped older sister Judy, played by Marta Kristen. This flick might be hard to track down, though.

★ *Gemini Affair* (1974)

k. d. lang The popular singer/songwriter is seen completely naked in this German drama about a woman who ends up in Alaska after escaping from East Germany after her lover is killed trying to scale the Berlin Wall. The woman, played by Rosal Zech, gets involved with lang, who has to pose as a man in order to get a job working on the Alaskan pipeline. (Say what?)

★ *Salmonberries* (1991, German)

Jennifer Jason Leigh If you're a Jennifer Jason Leigh fan, you're in luck . . . as this list of "revealing" movies illustrates!

★ *Fast Times at Ridgemont High* (1982); *Flesh + Blood* (1985); *Last Exit to Brooklyn* (1990); *Miami Blues* (1990); *Single White Female* (1992)

Ali MacGraw This movie made news when McGraw—ten years after the enormously successful *Love Story*—did a topless scene that prompted one Hollywood critic to proclaim that Ali MacGraw had the sexiest nipples in Hollywood. That claim alone makes it worth a rental, eh?

★ *Just Tell Me What You Want* (1980)

Mathilda May She is not one of the bigger name actresses, but Mathilda May is fondly remembered for this sci-fi film in which she plays a space vampire and spends a good deal of the movie walking around completely naked.

★ *Lifeforce* (1985)

Demi Moore Once again, we have the opportunity to experience two "versions" of an actress. Mrs. Bruce Willis (still?) has a nude, pre-implants shower scene with Rob Lowe in *About Last Night . . .* in which her less-than-bountiful chest is on full display. Ten years later, in *Striptease,* things have changed quite a bit and Demi's plastic surgeon's touch is quite evident.

★ *About Last Night . . .* (1986); *Striptease* (1996)

Julianne Moore This talented redhead is not averse to screen nudity, her most recent dabble being in *Boogie Nights* as seventies porn star Amber Waves. Even though her hard-core porn star is definitely a bold and sexually explicit characterization, many consider Moore's nude scene in Robert Altman's *Short Cuts* to be her ultimate expression of uninhibited nudism. Moore has to remove her skirt to clean it during an argument with her husband (played by Bruce Davison) and she's not wearing any panties. For close to five minutes, she walks around their living room and kitchen, naked from the waist down—with full frontal and rear views seen—as she cleans and irons her skirt. In the April 16, 1999, issue of *Entertainment Weekly,* director Robert Altman said, "One moment I loved was that nude scene with Julianne. I originally offered that part to Madeleine Stowe and told her, 'This is going to require you to be naked from the waist down for five minutes.' She called back and said, 'I can't.' So I called Julianne and said, 'Before I send you the script, let me tell you that you have to play naked from the waist down for five minutes.' She said, 'I can do that, and Bob, I have a bonus for you. I really am a redhead.'"

★ *Body of Evidence* (1992); *Short Cuts* (1993); *Boogie Nights* (1997)

Tatum O'Neal Ryan O'Neal's daughter, who won a Best Supporting

Actress Oscar for *Paper Moon,* shocked her fans when, seven years after her precocious debut in that charming Peter Bogdanovich movie, she did an explicit topless scene with Richard Burton in this otherwise forgettable flick.

★ *Circle of Two* (1980)

Gwyneth Paltrow This 1998 Best Actress Academy Award winner (for *Shakespeare in Love*) did a brief topless scene in *Flesh + Bone* and then did another one in her Oscar-winning role. It will be interesting to see if she will be as willing to do nudity in the future now that she has a statuette on her mantel.

★ *Flesh + Bone* (1993); *Hush* (1998); *Shakespeare in Love* (1998)

Alexandra Paul This gorgeous *Baywatch* babe has done several nude scenes in her films, and her TV fans who only know her from *Baywatch* should check some of them out, especially *8 Million Ways to Die* and *Sunset Grill.*

★ *American Nightmare* (1981, Canadian); *8 Million Ways to Die* (1986); *Millions* (1990); *Sunset Grill* (1992)

DeDee Pfeiffer DeDee is Michelle's *younger sister.* I can hear the video rentals being rung up already!

★ *Double Exposure* (1993)

Michelle Pfeiffer This stunning actress has a brief nude scene in *Into the Night*—she walks past an open doorway as Jeff Goldblum watches. This was early in her career, though, and she has not done any nudity since. Pfeiffer is married to TV wunderkind David E. (*The Practice*) Kelley and he supposedly based his character of Ally McBeal (from his other hit show) on his wife.

★ *Into the Night* (1985)

Kelly Preston Mrs. John Travolta has appeared nude in several films, her most recent being *Jerry Maguire* with Tom Cruise.

★ *Mischief* (1985); *Spellbinder* (1988); *A Tiger's Tale* (1988); *Jerry Maguire* (1996)

Julia Roberts This hugely popular (and highly paid) actress does not do nudity in her films—except for the time she did a brief nude scene in *Pretty Woman.* The opening shots of Julia ("Vivian") getting dressed in her hooker outfit were done by her body double Shelley Michelle. At about one and a half hours into the movie, however, Julia and Richard Gere are in bed together and her breast clearly can be seen—and we know it's her because her face can be seen at the same time. It's quick, but it's there.

★ *Pretty Woman* (1990)

Mimi Rogers This Showtime feature is notable for a couple of reasons, the first being that this is one of the rare times noted director Nicolas Roeg directed something for American television; and also for the fact that it might be one of the few (if any?) films in which a Hollywood star—Rogers—is seen being given a completely naked full body massage, including having her breasts handled and massaged, while having deep conversations with her masseur (played by the lucky Aussie Bryan Brown) about spirituality and the meaning of life. A keeper.

★ *Full Body Massage* (1995, Showtime)

Susan Sarandon This Oscar winner (for *Dead Man Walking*) had a memorable nude scene in *Atlantic City* that people still talk about: She washes her breasts with a lemon in front of a window as senior citizen Burt Lancaster clandestinely watches. The other three movies listed also contain some memorable topless scenes by Sarandon.

★ *Pretty Baby* (1978); *Atlantic City* (1981, French/Canadian); *The Hunger* (1983); *White Palace* (1990)

Cybill Shepherd This popular star (the TV series *Moonlighting* and many hit movies) made her film debut in *The Last Picture Show* and is remembered for her nude diving board scene. (This scene is why God invented the pause button.)

★ *The Last Picture Show* (1971)

Lori Singer This tall blond drink-of-water made her screen debut in the 1984 hit *Footloose.* After a string of flicks in which she remained mostly clothed, she did these two films appearing completely naked.

★ *Sunset Grill* (1992); *Short Cuts* (1993)

Mira Sorvino Paul Sorvino's daughter (and Oscar winner for *Mighty Aphrodite* in 1995) plays Marilyn Monroe in this winning HBO movie and flashes her breasts briefly. Interestingly, Ashley Judd plays Marilyn's alter ego. Norma Jean Baker, and has many more nude scenes than the Marilyn character does.

★ *Norma Jean & Marilyn* (1996, HBO)

Sissy Spacek This Best Actress Oscar winner (for *Coal Miner's Daughter* in 1980) plays the beleagured, psychokinetic daughter of a religious fanatic who gets her first period while naked in a high school shower. She thinks she's bleeding to death (her mother never prepared her) and her charming classmates compassionately pelt her with sanitary napkins while chanting "Plug it up!" Yikes. Spacek had guts to tackle this role so early in her career. (*Carrie* was her fourth film, after *Prime Cut* [1972], *Badlands* [1973], and *Ginger in the Morning* [1973]).

★ *Prime Cut* (1972); *Carrie* (1976)

Mary Steenburgen This Best Supporting Actress Oscar whipped off her waitress's uniform in this terrific comedy and stormed naked out of the bar where she had been working. Memorable.

★ *Melvin and Howard* (1980)

Sharon Stone The crotch shot is the scene everyone talks about when the subject of *Basic Instinct* is brought up. Stone claims she had no idea the scene would be so graphic; Paul Verhoeven the director claims she had full knowledge of the shot and approved it. Whatever. The scene made her a huge star.

★ *Basic Instinct* (1992)

Meryl Streep This was a very rare instance of this highly respected and enormously talented actress doing nudity. (In fact, she has not done skin since.) In *Silkwood,* she flashes her left breast very quickly in the lab facility where she and Cher work.

★ *Silkwood* (1984)

Sherry Stringfield This absolutely breathtaking blonde won a lot of hearts as Dr. Susan Lewis during the first two seasons of *ER*. Most of her new fans, though, do not know of her nude scene on *NYPD Blue* in 1993 and that is why we include it here, even though the episode is not available for rental on videotape. It is in syndication, however, so you might be able to catch this episode some day if you're vigilant. Stringfield's episode was a David Caruso installment (she played his estranged wife Laura) and in the scene to watch for, she gets out of bed naked and—as is typical for *NYPD Blue*'s nude scenes—we get to see her derrière for a few seconds.

★ *NYPD Blue: True Confessions* (October 12, 1993)

Sally Struthers Archie Bunker's little girl did a topless scene with Jack Nicholson back in 1970 before she starred in *All in the Family* (and also before she gained a great deal of weight). Struthers devotes her time these days to charity work, and touring as Miss Hannigan in *Annie*.

★ *Five Easy Pieces* (1970)

Lea Thompson This future star of the sitcom *Caroline in the City* made her film debut in 1983 in an under-appreciated high school football movie called *All the Right Moves*. Thompson played opposite another newcomer named Tom Cruise (it was only his fourth movie) and *All the Right Moves* now enjoys cult status because of Thompson and Cruise's love scene in which both young stars appear completely—and we're talking *completely*—nude for more than just a glimpse. This was the first and last time Lea Thompson did a topless or frontal nudity scene.

★ *All the Right Moves* (1983)

Uma Thurman The September 1996 issue of *Playboy* featured papparazzi photos of Uma Thurman on a nude beach. The cover tag line read, "Uma Thurman at the Beach—No Shirt, No Shoes, No Problem!" Reportedly, Thurman was livid that the mag had bought and published the pix, but they ran them anyway. What probably contributed to their decision was the fact that the comely actress had appeared topless in *Dangerous Liaisons* in 1988 and again in 1993 with Robert De Niro in *Mad Dog and Glory*. Whether this actually makes any difference or not is moot, but in all likelihood Thurman was probably upset with the *Playboy* spread because she had had no choice in whether or not the photos would run, the exact opposite of her *choosing* to do a nude scene in a movie (or two).

★ *Dangerous Liaisons* (1988); *Mad Dog and Glory* (1993)

Jeanne Tripplehorn Tripplehorn trained extensively for this film (her big-screen debut) because she wanted to look good naked. It worked.

★ *Basic Instinct* (1992)

Liv Tyler Liv's father is Steven Tyler, the lead singer of Aerosmith, and he was once quoted as saying he'd never allow his daughter to do nudity in a film—if he had anything to say about it, that is. Well, either he changed his mind or Liv overruled him, because in *Stealing Beauty*, she is seen naked and having sex.

★ *Stealing Beauty* (1996)

Julie Warner This talented actress (she eventually went on to her own sitcom) made a memorable film debut as the small-town girl who introduces herself to Michael J. Fox by walking out of a lake completely naked. When Fox can't keep his eyes in his skull and asks her if she'd like his shirt, she calmly tells him that if he's a doctor (he is), then she didn't have anything he hadn't seen before. This scene alone is worth the price of admission.

★ *Doc Hollywood* (1991)

Sigourney Weaver A story is told of a woman film critic attending a screening of *Half Moon Street,* in which Sigourney Weaver plays a hooker. After witnessing several topless scenes by the actress, the critic is reported to have said aloud (to much laughter and applause), "God, I am *so* sick and tired of her tits!" The scene of Weaver riding an exercise bike topless is legendary. And speaking of memorable scenes, many fans also love Sigourney's T-shirt and panties scenes in *Aliens* (1986).

★ *Half Moon Street* (1986)

JoBeth Williams Midway through her four-year stint on the soap *The Guiding Light,* JoBeth Williams made her feature film debut in this divorce drama, in which she walked naked out of bedroom into a hallway where she bumped right into Dustin Hoffman's young son. Williams then went on to the two roles she is probably best remembered for: Carol Ann's beleaguered mom in *Poltergeist* (1982), and the confused yuppie wife in *The Big Chill* (1983).

★ *Kramer vs. Kramer* (1979)

Debra Winger This sultry actress's résumé has some big hits in it, including *Urban Cowboy* (1980), *An Officer and a Gentleman* (1982), *Terms of Endearment* (1983), *Legal Eagles* (1986), and others. Winger appeared topless in her feature film debut (*Slumber Party '57*) and then did a much talked about scene with Richard Gere in *An Officer and a Gentleman.* Rumor has it that Winger's moans of passion during their nude love scene were actually her crying because of her distress over doing the steamy scene.

★ *Slumber Party '57* (1976); *An Officer and a Gentleman* (1982)

Sean Young Sean Young has a rep in Hollywood for being a tad "eccentric" but she is nevertheless a talented actress and her fans can check out the naked truth about this brunette beauty in these two thrillers.

★ *No Way Out* (1987); *Love Crimes* (1991)

- - - - - - - - - - - - - - -

Last night I literally had twenty minutes to relax, and I thought, *Jeopardy!* I ended up with *Entertainment* fucking *Tonight,* with myself on it. I'm still recovering.

Helen Hunt
Us, March 1998

- - - - - - - - - - - - - - -

The "Transvestites and Transsexuals" Movie List

These terrific flicks are definitely not a drag (even though they're mostly about guys *in* drag!)

I Was a Male War Bride (1949)
Glen or Glenda: Confessions of Ed Wood (1953)
Some Like It Hot (1959)
Psycho (1960)
Myra Breckenridge (1970)
Pink Flamingos (1972)
The Rocky Horror Picture Show (1975)
The *La Cage aux Folles* series (1978, 1981, 1986)
Dressed to Kill (1980)
Polyester (1981)
Tootsie (1982)
Victor/Victoria (1982)
The World According to Garp (1982)
The Year of Living Dangerously (1982)
Yentl (1983)

Just One of the Guys (1985)
Lust in the Dust (1985)
Hairspray (1988)
Torch Song Trilogy (1988)
Nobody's Perfect (1990)
Paris Is Burning (1991)
The Silence of the Lambs (1991)
Switch (1991)
The Crying Game (1992)
The Ballad of Little Jo (1993)
Just One of the Girls (1993)
M. Butterfly (1993)
Mrs. Doubtfire (1993)
The Adventures of Priscilla, Queen of the Desert (1994)
Ed Wood (1994)
It's Pat: The Movie (1994)
To Wong Foo, Thanks for Everything, Julie Newmar (1995)
Boys Don't Cry (1999)

For Your Consideration . . .

THE "W" LIST

Christopher Walken *The Deer Hunter* (1978); *True Romance* (1993)
Dee Wallace *E.T. The Extra-Terrestrial* (1982); *Cujo* (1983)
Jack Warden *The Verdict* (1982); *While You Were Sleeping* (1995)

Denzel Washington *Malcolm X* (1992); *Philadelphia* (1993)

Gedde Watanabe *Sixteen Candles* (1984); *Gung Ho* (1985)

Sam Waterston *September* (1988); *Crimes and Misdemeanors* (1989)

Sigourney Weaver The *Alien* series (1979–1997); *Copycat* (1995)

Forest Whitaker *Good Morning, Vietnam* (1987); *Lush Life* (1994)

Dianne Wiest *Hannah and Her Sisters* (1986); *Little Man Tate* (1991)

Gene Wilder *Young Frankenstein* (1974); *Blazing Saddles* (1974)

JoBeth Williams *The Big Chill* (1983); *Switch* (1991)

Robin Williams *Mrs. Doubtfire* (1993); *Good Will Hunting* (1997)

Bruce Willis The *Die Hard* series (1988–1995); *The Sixth Sense* (1999)

Debra Winger *An Officer and a Gentleman* (1982); *Terms of Endearment* (1983)

Henry Winkler *Night Shift* (1982); *Scream* (1996)

Mare Winningham *Threshold* (1983); *St. Elmo's Fire* (1985)

Kate Winslet *Titanic* (1997); *Hideous Kinky* (1998)

James Woods *Videodrome* (1983); *John Carpenter's Vampires* (1997)

Robin Wright *Forrest Gump* (1994); *Moll Flanders* (1996)

- - - - - - - - - - - - - - - - - -

And, of course, for John Holmes's movies

In 1953, studio honcho George Stevens told friends that he thought the new wide-screen cinematography was suitable only for photographing high school classes and snakes.

- - - - - - - - - - - - - - - - - -

It's All Relative:
Hollywood Family Connections

In the plumbing or painting business, they'll put "Smith & Sons" right on the trucks. (I even know of a local fuel oil company that has "& Daughters" emblazoned on the side of its tankers.)

But in Hollywood, family dynasties are not billboarded so publicly. In fact, some members of Tinseltown clans even go so far as to change their name (Nicolas Cage, Emilio Estevez, etc.) so that their family connections will not be so blatant.

Here is a look at dozens of Hollywood family ties, from mothers and fathers to cousins and even fathers-in-law.

(And just out of curiosity, did you ever wonder how show biz families decide whose movie to watch on cable? "Come on, dad, we've seen *Apocalypse Now* a thousand times . . . can't we watch *Men at Work* just once?" And we won't even hazard a guess about the Baldwins!)

Robert Alda is Alan Alda's father.
Alan Arkin is Adam Arkin's father.
Desi Arnaz is Lucie Arnaz's father.
James Arness and Peter Graves are brothers.

B

Alec Baldwin, Billy Baldwin, Daniel Baldwin, and Stephen Baldwin are
    brothers.
Martin Balsam is Talia Balsam's father.
John Barrymore is Diana Barrymore's father.
John Barrymore, Lionel Barrymore, and Ethel Barrymore are brothers
    and sister.

Maurice Barrymore is John Barrymore's, Lionel Barrymore's, and Ethel Barrymore's father.

Jason Bateman and Justine Bateman are brother and sister.

Warren Beatty and Shirley MacLaine are brother and sister.

Ed Begley is Ed Begley Jr.'s father.

John Belushi and James Belushi are brothers.

Edgar Bergen is Candice Bergen's father.

Noah Berry Sr. is Noah Berry Jr.'s father.

Dan Blocker is Dirk Blocker's father.

Pat Boone is Debbie Boone's father.

Lloyd Bridges is Beau Bridges's and Jeff Bridges's father.

Helen Broderick is Broderick Crawford's mother.

James Broderick is Matthew Broderick's father.

C

James Cagney and Jeanne Cagney are brother and sister.

Kirk Cameron and Candace Cameron are brother and sister.

Richard Carpenter and Karen Carpenter are brother and sister.

John Carradine is David Carradine's, Keith Carradine's, and Robert Carradine's father.

Jack Cassidy is David Cassidy's and Shaun Cassidy's father.

Lon Chaney is Lon Chaney Jr.'s father.

Charlie Chaplin is Geraldine Chaplin's and Josephine Chaplin's father.

Nick Clooney is George Clooney's father.

Rosemary Clooney is George Clooney's aunt.

Nat King Cole is Natalie Cole's father.

Jeanne Cooper is Corbin Bernsen's mother.

Carmine Coppola is Francis Ford Copppola's and Talia Shire's father.

Carmine Coppola is Nicolas Cage's grandfather.

Francis Ford Coppola is Nicolas Cage's uncle.

Francis Ford Coppola is Sofia Coppola's father.

Francis Ford Coppola and Talia Shire are brother and sister.

Bing Crosby is Gary, Dennis, Lindsay, and Philip Crosby's father.
Tony Curtis is Jamie Lee Curtis's father.

D

Arlene Dahl is Lorenzo Lamas's mother.
James Daly is Tim Daly's and Tyne Daly's father.
Dom DeLuise is Peter DeLuise's and Michael DeLuise's father.
Cecil B. DeMille is Agnes De Mille's uncle.
Catherine Deneuve is Christian Vadim's mother.
Gerard Depardieu is Guillaume Depardieu's father.
Bruce Dern is Laura Dern's father.
Colleen Dewhurst is Campbell Scott's mother.
Jimmy Dorsey and Tommy Dorsey are brothers.
Kirk Douglas is Michael Douglas's father.
Morton Downey is Morton Downey Jr.'s father.
Eddy Duchin is Peter Duchin's father.

E

Les Elgart and Larry Elgart are brothers.
Bob Elliott is Chris Elliott's father.

F

Nanette Fabray is Shelley Fabares's aunt.
Douglas Fairbanks is Douglas Fairbanks Jr.'s father.
John Farrow is Mia Farrow's father.
Eddie Fisher is Carrie Fisher's and Joely Fisher's father.
Henry Fonda is Peter Fonda's and Jane Fonda's father.
Peter Fonda is Bridget Fonda's father.
Joan Fontaine and Olivia de Havilland are sisters.

G

Zsa Zsa Gabor and Eva Gabor are sisters.
Clark Gable is John Clark Gable's father.
John Garfield is David and Julie Garfield's father.
George Gershwin and Ira Gershwin are brothers.
Andy Gibb, Barry Gibb, Robin Gibb, and Maurice Gibb are brothers.
Lillian Gish and Dorothy Gish are sisters.
Joel Gray is Jennifer Gray's father.
Woody Guthrie is Arlo Guthrie's father.

H

Alan Hale is Alan Hale Jr.'s father.
Barbara Hale is William Katt's mother.
George Hamilton is Ashley Hamilton's father.
Goldie Hawn is Kate Hudson's mother.
Helen Hayes is James MacArthur's mother.
Hedda Hopper is William Hopper's mother.
Jim Hutton is Timothy Hutton's father.
John Huston is Anjelica Huston's father.
Walter Huston is Anjelica Huston's grandfather.

I

Jules Irving is Amy Irving's father.

J

Ashley Judd and Wynonna Judd are sisters.
Naomi Judd is Ashley Judd's and Wynonna Judd's mother.

K

James Keach and Stacy Keach are brothers.
Klaus Kinski is Nastassja Kinski's father.

L

Diane Ladd is Laura Dern's mother.
Michael Landon is Michael Landon Jr.'s father.
Angela Lansbury is David Lansbury's aunt.
Bruce Lee is Brandon Lee's father.
Jack Lemmon is Chris Lemmon's father.
John Lennon is Julian Lennon's and Sean Lennon's father.
Gene Lockhart is June Lockhart's father.

M

Jeanette MacDonald and Blossom Rock are sisters.
Barbara Mandrell and Louise Mandrell are sisters.
Bob Marley is Ziggy Marley's father.
Dean Martin is Dean Paul Martin's father.
Mary Martin is Larry Hagman's mother.
Raymond Massey is Daniel Massey's and Anna Massey's father.
Marcello Mastroianni is Chiara Mastroianni's father.
Steve McQueen is Chad McQueen's father.
Audrey Meadows and Jayne Meadows are sisters.
Anne Meara is Ben Stiller's mother.
Vincente Minnelli is Liza Minnelli's father.
Robert Montgomery is Elizabeth Montgomery's father.
Henry Morgan and Alan Jay Lerner are cousins.
Vic Morrow is Jennifer Jason Leigh's father.

N

Ozzie Nelson is David Nelson's and Rick Nelson's father.
Paul Newman is Scott Newman's father.

O

Carroll O'Connor is Hugh O'Connor's father.
Ryan O'Neal is Griffin O'Neal's and Tatum O'Neal's father.
Maureen O'Sullivan is Mia Farrow's mother.

P

Gregory Peck is Tony Peck's father.
Michelle Pfeiffer and DeDee Pfeiffer are sisters.
River Phoenix and Joaquin Phoenix are brothers.
Priscilla Pointer is Amy Irving's mother.
Tyrone Power is Tyrone Power Jr.'s father.
Richard Pryor is Rain Pryor's father.

R

John Raitt is Bonnie Raitt's father.
Michael Redgrave is Lynn Redgrave's and Vanessa Redgrave's father.
Vanessa Redgrave and Lynn Redgrave are sisters.
Vanessa Redgrave is Natasha Richardson's and Joely Richardson's
    mother.
Carl Reiner is Rob Reiner's father.
Debbie Reynolds is Carrie Fisher's mother.
Tony Richardson is Natasha Richardson's and Joely Richardson's
    father.
Joan Rivers is Melissa Rivers's mother.
Jason Robards is Jason Robards Jr.'s father.

Eric Roberts and Julia Roberts are brother and sister.

Roberto Rossellini is Isabella Rossellini's father.

Boris Sagal is Katey Sagal's, Jean Sagal's, and Liz Sagal's father.

Edie Sedgewick and Kyra Sedgwick are cousins.

Charlie Sheen and Emilio Estevez are brothers.

Martin Sheen is Emilio Estevez's, Charlie Sheen's, and Renee Estevez's father.

Talia Shire is Nicolas Cage's aunt.

Frank Sinatra is Frank Sinatra Jr.'s, Nancy Sinatra's, and Tina Sinatra's father.

Paul Sorvino is Mira Sorvino's father.

Sylvester Stallone is Sage Stallone's father.

Connie Stevens is Joely Fisher's mother.

Stella Stevens is Andrew Stevens's mother.

Jerry Stiller is Ben Stiller's and Amy Stiller's father.

Lee Strasberg is Susan Strasberg's father.

Barbra Streisand is Jason Gould's mother.

Donald Sutherland is Kiefer Sutherland's father.

Jessica Tandy is Tandy Cronyn's mother.

Danny Thomas is Marlo Thomas's father.

Danny Thomas is Phil Donahue's father-in-law.

Arturo Toscanini is Vladimir Horowitz's father-in-law.

Steven Tyler is Liv Tyler's father.

Roger Vadim is Christian Vadim's father.

Dick Van Dyke and Jerry Van Dyke are brothers.

Dick Van Patten is Nels Van Patten's, Jimmy Van Patten's, and Vince
   Van Patten's father.
Melvin Van Peebles is Mario Van Peebles's father.
Jon Voight is Angelina Jolie's father

W

John Wayne is Patrick Wayne's father.
Ed Wynn is Keenan Wynn's father.

Z

Efrem Zimbalist Jr. is Stephanie Zimbalist's father.

- - - - - - - - - - - - - - - - - -

I tried to avoid lifetime achievement awards, because it always
means you are close to the end. It's hard for me to believe I'm 82. I
look in the mirror, and I say to myself, "How did that happen? There
must be some mistake."

Kirk Douglas
TV Guide, March 6, 1999

- - - - - - - - - - - - - - - - - -

85 Celebrities and Their Pets

Some stars take their pets everywhere (Joan Rivers likes to bring Spike
to tapings of talk show appearances); others keep their pets as far away
from the spotlight as possible.
   This list looks at 85 celebs and their pets. Following the star is their

companion animal of choice. When the names of the pet (or pets) are known, it's provided in parentheses.

Meow.

1. **Don Adams** Poodle (Brandy)

2. **Steve Allen** Springer Spaniel (Mr. T)

3. **Kirstie Alley** Cat (Elvis); Black Chicken (Billy Idol)

4. **June Allyson** Cocker Spaniel (Heathcliff)

5. **Anne Archer** Dog (Bordeaux)

6. **Lauren Bacall** Cocker Spaniel (Puddle)

7. **Catherine Bach** Persian Cat (Kitty)

8. **Lucille Ball** Toy Poodle (Tinker Toy)

9. **Tallulah Bankhead** Monkey (King Kong); Lion (Winston Churchill); Sealyham Terrier (Hitchcock)

10. **Brigitte Bardot** Dog (Gin)

11. **Drew Barrymore** Horse (Mocha Bailey)

12. **Orson Bean** Cat (Pussy Galore)

13. **Bonnie Bedelia** Cat (Brando)

14. **Candice Bergen** Cat (Furball)

15. **Linda Blair** Terrier (Pilsner)

16. **Dirk Bogarde** Mastiff (Candida)

17. **Johnny Carson** Yorkshire Terrier (Muffin)

18. **Kim Cattrall** Siamese Cat (Nellie Bly)

19. **Connie Chung** Snake (Geraldo)

20. **George Clooney** Potbellied Pig (Max)

21. **Doris Day** Dog (Barney Miller); Dog (Heineken)

22. **James Dean** Dachshund (Strudel)

23. **Bo Derek** Horse (Tarzan); Horse (Tanya Tucker)

24. **Susan Dey** Parakeet (Tweetie)

25. **Kirk Douglas** Spaniel (Cavalier King Charles)

26. **Michael Douglas** Borzoi

27. **Roger Ebert** Cat (Orange Cat)

28. **Erik Estrada** Persian Cat (Gucci)

29. **Douglas Fairbanks** Mastiff (Marco Polo); Terrier (Zorro)

30. **Corey Feldman** Dog (Twinky)

31. **Carrie Fisher** Rottweiler

32. **Michael J. Fox** Dalmatian

33. **Eddie Furlong** Cat (T2)

34. **Eva Gabor** Cat (Miss Puss Puss); Cat (Zsa Zsa)

35. **Mel Gibson** Australian Cattle Dog (Maverick)

36. **Kathie Lee Gifford** Dog (Regis); Bichon Frise (Chablis); Bichon Frise (Chardonnay)

37. **Whoopi Goldberg** Rhodesian Ridgeback

38. **Brian Austin** Green Boa Constrictor (Bo)

39. **Merv Griffin** Irish Setter (Poochie)

40. **Valerie Harper** Dog (Billy the Kid)

41. **David Hasselhoff** Cat (Kitty Kat)

42. **Tippi Hedren** Leopard (Cleopatra); Cheetah (Rhett Butler)

43. **Charlton Heston** Saint Bernard (Portia)

44. **Kate Jackson** Siberian Husky

45. **Michael Jackson** Chimpanzee (Bubbles); Ram (Mr. Tibbs)

46. **Victoria Jackson** Cat (Jolson)

47. **Shirley Jones** Dog (Cyrano)

48. **Stephen King** Welsh Corgi (Marlowe); Cat

49. **Ricki Lake** Dog (Zsa Zsa Gabor)

50. **Eriq LaSalle** Dog (Blue); Dog (Booda)

51. **Kelly LeBrock** Cat (Scratch)

52. **Liberace** Poodle

53. **Courtney Love** Dog (Bob Dylan)

54. **Meredith MacRae** Cat (Crumpet)

55. **Madonna** Chihuahua (Chiquita)

56. **Matthew McConaughey** Dog (Miss Hud)

57. **Ed McMahon** Cat (W. C. Fields)

58. **Sarah Miles** Skye Terrier (Gladys)

59. **Paul Newman** Fox Terrier

60. **Catherine Oxenberg** Cat (Tristan); Cat (Isolde)

61. **Luke Perry** Potbellied Pig (Jerry Lee)

62. **Maury Povich** Snake (Geraldo)

63. **Dick Powell** Cocker Spaniel (Heathcliff)

64. **Vincent Price** Dog (Brownie)

65. **Victoria Principal** Burmese Cat (Buns); Cat (Terra Catta)

66. **Dennis Quaid** Golden Retriever (Fawn Hall)

67. **Ronald Reagan** Scottish Terrier (Scotch); Scottish Terrier (Soda); Cockapoo (Muffin)

68. **Geraldo Rivera** Dog (Connie Chu); Canary (Maury Chirp)

69. **Tanya Roberts** Siamese Cat (Buns)

70. **Arnold Schwarzenegger** Labrador Retreiver (Conan); Labrador Retriever (Streudel)

71. **William Shatner** Doberman Pinscher

72. **Richard Simmons** Poodles (Lots of them)

73. **Jaclyn Smith** Poodle (Vivien Leigh)

74. **Aaron Spelling** Poodle (Muffin)

75. **Sylvester Stallone** Bullmastiff

76. **Sally Struthers** Cat (Joan Pawford)

77. **Loretta Swit** Dog (Croissant)

78. **Tiffani-Amber Thiessen** Golden Retriever (Bonnie); Golden Retriever (Clyde)

79. **Daniel J. Travanti** Cat (Kitty)

80. **Janine Turner** Poodle (Eclair)

81. **Jack Wagner** Golden Retriever (Elvis)

82. **Vanna White** Cat (Rhett Butler); Cat (Ashley)

83. **Robin Williams** Alaskan Malamute

84. **Oprah Winfrey** Dog

85. **Jane Wyman** Scottish Terrier (Scotch); Scottish Terrier (Soda)

For Your Consideration . . .

THE "Y" LIST

Dwight Yoakam *Sling Blade* (1996); *The Newton Boys* (1997)
Sean Young *Stripes* (1981); *No Way Out* (1987)

Silence is golden

At the 1998 Oscar ceremony, eighty-nine-year-old director Elia Kazan was awarded a lifetime achievement award by AMPAS but the controversy over his "anti-Communist" activities in the fifties had still not died down. (Some people defended Kazan's actions, however, claiming that many in Hollywood were actually Communists acting as spies for the Soviets and that all Kazan did was expose their treasonous deeds.) Comedian Chris Rock started things off by suggesting that Kazan not stand next to director Martin Scorsese backstage because Scorsese "hates rats." And when Kazan was brought out to receive his award (flanked by Scorsese and Robert De Niro), many in the audience (including Nick Nolte and Ed Harris) refused to applaud and simply sat with their arms crossed while others around them applauded and even stood up in honor of the director. Interestingly, Warren Beatty was one of the many who gave Kazan a standing ovation; Steven Spielberg and his wife Kate Capshaw clapped politely but did not stand. Outside the auditorium, protesters carried signs that read, "Kazan: Snitch" and "Elia Kazan: Benedict Arnold."

30 Great Music Documentaries
and Concert Films

1967 *Don't Look Back* Bob Dylan

1969 *Monterey Pop* The Animals; Booker T and the MGs; Country Joe and the Fish; Jimi Hendrix; Janis Joplin; Jefferson Airplane; The Mamas and the Papas; Otis Redding; Ravi Shankar; The Who

1969 *The Doors: Soft Parade, A Retrospective* The Doors

1970 *Gimme Shelter* The Rolling Stones

1970 *Let It Be* The Beatles

1970 *Sympathy for the Devil* The Rolling Stones

1970 *Woodstock* Joan Baez; Joe Cocker; Country Joe and the Fish; Crosby, Stills and Nash; Arlo Guthrie; Jimi Hendrix; Jefferson Airplane; Sha Na Na; Sly and the Family Stone; Ten Years After; The Who

1971 *Joe Cocker: Mad Dogs and Englishmen* Joe Cocker; Leon Russell; Rita Coolidge

1972 *Elvis on Tour* Elvis Presley

1976 *The Grateful Dead Movie* The Grateful Dead

1976 *The Song Remains the Same* Led Zeppelin

1978 *The Last Waltz* The Band; Eric Clapton; Neil Diamond; Bob Dylan; Joni Mitchell; Van Morrison; Muddy Waters; Neil Young

1981 *The Decline of Western Civilization 1* Circle Jerks; Black Flag; Fear

1982 *The Compleat Beatles* The Beatles

1984 *Stop Making Sense* The Talking Heads

1984 *That Was Rock* The Rolling Stones; James Brown; Ray Charles; The Ronettes; Marvin Gaye; The Miracles; Chuck Berry; Ike and Tina Turner; Jan and Dean; Lesley Gore

1984   *This Is Spinal Tap* Spinal Tap

1985   *Bring on the Night* Sting; Branford Marsalis; Miles Copeland

1987   *Chuck Berry: Hail! Hail! Rock 'n' Roll* Chuck Berry; Eric Clapton; Bo Diddley; Johnnie Johnson; Keith Richards; Little Richard; Linda Rondstadt

1987   *The Real Buddy Holly Story* Buddy Holly

1988   *Imagine* John Lennon

1988   *The Decline of Western Civilization Part II: The Metal Years* Alice Cooper; Chris Holmes; Megadeath; Ozzy Osbourne; Poison; Steven Tyler

1988   *Thelonius Monk: Straight No Chaser* Thelonius Monk

1988   *U2: Rattle and Hum* U2

1989   *Let's Get Lost* Chet Baker

1990   *Listen Up: The Lives of Quincy Jones* Quincy Jones; Dizzy Gillespie; Lionel Hampton; Frank Sinatra; Barbra Streisand; Miles Davis; Ella Fitzgerald; Ray Charles; Ice T; Melle Mel; Big Daddy Kane

1991   *For Those About to Rock: Monsters in Moscow* AC/DC; Metallica; The Black Crowes; Pantera; Electro Shock Therapy

1991   *Madonna: Truth or Dare* Madonna

1995   *The Beatles Anthology* The Beatles

1999   *Hype!* Pearl Jam; Stone Temple Pilots

167 Memorable Musical Movies

The Jazz Singer (1927)

42nd Street (1933)

Naughty Marietta (1935)

Top Hat (1935)

Broadway Melody of 1936 (1936)

San Francisco (1936)

Show Boat (1936)

Swing Time (1936)

Maytime (1937)

Shall We Dance? (1937)

Alexander's Ragtime Band (1938)

Broadway Melody of 1938 (1938)

Broadway Serenade (1939)

The Story of Vernon & Irene Castle (1939)

The Wizard of Oz (1939)

Broadway Melody of 1940 (1940)

New Moon (1940)

Pinocchio (1940)

Tin Pan Alley (1940)

Dumbo (1941)

Week-End in Havana (1941)

Footlight Serenade (1942)

For Me and My Gal (1942)

Star Spangled Rhythm (1942)

Yankee Doodle Dandy (1942)

You Were Never Lovelier (1942)

Best Foot Forward (1943)

Girl Crazy (1943)

Hello, Frisco, Hello (1943)

Presenting Lily Mars (1943)

Stormy Weather (1943)

Thank Your Lucky Stars (1943)

The Phantom of the Opera (1943)

Broadway Rhythm (1944)

Cover Girl (1944)

Meet Me in St. Louis (1944)

Pin-Up Girl (1944)

Shine On, Harvest Moon (1944)

Anchors Aweigh (1945)

Can't Help Singing (1945)

Rhapsody in Blue (1945)

Night and Day (1946)

The Dolly Sisters (1946)

The Jolson Story (1946)

Good News (1947)

Easter Parade (1948)

The Pirate (1948)

Words and Music (1948)

Jolson Sings Again (1949)

My Dream Is Yours (1949)

On the Town (1949)

Take Me out to the Ballgame (1949)

Annie Get Your Gun (1950)

Three Little Words (1950)

Young Man With a Horn (1950)

An American in Paris (1951)

The Great Caruso (1951)

Lullaby of Broadway (1951)

Show Boat (1951)

Singin' in the Rain (1952)

Stars and Stripes Forever (1952)

With a Song in My Heart (1952)

Calamity Jane (1953)

Kiss Me Kate (1953)

A Star Is Born (1954)

Brigadoon (1954)

Rose Marie (1954)

Seven Brides for Seven Brothers (1954)

Student Prince (1954)

The Glenn Miller Story (1954)

There's No Business Like Show Business (1954)

White Christmas (1954)

Young at Heart (1954)

Oklahoma (1955)

The Benny Goodman Story (1955)

Love Me or Leave Me (1955)

Carousel (1956)

High Society (1956)

The Eddy Duchin Story (1956)

The King and I (1956)

Les Girls (1957)

The Pajama Game (1957)

Damn Yankees (1958)

Gigi (1958)

King Creole (1958)

South Pacific (1958)

Can-Can (1960)

Little Shop of Horrors (1960)

West Side Story (1961)

Gypsy (1962)

The Music Man (1962)

The Wonderful World of the Brothers Grimm (1962)

Bye Bye Birdie (1963)

Viva Las Vegas (1963)

A Hard Day's Night (1964)

Mary Poppins (1964)

My Fair Lady (1964)

The Unsinkable Molly Brown (1964)

Beach Blanket Bingo (1965)

Help! (1965)

The Sound of Music (1965)

Camelot (1967)

How to Succeed in Business Without Really Trying (1967)

Magical Mystery Tour (1967)

Thoroughly Modern Millie (1967)

Chitty Chitty Bang Bang (1968)

Funny Girl (1968)

Oliver! (1968)

Star! (1968)

Hello, Dolly! (1969)

Paint Your Wagon (1969)

On a Clear Day You Can See Forever (1970)

Scrooge (1970)

Fiddler on the Roof (1971)

Cabaret (1972)

Oh! Calcutta! (1972)

American Graffiti (1973)

Jesus Christ, Superstar (1973)

Mame (1974)

Phantom of the Paradise (1974)

Funny Lady (1975)

Tommy (1975)

A Star Is Born (1976)

Saturday Night Fever (1977)

All You Need Is Cash (1978)

Grease (1978)

Thank God It's Friday (1978)

The Wiz (1978)

All That Jazz (1979)

Hair (1979)

The Muppet Movie (1979)

Rock 'n' Roll High School (1979)

The Rose (1979)

Coal Miner's Daughter (1980)

Fame (1980)

Idolmaker (1980)

One Trick Pony (1980)

Popeye (1980)

The Blues Brothers (1980)

Pippin (1981)

Annie (1982)

The Best Little Whorehouse in Texas (1982)

Yes, Giorgio (1982)

Eddie and the Cruisers (1983)

Flashdance (1983)

Yentl (1983)

Amadeus (1984)

Footloose (1984)

Purple Rain (1984)

Sweeney Todd: The Demon Barber of Fleet Street (1984)

This Is Spinal Tap (1984)

A Chorus Line (1985)

Little Shop of Horrors (1986)

The Singing Detective (1986)

Oliver & Company (1988)

The Little Mermaid (1989)

Cry-Baby (1990)

Beauty and the Beast (1991)

Sister Act (1992)

The Mambo Kings (1992)

Wayne's World (1992)

What's Love Got to Do With It? (1993)

The Lion King (1994)

Shine (1995)

Everyone Says I Love You (1996)

Evita (1996)

Spice World: The Movie (1997)

For Your Consideration . . .

THE "Z" LIST

Billy Zane *Dead Calm* (1989); *Titanic* (1997)
Renée Zellweger *Jerry Maguire* (1996); *Bridget Jones's Diary* (2001)
Catherine Zeta-Jones *The Phantom* (1996); *The Mask of Zorro* (1998).

Maybe his friends were afraid he wouldn't give it back?

According to Steven Spielberg, when he won a Best Director Oscar for *Schindler's List* (1993), and accepted the statuette, it was the first time he had ever held an Oscar in his hands.

Baseball Movies

Batter up!

Pride of the Yankees (1942)

The Babe Ruth Story (1948)

It Happens Every Spring (1949)

The Jackie Robinson Story (1950)

Bang the Drum Slowly (1956, 1973)

The Bad News Bears series (1976–1978)

The Bingo Long Traveling All-Stars and Motor Kings (1976)

Blue Skies Again (1983)

The Natural (1984)

Brewster's Millions (1985)

The Slugger's Wife (1985)

Amazing Grace & Chuck (1987)

Ironweed (1987)

Stealing Home (1988)

Field of Dreams (1989)

The *Major League* series (1989–1998)

Eight Men Out (1988)

Bull Durham (1988)

The Babe (1992)

A League of Their Own (1992)

Rookie of the Year (1993)

The Sandlot (1993)

Little Big League (1994)

The Scout (1994)

Angels in the Outfield (1952, 1994)

Ed (1996)

The Fan (1996)

For the Love of the Game (1999)

Perfect Game (2000)

61* (2001)

Football Movies

Hut!

Paper Lion (1968)

Brian's Song (1971)

The Longest Yard (1974)

Semi-Tough (1977)

Heaven Can Wait (1978)

North Dallas Forty (1979)

All the Right Moves (1983)

The Best of Times (1986)

Wildcats (1986)

The Last Boy Scout (1991)

The Program (1993)

Rudy (1993)

Jerry Maguire (1996)

The Waterboy (1998)

Any Given Sunday (1999)

Varsity Blues (1999)

The Replacements (2000)

Remember the Titans (2000)

The Current Occupations
of the 6 *Brady Bunch* Kids

1. **Barry Williams** born 1940. "Greg." *Currently:* Lecturing for schools and corporate events about his successful autobiographical book, *Growing Up Brady.*

2. **Maureen McCormick** born 1956. "Marcia." *Currently:* Acting. Starred as Barbara Mandrell in the CBS movie *Get to the Heart: The Barbara Mandrell Story;* costarring in *Fortune Hunters* with Corey Feldman.

3. **Christopher Knight** born 1957. "Peter." *Currently:* Vice president of graphics marketing for a computer firm.

4. **Eve Plumb** born 1958. "Jan." *Currently:* Acting. Recently appeared in the 1997 HBO movie *Breast Men* with David Schwimmer; also starred in the ABC kids' series, *Fudge.*

5. **Mike Lookinland** born 1960. "Bobby." *Currently:* First assistant camera operator on the CBS series *Promised Land.* (He was portrayed by his son in the recent *Brady Bunch* biopic, and he himself had a cameo in it as a photographer.)

6. **Susan Olsen** born 1961. "Cindy." *Currently:* Stay-at-home Mom.

Premiere Magazine's
25 "Most Dangerous" Movies

What, precisely, makes a movie "dangerous"? Here is a look at twenty-five films the respected movie magazine *Premiere* feels qualify, with a word or two as to why.

1929   *Un Chien Andalou* What else? The slitting of the eyeball with a razor scene, for starters.

1931   *M* Peter Lorre as a loathsome child-killer.

1932   *Freaks* Real ones.

1945   *The Lost Weekend* The DTs.

1960   *Peeping Tom* A killer who forces his female victims to watch their own deaths on video.

1965   *Repulsion* A woman's nervous breakdown, in color.

1967   *Bonnie and Clyde* The gruesome final slaughter scene (actually only 21 seconds of screen time).

1967   *Weekend* Cannibalism.

1970   *Gimme Shelter* A live murder caught on film.

1971   *A Clockwork Orange* The rape scene (although the eye clamps scene always makes me squirm.)

1975   *Salo, or The 120 Days of Sodom* Depraved violence, sexual torture, and sadism.

1976   *Seven Beauties* Life in a concentration camp.

1976   *Taxi Driver* Intense violence, underage prostitution, and a presidential assassination storyline.

1977   *Eraserhead* Where do I start?

1988   *Dead Ringers* Twin brother gynecologists. Creepy twin brother gynecologists.

1992   *Bad Lieutenant* Harvey Keitel in overdrive.

1992   *Romper Stomper* Skinheads and their, ahem, "antics."

1994   *Natural Born Killers* Frolicking serial killers.

1997   *In the Company of Men* Two corporate creeps destroy a deaf female co-worker.

1997   *Sick: The Life and Death of Bob Flanagan, Supermasochist* A cystic fibrosis patient who nails his own penis to a board. Yeah, I'd say this qualifies.

1997   *The Sweet Hereafter* Incest.

1998   *Happiness* Child molestation.

1999   *Boys Don't Cry* Transgender discrimination and torment.

2000   *Dancer in the Dark* The death penalty and what it really means.

2000   *Requiem for a Dream* Junkies.

I think I would add John's *Multiple Maniacs* (1970) to this list. To those of you who have seen it, you know why; to those of you who have not, I will not describe what's in it. I just ate.

Hollywood and Movie Web Sites

1. **The Internet Movie Database (www.imdb.com):** The most comprehensive movie Web site in existence. The IMDB is easy to use, and features a resident search engine so sophisticated, you can search for movies in almost an infinite number of variations. (You can even search for *crew members* instead of cast. My friend George Beahm's brother Paul is a stuntman and when I searched for Paul Beahm, the IMDB came up with *everything* he has appeared in . . . maybe even some things George didn't know about!) If there is one word to describe the Internet Movie Database, it is *indispensable.* You have to experience it to grasp the wonder of it all.

2. **E! (www.eonline.com):** The entertainment cable channel's Web site is one of the best entertainment sites around. (They really do live for this stuff, you know.) E! also offers a free e-mailed newsletter.

3. **ZENtertainment (www.zentertainment.com):** A free entertainment newsletter (and associated Web site) that is a digest of a huge amount of entertainment information sent weekly. (An example of ZENtertainment's completeness? When my book *The Lost Work of Stephen King* was due to be published, many media outlets reported this fact and many also reviewed it. ZENtertainment covered the release of the trade edition, but they also provided details on the very rare limited edition of the book, something published for collectors only.)

Other Noteworthy Entertainment Sites

chamber.hollywood.com (the Hollywood Chamber of Commerce)

www.canoe1.canoe.ca/Jam (Jam!)

www.cnn.com/SHOWBIZ/index.html (CNN entertainment news)

www.edrive.com (eDrive)

www.enn2.com (Entertainment Network News)

www.mrshowbiz.com (Mr. Showbiz)

www.mtv.com/news/headlines (MTV News Online)

www.oscar.com (the Academy Awards)

www.pathfinder.com/ew (*Entertainment Weekly* Online)

www.pathfinder.com/people (*People Weekly* Online)

www.premieremag.com (*Premiere* magazine)

www.showbizwire.com (the Showbiz Wire)

www.whitesguidetomovies.com (*White's Guide to the Movies* magazine)

www.hollywood.com (Hollywood Online)

www.hollywoodreporter.com (*The Hollywood Reporter*)

www.variety.com (*Daily Variety*)

Entertainment Newsgroups

alt.movies; rec.arts.movies.current-films; rec.arts.movies.past-films; rec. arts. movies.production; rec.arts.movies.misc

About the Author

Stephen J. Spignesi is a full-time writer who specializes in popular culture subjects, including historical biography, television, film, American and world history, and contemporary fiction.

Mr. Spignesi—christened "the world's leading authority on Stephen King" by *Entertainment Weekly* magazine—has written many authorized entertainment books and has worked with Stephen King, Turner Entertainment, the Margaret Mitchell Estate, Andy Griffith, Viacom, and other entertainment industry personalities and entities on a wide range of projects. Mr. Spignesi has also contributed essays, chapters, articles, and introductions to a wide range of books.

Mr. Spignesi's 30 books have been translated into several languages and he has also written for *Harper's, Cinefantastique, Saturday Review, Mystery Scene, Gauntlet,* and *Midnight Graffiti* magazines; as well as the *New York Times, New York Daily News, New York Post, New Haven Register,* the French literary journal *Ténèbres,* and the Italian online literary journal *Horror.It.* Mr. Spignesi has also appeared on CNN, MSNBC, Fox News Channel, and other TV and radio outlets; and also appeared in the 1998 E! documentary, *The Kennedys: Power, Seduction, and Hollywood,* as a Kennedy family authority; and in the A&E *Biography* of Stephen King that aired in January 2000. Mr. Spignesi's 1997 book *JFK Jr.* was a *New York Times* bestseller. Mr. Spignesi's *Complete Stephen King Encyclopedia* was a 1991 Bram Stoker Award nominee.

In addition to writing, Mr. Spignesi lectures on a variety of popular culture and historical subjects and teaches writing in the Connecticut area. He is the founder and editor-in-chief of the small press publishing company, the Stephen John Press, which recently published the acclaimed feminist autobiography *Open Windows.*

Mr. Spignesi is a graduate of the University of New Haven, and lives in New Haven, Connecticut, with his wife, Pam, and their cat, Carter, named for their favorite character on *ER.*